Communications
in Computer and Information Science 490

Lynn Batten   Gang Li   Wenjia Niu
Matthew Warren (Eds.)

Applications and Techniques in Information Security

5th International Conference, ATIS 2014
Melbourne, VIC, Australia, November 26-28, 2014
Proceedings

 Springer

Volume Editors

Lynn Batten
Gang Li
Deakin University
School of Information Technology
Melbourne Campus at Burwood
221 Burwood Highway, Burwood, VIC 3125, Australia
E-mail: {lynn.batten, gang.li}@deakin.edu.au

Wenjia Niu
Chinese Academy of Sciences
Institute of Information Engineering
National Engineering Laboratory for Information Security Technology
89 Minzhuang Road, Haidan District, Beijing 100093, China
E-mail: niuwenjia@iie.ac

Matthew Warren
Deakin University
School of Information and Business Analysis
Melbourne Campus at Burwood
221 Burwood Highway, Burwood, VIC 3125, Australia
E-mail: matthew.warren@deakin.edu.au

ISSN 1865-0929   e-ISSN 1865-0937
ISBN 978-3-662-45669-9   e-ISBN 978-3-662-45670-5
DOI 10.1007/978-3-662-45670-5
Springer Heidelberg New York Dordrecht London

Library of Congress Control Number: 2014954830

Typesetting: Camera-ready by author, data conversion by Scientific Publishing Services, Chennai, India

Printed on acid-free paper

Springer is part of Springer Science+Business Media (www.springer.com)

Invited Speeches

Near-field Privacy

Lejla Batina

Institute for Computing and Information Sciences (iCIS)
Radboud University Nijmegen, The Netherlands
lejla@cs.ru.nl

Abstract. With the expansion of various privacy-sensitive RFID applications a clear need for new identification schemes has been established. In the past few years a plenitude of identification protocols has been proposed addressing different real-life scenarios and relying on both symmetric-key and asymmetric-key cryptography. In this talk we first survey some prominent solutions for privacy-sensitive RFID identification protocols and discuss their properties and hardware requirements. In the second part of this talk we discuss some recent work on privacy-friendly attribute matching.

Keywords: RFID, cryptography, privacy.

Towards Protecting Service Accessibility of Anonymous Communication Systems: Catch Me if You Can!

Jinqiao Shi

National Engineering Laboratory for Information Security Technologies,
Institute of Information Engineering,
Chinese Academy of Sciences, P.R. China
shijinqiao@iie.ac.cn

Abstract. Nowadays, Internet has become an important infrastructure for human society, and the security and privacy issues on Internet have drawn significant attention from both industries and governments. Service accessibility is one of the most basic and important requirements for Internet services, which means the ability to access and benefit from some system or entity. With more and more real world access-denial attacks against Internet service such as Internet censorship, service accessibility under attack has become one severe security threat on Internet, which has aroused wide interests from individuals, researchers, commercial companies and even governments.

The conflict of Internet service accessibility has arisen for more than ten years. And during this period, quite a lot of work has have been made to win the battle between attack and protection of Internet service accessibility, both in research and practice. For example, to protect service accessibility from sophisticated attacks such as IP address blocking, DNS redirecting, content filtering, domain hijacking, connection reset and so on, the architecture of accessibility-enabling systems has evolved from single access-point to multiple dynamic access-points. And the infrastructures of such systems are based on volunteered nodes, dedicated nodes and even commercial cloud computing platform. Many security techniques have been imported to protect accessibility such as traffic encryption, multi-hop routing, protocol camouflaging, and end-to-middle proxy. And many systems has been developed and deployed to help access Internet service, such as the most famous anonymous communication system Tor. However, there are still some research challenges such as proxy distribution with enumeration attacks from insider attackers.

In this talk, we will take anonymous communication systems as an example and present the cat-and-mouse games between the attacker and defender of service accessibility. We will introduce the general model on network service accessibility, give a thorough analysis of related work on the key procedures of accessibility confrontation, and discuss the future of service accessibility.

Keywords: service accessibility, anonymous communication system, privacy.

Table of Contents

Applications

Curbing Cyber Crimes

Data Privacy

Digital Forensics

Security Implementations

System-Level Permission Management Mechanism
of Android Device

Dali Zhu, Zheming Fan, and Na Pang

Institute of Information Engineering, Chinese Academy of Sciences, Beijing, China, 100093
{zhudali,fanzheming,pangna}@iie.ac.cn

Abstract. As the existing Android operating system doesn't grant users the permission to manage system hardware. A system-level permission management mechanism of android device is proposed to solve this problem. This mechanism is based on the existing system. The existing Android system framework layer and application layer are modified and extended by using a control terminal application to control hardware and authorization, the system boot process, SystemProperty and Camera class to implement new system-level permission management mechanism of Android device. Via the mechanism, the security of Android system is improved, a new layer of protection is increased, the control function of hardware resource access is attached, and security threat for the platform is reduced from the system level. Experimental results show that the feasibility of this system privilege management mechanism is high.

Keywords: Android, permission management, system Framework, security mechanism, properties.

1 Introduction

With the development of mobile Internet, the functionality and ability in data processing of smart phone is promoted. Users can make online transfers, register information, send e-mail and handle business by using smart phone. Android is a smart phone platform launched by Google company. Open system, equality of application, no boundaries between applications, fast and easy of application development are advantages of Android platform. The privacy leaks and all kinds of malicious chargeback software are the most dangerous security threats. The malicious software exploits the vulnerabilities of previous permission mechanism to attacks to mobile phones. What's more, it might call hardware for spying privacy invisibly in the background.

In recent years, with the rapid development of the Android platform, the research on Android security-related becomes more and more. An existing android application permission management mechanism has been implemented in paper [1] and a fine-grained android application permission management model is proposed and users can distribute application permissions which android system installed as needed under certain restrictions. However, due to the use of SQLite database, it is relatively

L. Batten et al. (Eds.): ATIS 2014, CCIS 490, pp. 1–12, 2014.

insecure to protect the data itself for permission. A security service for Android has been proposed in paper [2], which performs lightweight certification of applications to mitigate malware at installing time. Certain properties in system security policy and permission requests of applications are conservatively combined in the security rules. The application can be installed on mobile phones only when the application meets the system security policy. A strategy implementation framework for different applications is proposed in paper [3]. So that mobile phone users can selectively grant or revoke permission to access.

Although these methods have been studied application permissions from different aspects, they are only limited to the application scope of judging on application level. Meanwhile, a relatively narrow range of security threats originate from by these traditional methods. The traditional mechanism of permission management can only accept all the permission of application or refuse all. The permission audit made by user of Android system permission mechanism is the only factor to choosing whether to install. Moreover, it is unsafe that once the program was installed on, the application would get all permissions it request. A specific function or setting on mobile phone cannot be managed by Android mechanism. Great disadvantages lie in this traditional model, and meanwhile this extensive management strategy has been unable to meet our needs in many scenes.

2   Background and Related Technology

Android is a mobile operating system based on the Linux kernel and currently developed by Google. With a user interface based on direct manipulation, Android is designed primarily for touchscreen mobile devices. It has been developing rapidly in recent years. Nowadays, Android system is carried into more and more intelligent mobile phones as their mobile phone operating system. Smart phone becomes a carrier storing a large number of important information, and it has also become a prime target for malicious attacks.   The privacy leaks and all kinds of malicious chargeback software are the most dangerous security threats. The malicious software exploits the vulnerabilities of previous permission mechanism to attacks to mobile phones.

Android applications run in a sandbox, an isolated area of the system that does not have access to the rest of the system's resources, unless access permissions are explicitly granted by the user when the application is installed. Before installing an application, system displays all required permissions. The user can choose to accept or refuse them, installing the application only if they accept. There are still so many weaknesses lying in the traditional strategy which is used to protect system's hardware.

2.1   Init Process of Android System

Init executable program is the first program in user space when system booting, running as a daemon process. Init process is the entrance into Android system when it starts from the standard Linux boot, responsible for system ini-tialization's the back-ground loop. Init executable program's source code location is system/core/init. Init executable program will analysis the init script located in the same root directory, executing the function of the script. The reason for this strategy is to make init ex-ecutable program's function remain fixed and custom work is performed by Init script. The key function of the Init executable program is to analysis and execute the init.c script. After the analysis of complete init.c script, it executes some of the "built-in" action. The properties processing in init script calls the interface provided by _system_properties.h supported by Bionic Libc. Related content of properties processing in Init is defined in proper-ty_service.h and implemented in proper-ty_service.c. In related content of prop-erty, handle_property_set_fd() is used for setting property as a routine work. The setting of properties may come from the vari-ous aspects of the procedure, but is not only limited to init process. No matter what is the property setting's reason, the system will send messages through a Socket. In this situation, fuction "the handle_property_set_fd ()" will receive this message and com-plete process of final setting work of properties . Specific process is shown in Fig.1.

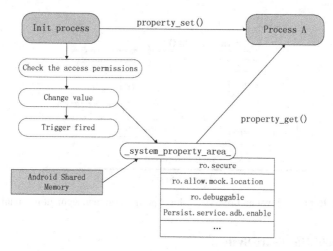

Fig. 1. Android system property service

3   System-Level Permission Management Mechanism

Since the hardware of the Android system is generally invoked in singleton pattern, a new privilege audit mechanism to various hardware classes attached to application framework for checking and authorization is proposed. But the problem lies in that the static global variable cannot be created which can be used permanently instead of local variables of various hardware classes, since the system framework only provides API to the upper and is unable to create a static global variable. It's obvious that it is not available to store data from the perspective of safety. So the android system prop-erty is chosen to store the data. From a security point of view, it's invisible to assign and alter the system properties when system initialize to the applications, so it has a strong safety. Meanwhile, a management program using to manage the device permissions is absolutely necessary. Since the program should call for the @hide API in the system,   permission of the application is improved to become "android.uid.system" and made to be a system-level application.

3.1   Running Process of Permission Management Mechanism

Firstly, using function setprop and getprop to create attributes and read system properties "persist.sys.hardware_prop" in the process of starting initialization init.c is envisioned by the permission management mechanism. A checking mechanism in the application framework is attached so that the application needs to be checked whenever it requests access to a variety of hardware instances. It's effective to protect hardware to prevent illegal call of privacy. Moreover, a variety of appropriate authority protection strategies in the hypervisor can be set to manage own hardware. Operation process is shown in Fig.2.

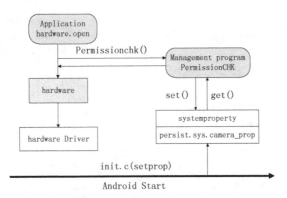

Fig. 2. Running flow chart of System-level permission management mechanism

3.2   Android Hardware System

Calling mode of Android hardware system is as generally follows: Applications call the API provided by the application framework to obtain instances of hardware, then calling on Linux kernel driver for C framework through JNI (Java Native Interface).Here, the camera is taken as an example to explain the new permission management model which is designed on Android system-level.

The underlying hardware of the camera system is the camera device which is used for inputting video data to the system. Camera system provides three functions as viewfinder, video recording and photo shooting to the top of the interface. It also provides the various interfaces for control class. The camera system provides interfaces in Java layer and camera class in local Interface's Java framework. These interfaces are used for building program like cameras and scanning.

3.3   The Android Camera System Architecture

The camera system in Android system includes camera device layer, camera hardware abstraction layer, audio service, camera native library, Java framework classes of camera, and calling for camera system from application layer. Firstly camera system is based on singleton pattern. Applications use the android.hardware.Camera class provided by the Android framework to access the camera service. The camera service can be used for the Java application layer to build program like cameras and scanning. Camera JNI provides local support for upper Java class which connecting framework layer and the lower layer of Camera services. It contains a capability which calling Java reversely to transmit information and data. Camera service is an independent part. It is one of the typical local system services. Architecture of camera system is shown in Fig.3.

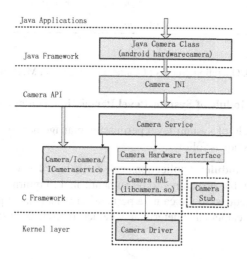

Fig. 3. System architecture of camera

3.4   System-Level Permission Management Mechanism Implementation

The camera system is taken as an example to explain the new permission management model which is designed on Android system-level and a control terminal application is used to control hardware and authorization from system level. SystemProperty and Camera class are designed to implement new system-level permission management mechanism of Android device during startup of the system. Operation process of camera management mechanism is shown in Fig.4.

Using function setprop and getprop to create attributes and read system properties "persist.sys.hardware_prop" in the process of starting initialization init.c is envisioned by the permission management mechanism. A checking mechanism in the application framework is attached so that the application needs to be checked whenever it requests access to a variety of hardware instances.

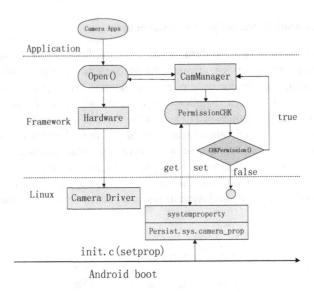

Fig. 4. Operation process of Camera Management Mechanism

3.5   Functional Module of System-Level Permission Management Mechanism

The functional module of system-level permission management mechanism is shown as above. The details are as follows.

Camera Interface Module: Applications call for it in order to get each instance of the hardware system, but it requires to be authenticated to return the correct instance. This module sends request to the camera permission management program module to obtain permission to camera and determine whether to return an instance. (Module1).

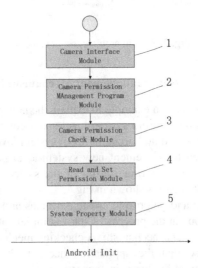

Fig. 5. Functional Module of System-level Permission Management Mechanism

Camera Permission Management Program Module: It's responsible for setting various suitable calling rules to manage the hardware to prevent illegal calling. It responds to the auditing request for the camera interface module to return the permissions. It calls the camera permission auditing module to get the camera permission value of the system properties and audits whether it conforms to the rules. Then it returns the results to the hardware auditing module to review calling permission. (Module2).

Camera Permission Check Module: It obtains the camera permission value of the system property and audits whether it conforms to the rules of calling setting. It only calls the permission reading and setting module to get the value of the system properties. (Module3).

Permission Reading and Setting Module: It communicates with the system property in the camera permission auditing module to ensure that the reading and setting module accesses to the system properties correctly and efficiently. (Module4).

System Property Configuration Module: It calls the related system property to initialize and assign at system startup, then reading and modifying it. (Module5).

3.6   Source Code of System-Level Permission Management Mechanism

Applications call for it in order to get each instance of the hardware system, but it requires to be authenticated to return the correct instance. This module sends request to the camera permission management program module to obtain permission to camera and determine whether to return an instance.

It's effective to protect hardware to prevent illegal call of privacy. Core source code is as follows:

- **Source code of authentication mechanism of Camera**

Android.hardware.Camera class provides a Camera instance for application layer: it is a bridge between camera apps and camera driver. It is also responsible for communicating among camera apps and CamManager. When the application requests framework layer function open () for an instance, the function does not directly return the instance. On the contrary, the function sends the request to the system management program CamManager. In the management program, if feedback permission is not obtained, the function open() is in a wait state. A direct request timed out or results for false from the function leads to returning an empty. Only when the return value of true within the specified time range, the function open() return the instance of the camera to the application. So that applications can use the instance to call system camera driver by JNI.

```
public static Camera open() {
        int numberOfCameras = getNumberOfCameras();
        CameraInfo cameraInfo = new CameraInfo();
   if ( PermissionChkHelper.getPermission() == true )
```

```
for (int i = 0; i < numberOfCameras; i++) {
    getCameraInfo(i, cameraInfo);
    if (cameraInfo.facing == CameraIn-
fo.CAMERA_FACING_BACK) {
        return new Camera(i);
    }
}
return null;
}
```

- **Core source code of management program**

PermissionChkHelper manages the authority list under the new mechanism and connects applications with the android runtime and provides feedback to android.hardware.Camera:

When the system level permission management program CamManager received authority verification request, our program opens PermissionCHK class call the function getSystemProperty () to read the value of the system attribute. Once the program obtains permission value, the program returns the value to the framework layer camera type. If the permission of the camera check passes, the program returns an instance for camera apps which apply to access camera driver. Moreover, the specific system attribute prefix must be "persist.sys"

Management program is also responsible for setting suitable call rules for camera systems to manage hardware to prevent illegal calls. The discrete time period and specific location setting   can be used as factors to manage the camera calling permission. Moreover, black and white lists are built by recognition of an application package name to manage permission, etc.

The use of @hide in the notes can hide methods, properties and the whole class. The use of @hide content appears in the source code of JAVA, but it not be regarded as an Android system of API. Because the use of @hide hidden content does not belong to the Android API platform, the @hide interface cannot be called in the SDK development environment. On the contrary, in the source code development environment, the @hide hidden content still can be called and used.

```
/**
*  hide for application
* @hide
*/
public static void setPermission(boolean per) {
if( per == true)
    SystemProper-
ties.set("persist.sys.tylorvan_permission", "1");
    else
    SystemProper-
ties.set("persist.sys.tylorvan_permission", "0");}
    public static boolean getPermission() {
```

```
  if(SystemProperties.get("persist.sys.camera_prop","-
1")
    .compareTo("1") == 0)
      return true;
    else return false;
  }
```

- **System Level App SysUninstall**

For the protection of the security mechanism and considering the program to call to @hide interface of system, the system level application sysuninstall need to be set to "android.uid.system" become the system level application. At the same time, once the application becomes system level programs, it cannot be uninstalled and disabled. Even the Android system be formatted, the program still cannot be uninstalled. So the protection mechanism still exists. The systuninstall provide a stable running environment for the system-level management program CamManager.

AndroidManifest.xml is used to set the android permission to "android.uid.system" become the system level application. The core code of   AndroidManifest.xml is as follows:

```
<?xml version="1.0" encoding="utf-8"?>
<manifest …
  android:sharedUserId="android.uid.system">
  <original-package andro-
id:name="com.tylorvan.sysuninstall" />
    <application
        android:allowBackup="true"
        android:icon="@drawable/ic_launcher"
        android:theme="@style/AppTheme" >
        ……
    </application>
```

</manifest>

Android.mk is used to build the system level program sysuninstall in the source code environment in android system level. Core code of Android.mk is follows:

```
###################################################

LOCAL_PATH := $(call my-dir)

include $(CLEAR_VARS)

LOCAL_MODULE_TAGS := optional

LOCAL_SRC_FILES := $(call all-java-files-under, src)
```

```
LOCAL_STATIC_JAVA_LIBRARIES := libarity android-support-
v4 guava

LOCAL_PACKAGE_NAME := sysuninstall

LOCAL_CERTIFICATE := platform

include $(BUILD_PACKAGE)
#################################################
```

4   Experiments and Results

The original android phone Nexus4 is selected for testing, equipped with Android 4.4.2 system. The system will not be able to use the camera when The management terminal prohibit it, furthermore only when the state is set to allow the camera be used properly. Our system-level program sysunistall cannot be uninstalled as expected. Protection mechanisms remain effective even if after formatting, while management terminal is also normal used and cannot be uninstalled maliciously.

Our application's Interface and application uninstall interface in Android setting is shown in Fig.6

Fig. 6. Authorization interface of management terminal

The top 20 camera applications from Google Play Downloads Center which locate 20 and the system itself are selected to be tested. The results show that the camera cannot be called by the 21 applications when they are set to be disabled and the camera can be called when they are set to be abled. The specific results are shown in Table 1.

Table 1. Camera Apps' Effectiveness in System-level Permission Management Mechanism

	Google Camera	Camera for Android	HD Camera Ultra	Candy Camera	Camera360 Ultimate	Magic Effects Camera	Selfie Camera
Allow	√	√	√	√	√	√	√
Forbid	×	×	×	×	×	×	×

	Grid Camera	Twin Camera	Camera 720	Camera Nexus 7	Silent Camera	Wink Camera	Cartoon Camera
Allow	√	√	√	√	√	√	√
Forbid	×	×	×	×	×	×	×

	Google Camera	Camera HD	Night Camera	Beauty Camera	Camera Effect	PIP Camera	Camera FV-5
Allow	√	√	√	√	√	√	√
Forbid	×	×	×	×	×	×	×

Notice: √ is for that the camera app running correct in corresponding permission.
× is for the camera app running correct in corresponding permission.

The system management interface of the "Camera 360" is an example of these testing applications, which is at the first list of camera application and has been downloaded 20.34 million times before. The comparison between before and after authorization of management terminal application is shown in Fig.7.

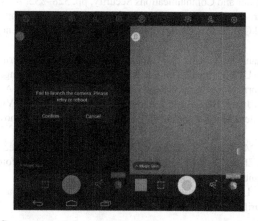

Fig. 7. Contrast interface on whether management terminal authorizes

5   Conclusion

In this paper, the camera is taken as an example to explain the new permission management model which is designed on Android system-level. This security system is particularly applicable in some of the need for strict control of the phone hardware or special requirements, such as private agencies and units. In addition, the system-level permission management model is proposed to achieve management based on the security management strategy developers in some android embedded systems. Through the mechanism, it will be safe and easy to manage android hardware devices. For example, cameras can be turned off automatically when it is in some secret places so that work efficiency and keep secret can be improved.

At present, the software development and test have been completed. All the features of the initial design have reached and a unique system-level permission management mechanism has been built. Another way to call Android is double call. One is to control the switch of hardware and the other is to control the interaction of information, such as Bluetooth and WIFI. In the future, multi-line calling to the android system and attaching more android hardware re-sources to this security mechanism will be the key point.

References

1. Bao, K.-j., Peng, Z.: An Extended Android Application Permission Management Model. Computer Enginieering 18, 15 (2012)
2. Enck, W., Ongtang, M., McDaniel, P.: On lightweight mobile phone application certification. In: Proceedings of the 16th ACM Conference on Computer and Communications Security, pp. 235–245. ACM Press, USA (2009)
3. Nauman, M., Khan, S., Zhang, X.: Apex:Extending android permission model and enforcement with user-defined runtime constraints. In: Proceedings of the 5th ACM Symposium on information, Computer and Communications Security, pp. 328–332. ACM, USA (2010)
4. Di Cerbo, F., Girardello, A., Michahelles, F., Voronkova, S.: Detectionof Malicious Applications on Android OS. In: Proceeding of the 4th International Conference onComputational Forensics (2011)
5. Nauman, M., Khan, S., Zhang, X.: Apex: Extending AndroidPermission Model and Enforcement with User-Defined Runtime Constraints. In: Proceedings of the 5th ACM Symposium on Information, Computer and Communications Security, ASIACCS (2010)
6. Han, K.S., Lee, Y., Jiang, B., GyuIm, E.: Android Permission System Violation: Case Study and Refinemen. International Journal of E-Entrepreneurship and Innovation (IJEEI) 4(1), 16–27 (2013)
7. Banuri, H., Alam, M., Khan, S., Manzoor, J., Ali, B., Khan, Y., Yaseen, M., Tahir, M.N., Ali, T., Alam, Q., Zhang, X.: An Android runtime security policy enforcement framework. Personal and Ubiquitous Computing 16 (2012)
8. Fang, Z., Han, W., Li, Y.: Permission based Android security: Issues and countermeasures. Computers & Security (2014)

Enhancing Security of the Android Platform via Multi-level Security Model

Ji-Soo Oh[1], Min-Woo Park[1], and Tai-Myoung Chung[2],*

[1] Department of Electrical and Computer Engineering
Sungkyunkwan University, Suwon, Korea
{jsoh,mwpark}@imtl.skku.ac.kr
[2] College of Information and Communication Engineering
Sungkyunkwan University, Suwon, Korea
tmchung@skku.edu

Abstract. The recent trend towards interconnection of all networked objects lets smartphones consolidates its position as a global interface between user and Internet. Smartphones are getting closer to our daily life, and at the same time security threats to privacy of smartphone users continue to proliferate at a rapid rate. Android is the most popular target of attackers among other mobile platforms. Although the Android provides permission based security model, there are still many security weak points which may lead to invasion of smartphone user's privacy. In this paper, we propose multi-level security model for enhancing Android security. Our security framework assigns security level to application at installation and performs runtime monitoring. We describe an implementation of our security framework, and finally evaluate the security and performance.

Keywords: Android, Mobile Phone Security, Permission Mechanism.

1 Introduction

The Information and Communication Technology is evolving to connect all physical objects (things) surrounding us, called Internet of Things (IoT). As we are moving towards the IoT, smartphones come to be the universal interface between IoT and users. Smartphones are going to play important roles in the vision of global infrastructure of networked objects. However, as smartphones are getting closer to our private and daily life, more and more malwares are watching for a chance to attack. Although various companies provide a lot of tools for protecting mobile devices from malware, [1] has found that 80% of smartphone remain unprotected from malware attacks. Especially, the Android operating system is the most popular prey for attackers, due to increased market share and the openness of Android. According to statistics of [2], 98.05% of known mobile malware targeted Android smartphone users in 2013.

---

* Corresponding author.

L. Batten et al. (Eds.): ATIS 2014, CCIS 490, pp. 13–24, 2014.
© Springer-Verlag Berlin Heidelberg 2014

The main security mechanism of Android is permission-based security model. Android regulates access to applications, sensitive data and system resources via permission labels. However, Android platform has several security short-comings. First, Attackers exploit vulnerabilities of permission checking in Intent mechanism which is used for communication between applications. There are two main types of vulnerabilities: Intent-based attack and privilege escalation attack. Second, malicious applications can be easily uploaded on the official market store, because anyone can register as an Android developer by simply paying a fee of $25. Moreover, developers can also distribute their application through unauthorized link. Lastly, Android users frequently install applications without worries about unnecessary permissions. Malicious applications tend to request more permissions than benign ones [3].

In this paper, we propose multi-level security framework to reduce the vulner-abilities of the Android platform. Our security framework assigns security level to all of installed applications and regulates Inter-Component Communication (ICC) depending on the security levels. Security administrators have to configure security level assignment policy at the time of platform development. They can adopt our security framework for reflecting their different security requirements. This framework based on multi-level security model can prevent Intent-based attack and privilege escalation attack.

The remainder of this paper is organized as follows. In section 2, we explain Intent mechanism which is Android's message passing system, security enforce-ment of Android and vulnerabilities of Intent. Section 3 describes our multi-level security framework. We show implementation of our framework in section 4 and evaluation in section 5. Finally we conclude the paper in section 6.

2   Android

2.1   Intent Mechanism

The Intent is a special message among components that is used to request or inform to other component. Android can provide Inter-Component Communica-tion (ICC) by using this Intent mechanism. The Intents can be divided into two groups: an explicit Intent and an implicit Intent. An explicit Intent designates the exact recipient by its component name. On the other hand, an implicit Intent does not name a target. When an implicit Intent occurs, Android finds the best component to handle the implicit Intent by comparing the contents of the Intent to the Intent filters. Explicit Intents are typically used for application-internal messages and implicit Intents are often used to activate components in other applications. The Broadcast Intent is a kind of an implicit Intent which is sent to all matched receivers. Broadcast intents are divided into normal broadcasts and ordered broadcasts. Any receivers which subscribe to a normal broadcast executes at the same time, while the ordered broadcasts are serially delivered to receivers in order of priority [4].

Android communicates with Activities, Services, and Broadcast Receivers through Intent mechanism. (Fig. 1) depicts three types of ICC. First, any component can start an Activity for a result by using both implicit Intent and explicit Intent (Fig. 1a). Second, any component can call a Service for background processing (Fig. 1b). Lastly, Activity, Service, and system send a Broadcast Intent, and related Broadcast Receivers serve for receiving event notifications (Fig. 1c) [5].

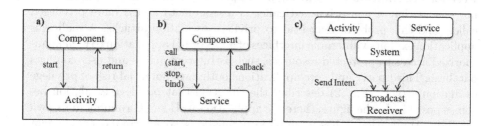

Fig. 1. Three types of Intent communication

2.2   Security Enforcement

Android's core security mechanism is permission-based security model. Applications declare the permissions they require, and smartphone user confirms the permissions at installation time. At runtime, Android mediates ICC based on the permission model using a reference monitor. The Android's reference monitor enforces mandatory access control (MAC) on ICC calls by reasoning about permissions assigned to applications [7]. If a component requests to send an Intent, the reference monitor checks permission assignments, and it allows ICC to proceed or denies ICC calls if the caller does not have the required permission. Traditional MAC policy regulates access on the basis of classification of the users and objects which have security levels. But, the MAC enforcement of Android's reference monitor does not provide information flow, so that there are various vulnerabilities in the security model. In the following, we explain two main types of vulnerabilities which are Intent-based attack and privilege escalation attack.

2.3   Intent Vulnerabilities

Intent-Based Attack. Due to the nature of Android, the implicit Intents can be delivered to unintended recipient by declaring an Intent filter, so that attackers could launch the Intent-based attack. The attackers receive unnecessary implicit Intents to invade smartphone user's privacy, because Intents may contain sensitive data of smartphone user. First of all, malicious applications can eavesdrop on broadcast Intents, and they intercept contents in these Intents. Denial of service attack on ordered broadcasts can also be launched by malicious applications. The malware receives the ordered broadcast Intent first by setting itself high priority and impedes delivery to other benign receivers by aborting it. These attacks occur in a type of ICC explained in the (Fig. 1c). Furthermore, malicious applications can launch Activity and Service hijacking attacks. The malware intercepts a request that starts an Activity or a Service using implicit Intent, and then it starts attacker's component in place of the intended one. This hijacking attack takes place in cases described in (Fig. 1a) and (Fig. 1b) [8].

Privilege Escalation Attack. Android's permission-based security model does not ensure that a non-privileged caller is restricted to access more privileged callee, and this problem may lead to privilege escalation attacks. A malicious application exploits vulnerable interfaces of a privileged application to gain unauthorized access to protected resources, such as Internet access and user contacts database. Third party and core applications both have potential risk of privilege escalation attack. (Fig. 2) describes the situation that privilege escalation becomes possible. In the figure, there are application A, B and C running in its own sandbox. Application A has no granted permissions, so A's components cannot access to application C because of Android permission mechanism. But in this case component C1 in application A can access component C3 in application C. Component C2 is not guarded by any permissions, so that it is accessible by any other components including application A. Moreover, C2 can access C3 because the application B is granted P1 permission. Therefore, component C1 is able to access C3 via C2 without any requested permission.

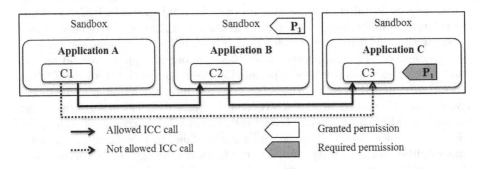

Fig. 2. Privilege Escalation Attack on Android [6]

3 Multi-level Security

In this section, we explain the design and architecture of the multi-level security model for Android platform. Android's security model provides MAC enforcement to control ICC via reference monitor. The reference monitor protects applications and system resources by mediating ICC based on application permissions, but there are various vulnerabilities which threaten smartphone users. To reduce the vulnerabilities, we introduce the concept of the security level to Android platform. Our security framework assigns security level to application at installation and performs runtime monitoring. When a company wants to provide secure platform to employees or when platform developer takes on the work for handling sensitive information, they can adopt our security framework into their system.

3.1 Architecture

The overall architecture of our security framework is described in (Fig. 4). The application framework in Android platform provides high-level building blocks for supporting applications. Package Installer, Package Manager, and Activity Manager are contained in the application framework, and they are involved in application installation and Intent mechanism. Therefore, we extend the application framework for enhancing Android security. In our proposal, we newly add Level Manager, Security level assignment policy, and Security Levels database into the application framework. Furthermore, to apply new modules into the platform properly, we modified Package Manager and Activity Manager.

Operation of our security framework is composed of application installation and ICC call handling. At installation procedure, our framework assigns proper security level to applications depending on the pre-defined policy which differs based on security requirements. In general, applications which handle sensitive resources must be assigned high level, and applications which have a potential threat must be assigned low level. At runtime, the modified reference monitor regulates ICC establishment according to the multi-level security rules as well as permission labels.

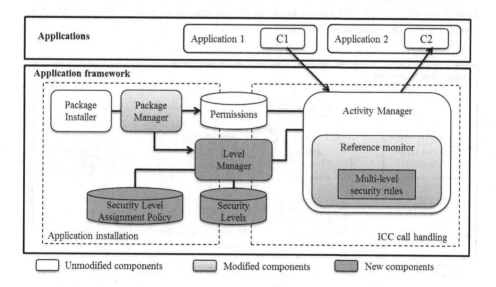

Fig. 3. Overall architecture of the multi-level security framework

3.2   Application Installation

First of all, security administrators have to configure security level assignment policy with their different security requirements at the time of platform development. The security level assignment policy is very important in our framework, since the policy affects security strength of the system. More fine-grained security level may satisfy more security requirements, but it increases complexity of definition and management. The policy includes rules for deciding application's security level, the number of security levels, and so on. After that, security administrators determine security levels of pre-installed applications depending on the policy, while the security levels of third-party applications are set at application installation by Level Manager. Security levels of both pre-installed and third party applications are stored in the Security Levels database.

When a smartphone user wants to download an Android application, the platform starts procedure of application installation. Firstly, Package Installer which provides user interface for installation shows required permissions list of the application. At this point, the user decides whether or not to grant all requested permissions. If the user allows, Package Manager starts installing APK file of the application. Package Manager is responsible for handling information about all applications loaded in the platform, so it parses the manifest file and extracts package information like permissions or Intent filters. At last, Package Manager calls Level Manager API and passes the parsed information as a parameter. Level Manager determines security level of the application according to the package information and security level assignment policy. After the process is complete, Level Manager subsequently stores the security level into the Security Levels database. (Fig. 5) shows an application installation part of (Fig. 4) and describes entire procedure briefly.

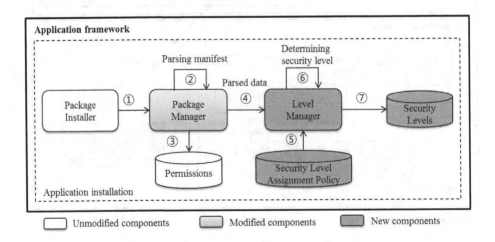

Fig. 4. Procedure of application installation

3.3   ICC Call Handling

The key part of the Android's security mechanism is a reference monitor in the application framework. When a component initiates ICC, the reference monitor checks permissions assigned to its containing application and provides MAC enforcement. Therefore, we modify the reference monitor for handling ICC establishment depending on the security levels as well as permissions. We control implicit Intent and explicit Intent differently according to the multi-level security rules. The rules are as follows: Implicit Intent from high level component cannot flow to low level component, while low level component is restricted to send explicit Intent to high level component. The framework has an exception that normal broadcast Intent from system is always allowed because it is free from risk. The multi-level security rules are described in (Fig. 5) as a flow chart.

Intent-based attack is caused by delivery of implicit Intent to malicious application, and on the contrary, privilege escalation attack occurs in the way malicious application sends Intents for exploiting vulnerability of benign application. Therefore, we set information flow in the opposite direction to prevent Intent-based attack and alleviate privilege escalation attack at the same time. There is a limitation that our framework hard to prevent from privilege escalation using implicit Intent.

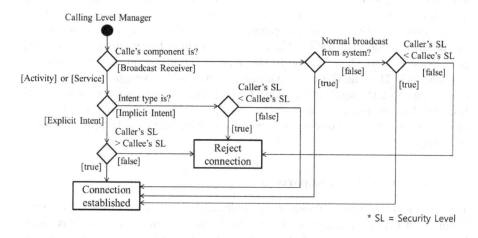

Fig. 5. Flow chart of ICC call handling

4   Implementation

We implement multi-level security framework based on the Android 4.4.2 sources. We extend the Activity Manager and Package Manager in application framework and add Level Manager. In the following, we explain in detail how Android was modified to implement our prototype as presented in section 3.

4.1   Security Level Assignment

We implement the procedure of security level assignment by redesigning the application installation modules in application framework. As presented in section 3.2, when a smartphone user downloads a third-party application, Package Manager is called by Package Installer. installPackageLI() of PackageManagerService API stores meta-data of the application in the middle of installation. This method parses the manifest via PackageParser. parsePackage() and keeps it as an object of Package class. After that, this Package object is passed to levelAssignment() of Level Manager as a parameter. Any other information of the application can also be passed according to the security level assignment policy of the system.

levelAssignment() analyzes passed information and decides security level according to the pre-defined policy. For implementation of our prototype we define sample policy which can generally be used. This policy is based on three level security: pre-installed application, trusted third-party application and untrusted third-party application. Our prototype can be used appropriately in case several specialized applications are pre-installed exclusively for finance or health-care, so the Android device need high security to handle critical information like user's medical records.

Third-party applications are classified as trusted or untrusted applications via a simple checklist listed in (Fig. 6). If user downloads Android application via unauthorized way, there is a possibility of downloading malicious application. So, we check whether installer application is Google official market or not using package name of installer. Moreover, we confirm the number of requested permission is more than 11, due to the average number requested by malicious application is 11 while the average number requested by benign application is 4. Lastly, we check the application requests the permissions that malicious applications tend to request more frequently [3]. After determination of security level, Level Manager stores the security level and package name of the applications in Hashmap.

4.2   Security Level Comparison

We modify the reference monitor to implement comparison of security levels. When an ICC establishment starts, we check whether component name is specified in Intent or not to identify Intent type. The Intent type and package names of caller and callee are passed to comparingLevels() of Level Manager as parameters, and then the method performs comparison of security levels. In case of broadcast Intent, if the caller of ICC is Android system, the procedure of security level comparison is skipped. Android provides three types of ICC like (Fig. 1), and there are various APIs for each ICC type.

Accordingly, we add a process of calling comparingLevels() into such APIs (Fig. 7). First, we modify startActivityMayWait() of ActivityStackSupervisor API for in case of (Fig. 1a), because the method is commonly called by some

Three level security

	Applications	Security level	
⬆ Implicit Intent ⬇	Pre-installed application	1	⊓ Explicit Intent ⬇
	Trusted third-party application	2	
	Untrusted third-party application	3	

Checklist for third-party applications

- Installer package name != "com.android.vending"
- The number of requested permissions >= 11
- The permissions contains more than 5 of the followings
    1. android.permission.INTERNET   6. android.permission.READ_SMS
    2. android.permission.READ_PHONE_STATE   7. android.permission.WRITE_SMS
    3. android.permission.ACCESS_NETWORK_STATE   8. android.permission.SEND_SMS
    4. android.permission.ACCESS_WIFI_STATE   9. android.permission.RECEIVE_SMS
    5. android.permission.RECEIVE_BOOT_COMPLETED   10. android.permission.VIBRATE

Fig. 6. Sample policy for implementation of the security framework

methods which start Activity. Second, we modify startServiceLocked() and bind-ServiceLocked() of ActiveService API for in case of (Fig. 1b). Lastly, broad-castIntentLocked() of ActivityManagerService API is modified for delivery of broadcast Intent. When modified APIs perform ICC establishment, comparing-Levels() of Level Manger is called. The method gets security levels of caller and callee which are mapped with each of their package names in the Hashmap. If caller and callee have the same security level, then it allows ICC. If not, then the method performs comparison of security levels according to the multi-level security rules.

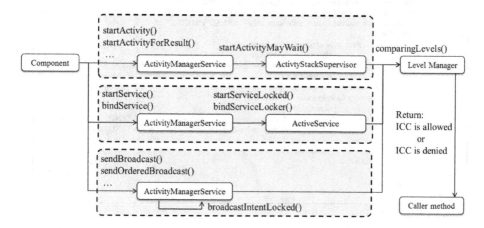

Fig. 7. Calling comparingLevels() method

5   Evaluation

5.1   Security Analysis

We assume that a smartphone user downloads a malicious application through Social Network Service (SNS), and the application tries Intent-based attack to eavesdrop the user's SMS. This application requests several sensitive permissions for collecting and leaking the SMS information, and the user grants them without any concern. The manifest of the malicious application is presented in (Fig. 8).

To evaluate our framework's security capabilities, we show that our prototype can prevent the malicious application's Intent-based attack. We manually inspect the manifest based on the sample policy as presented in section 4.1. First, this malicious application is installed via unauthorized link which is SNS not Google official market. Second, it requires 11 permissions for eavesdropping SMS and for surveillance of the smartphone's status. Third, 8 of requested permissions are included in the list of dangerous permissions which is specified in the sample policy. Accordingly, the application is assigned security level 3, and it can only receive implicit Intent from other untrusted third-party applications. As a result, our prototype protects the sensitive information of the smartphone from the eavesdropper's Intent-based attack.

```
<? xml version="1.0" encoding="utf-8"?>
<manifest>
          <uses-permission android:name="android.perimission.INTERNET" />
          <uses-permission android:name="android.perimission.WRITE_SMS" />
          <uses-permission android:name="android.perimission.BROADCAST_SMS" />
          <uses-permission android:name="android.perimission.READ_SMS" />
          <uses-permission android:name="android.perimission.RECEIVE_SMS" />
          <uses-permission android:name="android.perimission.RECEIVE_MMS" />
          <uses-permission android:name="android.perimission.SEND_SMS" />
          <uses-permission android:name="android.perimission.ACCESS_NETWORK_STATE" />
          <uses-permission android:name="android.perimission.ACCESS_WIFI_STATE" />
          <uses-permission android:name="android.perimission.READ_PHONE_STATE" />
          <uses-permission android:name="android.perimission.READ_PROFILE" />
          <application>
                    <receiver android:name=".SmsReceiver">
                              <intent-filter android:priority="1000">
                                        <action android:name="android.provider.Telephony.SMS_DELIVER />
                              </intent-filter>
                    </receiver>
                    <activity android:name=".SmsActivity">
                              <intent-filter>
                                        <action android:name="android.intent.action.SEND" />
                                        <action android:name="android.intent.action.SENDTO" />
                                        ...
                              </intnet-filter>
                    </activity>
                    ...
          </application>
</manifest>
```

Fig. 8. Manifest of the malicious application

5.2   Performance Evaluation

We evaluate performance of our prototype using Android Debug Bridge (ADB) which is a versatile command line tool that lets developer communicate with connected Android-powered device [4]. We use vmstat command at ADB shell. Vmstat provides information about resource usage statistics of Android device.

We compare our prototype with the original Android platform by observing CPU utilization during installation of APK files of Chrome and Facebook. Line graphs in (Fig. 9) shows results of the comparison. The dark lines represent our prototype and the light lines represent the original platform. In both cases of Chrome and Facebook, the basic shapes of the dark line and the light line are similar. However, as we can see, our prototype has a lightweight overhead on the whole graphs. Therefore, our multi-level security framework improves security of Android platform with less system loads.

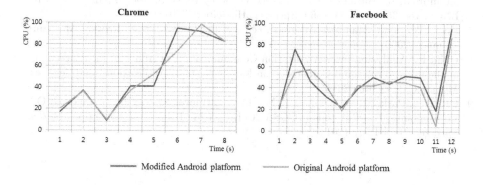

Fig. 9. CPU utilization during installing APK files

6   Conclusion

In this paper, we explain Android's security mechanism and main vulnerabilities which are Intent based attack and privilege escalation attack. To address the problems we propose multi-level security model for Android platform. Our security framework assigns proper security level to applications and controls ICC depending on the security levels. We describe an implementation of the framework's prototype in detail and an evaluation on security and performance.

Further, we plan to extend our security framework to reduce other security threats in Android. There are several vulnerabilities that we do not considered in this paper, so we aim to build a security framework which handles all possible threats in Android platform.

Acknowledgments. This work was supported by the ICT R&D program of MSIPIITP. [2014-044-072-003 , Development of Cyber Quarantine System using SDN Techniques].

References

1. Juniper Research, Mobile Security. BYOD, mCommerce, Consumer & Enterprise 2013-2018 (October 2013)
2. Funk, C.: Kapersky security Bulletin 2013 (December 2013)
3. Zhou, Y.: Dissecting Android Malware: Characterization and Evolution (May 2012)
4. Android Developers Google, http://developer.android.com/
5. Enck, W.: On Lightweight Mobile Phone Application Certification. In: Proceedings of the 16th ACM Conference on Computer and Communications Security (CCS) (November 2009)
6. Davi, L., Dmitrienko, A., Sadeghi, A.-R., Winandy, M.: Privilege escalation attacks on android. In: Burmester, M., Tsudik, G., Magliveras, S., Ilić, I. (eds.) ISC 2010. LNCS, vol. 6531, pp. 346–360. Springer, Heidelberg (2011)
7. Enck, W.: Understanding Android Security. IEEE Security & Privacy Magazine (January 2009)
8. Chin, E.: Analyzing Inter-Application Communication in Android. In: Proceedings of the 9th International Conference on Mobile System, Applications, and Services, MobiSys 2011 (June 2011)
9. Oh, J.-S., Park, M.-W., Chung, T.-M.: The multi-level security for the android OS. In: Murgante, B., et al. (eds.) ICCSA 2014, Part IV. LNCS, vol. 8582, pp. 743–754. Springer, Heidelberg (2014)

A Competitive Three-Level Pruning Technique for Information Security

Morshed Chowdhury[1], Jemal Abawajy[1], Andrei Kelarev[1],
and Kouichi Sakurai[2]

[1] School of Information Technology, Deakin University
221 Burwood Hwy, Melbourne 3125, Australia
{morshed.chowdhury,jemal.abawajy}@deakin.edu.au,
andreikelarev-deakinuniversity@yahoo.com
[2] Department of Informatics, Kyushu University-Ito Campus, Fukuoka, Japan
sakurai@csce.kyushu-u.ac.jp

Abstract. The reduction of size of ensemble classifiers is important for various security applications. The majority of known pruning algorithms belong to the following three categories: ranking based, clustering based, and optimization based methods. The present paper introduces and investigates a new pruning technique. It is called a Three-Level Pruning Technique, TLPT, because it simultaneously combines all three approaches in three levels of the process. This paper investigates the TLPT method combining the state-of-the-art ranking of the Ensemble Pruning via Individual Contribution ordering, EPIC, the clustering of the K-Means Pruning, KMP, and the optimisation method of Directed Hill Climbing Ensemble Pruning, DHCEP, for a phishing dataset. Our new experiments presented in this paper show that the TLPT is competitive in comparison to EPIC, KMP and DHCEP, and can achieve better outcomes. These experimental results demonstrate the effectiveness of the TLPT technique in this example of information security application.

Keywords: pruning techniques, ensemble classifiers, phishing, k-means, directed hill climbing.

1 Introduction

Pruning reduces the size of large ensembles at the same time improving their performance. The reduction of size is crucial for the development of effective classifiers required for the security of dynamic and distributed web services (cf. [34]), wireless sensor networks (cf. [11,33,41,42,43,48]) and smartphones (cf. [29,32]), which have been actively investigated recently.

This paper introduces and investigates a new pruning method called Three-Level Pruning Technique, TLPT. According to the taxonomy given in [44], pruning algorithms belong to the following three categories: ranking based, clustering based, and optimization based methods. The TLPT is a general technique which operates as a three-level process. It consecutively invokes ranking, clustering and

L. Batten et al. (Eds.): ATIS 2014, CCIS 490, pp. 25–32, 2014.

optimization based methods at each of the three levels, respectively. First, it ranks all instances of the base classifiers in the ensembles and selects a percentage of the higher ranked classifiers for further analysis. Second, it applies an appropriate clustering algorithms to the selected base classifiers. Finally, within each of the formed clusters it utilizes an optimization strategy to choose base classifiers for the final ensemble.

The aim of this paper is to demonstrate the competitiveness of the TLPT pruning in comparison to other pruning techniques. In this paper, we use the state-of-the-art ranking heuristic of the Ensemble Pruning via Individual Contribution ordering, EPIC [28]. The EPIC ranking heuristic combines accuracy, diversity and predictions in the minority group to rank individual contribution of classifiers. Further, we invoke clustering used in the K-Means Pruning, KMP [12]. The KMP applies the well-known standard k-means clustering algorithm and then selects in each cluster the single base classifier that is most distant to the rest of the clusters [12]. Finally, the optimisation algorithm Directed Hill Climbing Ensemble Pruning, DHCEP [44], is applied to each cluster obtained previously. For each cluster, DHCEP uses its greedy search strategy by adding to each subensemble the next base classifier that belongs to the same cluster and makes the most significant improvement to the whole ensemble.

We undertake a case study of the effectiveness of TLPT in the particular application of phishing email detection, since this is an important area and there is a ready large classifier suitable for such experiments, see Section 4. Our tests compare the performance of the TLPT pruning with three pruning algorithms: EPIC [28], KMP [12], and DHCEP [44]. The TLPT method produced better results.

Sections 2 and 3 give a brief overview of the previous work. Section 4 is devoted to the large ensemble classifier used in our experiments. The outcomes of the experimental evaluation are presented in Section 5. Finally, conclusions are given in Section 6.

2   Previous Work on Pruning

We refer to [44] for a taxonomy of ensemble pruning methods and a vast account of previous work on pruning. A pruning algorithm based on frequent patterns and Boolean matrices is studied in [51]. A Modified Backtracking Ensemble Pruning algorithm, ModEnPBT, is proposed in [9]. It is a backtracking optimization algorithm relying on a depth-first search. Harmony search is a music inspired algorithm to prune and select the best combination of classifiers. The paper [37] compares the effectiveness of the Harmony search pruning and ensembles produced by the AdaBoost and Bagging. Harmony search is also used to prune parallel ensembles for malware detection in [38]. A genetic algorithm-based ensemble pruning algorithm is presented in [4]. Margin-based ordered aggregation for ensemble pruning is studied in [13]. A competitive ensemble pruning based on cross-validation is proposed in [8]. Diversity regularized ensemble pruning is studied in [26]. The classifiers are combined by voting and the pairwise diversity is measured to select base classifiers. The paper [50] investigates pruning ensembles created with both labelled and unlabeled data.

3 Previous Work on Phishing

The readers are referred to [15,16,23,24,25] for more information. The papers [14] and [5] investigated a hybrid feature selection approach based on a combination of content-based and behaviour-based features. The paper [25] is devoted to unsupervised authorship analysis of phishing webpages that aims to enable advanced analysis of phishing attacks beyond basic exploratory studies. The paper [21] analyses the results of a phishing exercise conducted to train users cultivating users resistance against phishing attacks. A different game design framework for training users against phishing was investigated in [6]. The article [35] investigated both phishing emails and webpages. A robust technique counteracting phishing was proposed in [7]. It is based on new inputs not considered previously in a single protection platform. The paper [27] proposes a new phishing webpage detection approach based on so-called transductive support vector machine, TSVM, which is a semi-supervised learning method. A behaviour-based model for trustworthiness testing was proposed in [36]. The model was described using the notion of a Finite State Machine.

4 Automatically Generated Multi-level Meta Classifier

The Automatically Generated Multi-Level Meta Classifiers, AGMLMC, can produce ensembles combining a large number of the base classifiers. Here we use AGMLMC that is generated by combining AdaBoost, Bagging and SMO classifier, because it achieved good performance in our previous journal article [1] and contains 400 base classifiers.

Note that other efficient multi-tier classifiers and multi-classifier systems for different tasks have been explored recently, for example, in [3,2,10,15,16,20,22,39,49]. The authors have shown in [1] that this AGMLMC classifier achieved good performance in comparison with several other hierarchical classifiers.

The AGMLMC classifier uses AdaBoost meta classifier. It generates and invokes several classifiers in succession. Each classifier is trained on the instances that have turned out more difficult for the preceding classifier. To this end all instances are assigned weights, and if an instance turns out difficult to classify, then its weight increases, [47]. Bagging (bootstrap aggregating), generates a collection of new sets by resampling the given training set at random and with replacement. These sets are called bootstrap samples. New classifiers are then trained, one for each of these new training sets. They are amalgamated via a majority vote [47]. The AGMLMC classifier uses SMO base classifier available in WEKA. SMO invokes Sequential Minimal Optimization in order to train a support vector machine. Let us refer to [31,47] for more information on AdaBoost, Bagging and SMO incorporated in the AGMLMC classifier.

5   Experimental Evaluation of Pruning Methods

This paper concentrates on the effectiveness of the TLPT technique and its competitiveness in comparison to the underlying basic pruning methods. This is why we use ready features extracted during work on our previous journal article [1] for the same data set. We refer to [1] also to the corresponding links to publicly available data. Let us include a concise overview in this section.

Our new experiments used a collection of simple features extracted during work on the paper [1]. The extraction of features is very important for applications, for example, see [17,18,19,30,40,45,46].

Our TLPT method accepts the required pruning percentage and number of clusters used at the clustering stage as parameters, and then applies the DHCEP algorithm to each of the clusters.

Table 1. F-measure of the pruned classifiers produced by the TLPT pruning algorithm for various percentages of the base classifiers in the resulting pruned ensemble classifiers

Pruning	TLPT		
percentage	5 clusters	10 clusters	15 clusters
20%	0.89	0.92	0.88
30%	0.93	0.95	0.92
40%	0.95	0.97	0.94
50%	0.96	**0.98**	0.95
60%	0.95	0.97	0.94
70%	0.93	0.94	0.92
80%	0.89	0.90	0.88
90%	0.85	0.85	0.84

Next, we include the results of experiments. All tables of outcomes in this paper include the F-measure, since it combines precision and recall into a single number evaluating performance of the whole system, [47]. The F-measure is equal to the harmonic mean of precision and recall

$$\text{F-measure} = \frac{2 \times \text{recall} \times \text{precision}}{\text{recall} + \text{precision}} \qquad (1)$$

The weighted average F-measure is contained in the standard WEKA output for all classifiers.

The F-measures of the pruned classifiers produced by the pruning algorithms for various percentages of the base classifiers are given in Table 1. For comparison, Table 2 includes the results obtained by the three standard algorithms. The table compares the performance of the TLPT method with the well-known DH-CEP, EPIC, and KMP phishing algorithms. The best outcomes were obtained by

Table 2. F-measure of the pruned classifiers produced by the standard pruning algorithms

Pruning percentage	DHCEP	EPIC	KMP
20%	0.82	0.86	0.76
30%	0.87	0.90	0.83
40%	0.89	0.92	0.86
50%	0.90	0.92	0.87
60%	0.89	0.91	0.87
70%	0.88	0.89	0.86
80%	0.86	0.87	0.84
90%	0.83	0.84	0.82

the TLPT pruning method for a 50% reduction in the number of base classifiers using 10 clusters at the clustering stage.

These results demonstrate that TLPT technique can be competitive in comparison to other methods and deserves investigation for other data sets too.

6 Conclusion

We introduced the TLPT method for pruning of large ensemble classifiers and carried out a case study of its performance for various percentages of reduction in the number of base classifiers. The experiments show that, for our dataset and large AGMLMC ensemble made up of 400 base classifiers, the TLPT methods consistently performed better than DHCEP, EPIC, and KMP phishing algorithms. The TLPT pruning turned out capable of maintaining high values of the F-measure of the ensemble for significant percentage of pruning reducing the size of the ensemble up to 20% of the original number of the base classifiers. The best F-measure of the pruned ensemble was achieved by the TLPT pruning method for a 50% reduction in the number of base classifiers using 10 clusters at the clustering stage. The outcomes obtained show that the TLPT technique can be effective.

Acknowledgments. The authors are grateful to three referees for thorough reports that have helped us to improve this paper. The second author was supported by Discovery grant DP0880501 from the Australian Research Council. The third author was supported by ARC Discovery grant DP0449469.

References

1. Abawajy, J., Kelarev, A., Chowdhury, M.: Automatic generation of meta classifiers with large levels for distributed computing and networking. Journal of Networks (to appear, 2014) (accepted in final form)

2. Abawajy, J., Kelarev, A., Chowdhury, M., Stranieri, A., Jelinek, H.F.: Predicting cardiac autonomic neuropathy category for diabetic data with missing values. Computers in Biology and Medicine 43, 1328–1333 (2013)
3. Abawajy, J.H., Kelarev, A.V., Chowdhury, M.: Multistage approach for clustering and classification of ECG data. Computer Methods and Programs in Biomedicine 112, 720–730 (2013)
4. Abdi, L., Hashemi, S.: GAB-EPA: A GA based ensemble pruning approach to tackle multiclass imbalanced problems. In: Selamat, A., Nguyen, N.T., Haron, H. (eds.) ACIIDS 2013, Part I. LNCS, vol. 7802, pp. 246–254. Springer, Heidelberg (2013)
5. Ahamid, I.R., Abawajy, J., Kim, T.H.: Using feature selection and classification scheme for automating phishing email detection. Studies in Informatics and Control 22, 61–70 (2013)
6. Arachchilage, N.A.G., Love, S.: A game design framework for avoiding phishing attacks. Computers in Human Behavior 29, 706–714 (2013)
7. Barraclough, P.A., Hossain, M.A., Tahir, M.A., Sexton, G., Aslam, N.: Intelligent phishing detection and protection scheme for online transactions. Expert Systems with Applications 40, 4697–4706 (2013)
8. Dai, Q.: A competitive ensemble pruning approach based on cross-validation technique. Knowledge-Based Systems 37, 394–414 (2013)
9. Dai, Q., Liu, Z.: ModEnPBT: A modified backtracking ensemble pruning algorithm. Applied Soft Computing 13, 4292–4302 (2013)
10. Dazeley, R., Yearwood, J.L., Kang, B.H., Kelarev, A.V.: Consensus clustering and supervised classification for profiling phishing emails in internet commerce security. In: Kang, B.-H., Richards, D. (eds.) PKAW 2010. LNCS, vol. 6232, pp. 235–246. Springer, Heidelberg (2010)
11. Doss, R., Chandra, D., Pan, L., Zhou, W., Chowdhury, M.: Dynamic addressing in wireless sensor networks without location awareness. Journal of Information Science and Engineering 26, 443–460 (2010)
12. Giacinto, G., Roli, F., Fumera, G.: Design of effective multiple classifier systems by clustering of classifiers. In: Proceedings of the 15th International Conference on Pattern Recognition, pp. 160–163 (2000)
13. Guo, L., Boukir, S.: Margin-based ordered aggregation for ensemble pruning. Pattern Recognition Letters 34, 603–609 (2013)
14. Hamid, I.R.A., Abawajy, J.: Hybrid feature selection for phishing email detection. In: Xiang, Y., Cuzzocrea, A., Hobbs, M., Zhou, W. (eds.) ICA3PP 2011, Part II. LNCS, vol. 7017, pp. 266–275. Springer, Heidelberg (2011)
15. Islam, R., Abawajy, J.: A multi-tier phishing detection and filtering approach. Journal of Network and Computer Applications 36, 324–335 (2013)
16. Islam, R., Abawajy, J., Warren, M.: Multi-tier phishing email classification with an impact of classifier rescheduling. In: 10th International Symposium on Pervasive Systems, Algorithms, and Networks, ISPAN 2009, pp. 789–793 (2009)
17. Islam, R., Tian, R., Batten, L., Versteeg, S.: Classification of malware based on string and function feature selection. In: CTC 2010: Proceedings of the Second Cybercrime and Trustworthy Computing Workshop, pp. 9–17 (2010)
18. Islam, R., Tian, R., Batten, L.M., Versteeg, S.: Classification of malware based on integrated static and dynamic features. Journal of Network and Computer Applications 36, 646–656 (2013)
19. Islam, R., Tian, R., Moonsamy, V., Batten, L.: A comparison of the classification of disparate malware collected in different time periods. Journal of Networks 7, 956–955 (2012)

20. Islam, R., Zhou, W., Chowdhury, M.U.: Email categorization using (2+1)-tier classification algorithms. In: Proceedings – 7th IEEE/ACIS International Conference on Computer and Information Science, IEEE/ACIS ICIS 2008, In conjunction with 2nd IEEE/ACIS Int. Workshop on e-Activity, IEEE/ACIS IWEA 2008, pp. 276–281 (2008)

21. Jansson, K., von Solms, R.: Phishing for phishing awareness. Behaviour & Information Technology 32, 584–593 (2013)

22. Jelinek, H.F., Abawajy, J.H., Kelarev, A.V., Chowdhury, M.U., Stranieri, A.: Decision trees and multi-level ensemble classifiers for neurological diagnostics. AIMS Medical Science 1, 1–12 (2014)

23. Kelarev, A., Brown, S., Watters, P., Wu, X.W., Dazeley, R.: Establishing reasoning communities of security experts for internet commerce security. In: Technologies for Supporting Reasoning Communities and Collaborative Decision Making: Cooperative Approaches, pp. 380–396. IGI Global (2011)

24. Layton, R., Brown, S., Watters, P.: Using differencing to increase distinctiveness for phishing website clustering. In: Cybercrime and Trustworthy Computing Workshop, CTC-2009, Brisbane, Australia (2009)

25. Layton, R., Watters, P., Dazeley, R.: Unsupervised authorship analysis of phishing webpages. In: 2012 International Symposium on Communications and Information Technologies, ISCIT 2012, pp. 1104–1109 (2012)

26. Li, N., Yu, Y., Zhou, Z.-H.: Diversity regularized ensemble pruning. In: Flach, P.A., De Bie, T., Cristianini, N. (eds.) ECML PKDD 2012, Part I. LNCS, vol. 7523, pp. 330–345. Springer, Heidelberg (2012)

27. Li, Y., Xiao, R., Feng, J., Zhao, L.: A semi-supervised learning approach for detection of phishing webpages. Optik – Int. J. Light Electron Opt. (2013), doi:10.1016/j.ijleo.2013.04.078

28. Lu, Z., Wu, X., Zhu, X., Bongard, J.: Ensemble pruning via individual contribution ordering. In: Proceedings of the 16th ACM SIGKDD International Conference on Knowledge Discovery and Data Mining, KDD 2010, pp. 871–880 (2010)

29. Moonsamy, V., Rong, J., Liu, S., Li, G., Batten, L.: Contrasting permission patterns between clean and malicious Android applications. In: Proceedings of the 9th International Conference on Security and Privacy in Communication Networks, SECURECOMM 2013, pp. 69–85 (2013)

30. Moonsamy, V., Tian, R., Batten, L.: Feature reduction to speed up malware classification. In: Laud, P. (ed.) NordSec 2011. LNCS, vol. 7161, pp. 176–188. Springer, Heidelberg (2012)

31. Negnevitsky, M.: Artificial Intelligence: A Guide to Intelligent Systems, 3rd edn. Addison Wesley, New York (2011)

32. Nguyen, A., Pan, L.: Detecting SMS-based control commands in a botnet from infected Android devices. In: Proceedings of the 3rd Workshop Applications and Technologies in Information Security, ATIS 2012, pp. 23–27 (2012)

33. Niu, W., Lei, J., Tong, E., Li, G., Shi, Z., Ci, S.: Context-aware service ranking in wireless sensor networks. Journal of Network and Systems Management 22, 50–74 (2014)

34. Niu, W., Li, G., Tang, H., Shi, Z.: Multi-granularity context model for dynamic web service composition. Journal of Network and Computer Applications 34, 312–326 (2011)

35. Ramanathan, V., Wechsler, H.: Phishing detection and impersonated entity discovery using Conditional Random Field and Latent Dirichlet Allocation. Computers & Security 34, 123–139 (2013)

36. Shahriar, H., Zulkernine, M.: Trustworthiness testing of phishing websites: A behavior model-based approach. Future Generation Computer Systems 28, 1258–1271 (2012)
37. Sheen, S., Aishwarya, S.V., Anitha, R., Raghavan, S.V., Bhaskar, S.M.: Ensemble pruning using harmony search. In: Corchado, E., Snášel, V., Abraham, A., Woźniak, M., Graña, M., Cho, S.-B. (eds.) HAIS 2012, Part II. LNCS, vol. 7209, pp. 13–24. Springer, Heidelberg (2012)
38. Sheen, S., Anitha, R., Sirisha, P.: Malware detection by pruning of parallel ensembles using harmony search. Pattern Recognition Letters 34, 1679–1686 (2013)
39. Stranieri, A., Abawajy, J., Kelarev, A., Huda, S., Chowdhury, M., Jelinek, H.F.: An approach for ewing test selection to support the clinical assessment of cardiac autonomic neuropathy. Artificial Intelligence in Medicine 58, 185–193 (2013)
40. Sun, L., Versteeg, S., Boztaş, S., Yann, T.: Pattern recognition techniques for the classification of malware packers. In: Steinfeld, R., Hawkes, P. (eds.) ACISP 2010. LNCS, vol. 6168, pp. 370–390. Springer, Heidelberg (2010)
41. Tissera, M., Doss, R., Li, G., Batten, L.: Information discovery in multidimensional wireless sensor networks. In: Proceedings of International Conference on information Networking, ICOIN 2013, pp. 54–59 (2013)
42. Tong, E., Niu, W., Li, G., Tang, D., Tang, H., Ci, S.: Bloom filter - based workflow management to enable QoS guarantee in wireless sensor networks. Journal of Network and Computer Applications 39, 38–51 (2014)
43. Tong, E., Niu, W., Li, G., Tang, H., Tang, D., Ci, S.: Hierarchical workflow management in wireless sensor network. In: Anthony, P., Ishizuka, M., Lukose, D. (eds.) PRICAI 2012. LNCS, vol. 7458, pp. 601–612. Springer, Heidelberg (2012)
44. Tsoumakas, G., Partalas, I., Vlahavas, I.: An ensemble pruning primer. In: Okun, O., Valentini, G. (eds.) Applications of Supervised and Unsupervised Ensemble Methods. SCI, vol. 245, pp. 1–13. Springer, Heidelberg (2009)
45. Vu, H.Q., Liu, S., Li, Z., Li, G.: Microphone identification using one-class classification approach. In: Applications and Techniques in Information Security, ATIS 2011, pp. 29–37 (2011)
46. Wang, X., Niu, W., Li, G., Yang, X., Shi, Z.: Mining frequent agent action patterns for effective multi-agent-based web service composition. In: Cao, L., Bazzan, A.L.C., Symeonidis, A.L., Gorodetsky, V.I., Weiss, G., Yu, P.S. (eds.) ADMI 2011. LNCS, vol. 7103, pp. 211–227. Springer, Heidelberg (2012)
47. Witten, I.H., Frank, E.: Data Mining: Practical Machine Learning Tools and Techniques. Elsevier/Morgan Kaufman, Amsterdam (2011)
48. Xu, Y., Niu, W., Tang, H., Li, G., Zhao, Z., Ci, S.: A policy-based web service redundancy detection in wireless sensor network. Journal of Network and Systems Management 21, 1–24 (2013)
49. Yearwood, J., Webb, D., Ma, L., Vamplew, P., Ofoghi, B., Kelarev, A.: Applying clustering and ensemble clustering approaches to phishing profiling. In: Kennedy, P.J., Ong, K., Christen, P. (eds.) Data Mining and Analytics 2009. Proc. 8th Australasian Data Mining Conference, AusDM 2009. CRPIT, vol. 101, pp. 25–34. ACS, Melbourne (2009)
50. Zhang, G., Zhang, S., Wang, C., Cheng, L.: Ensemble pruning for data dependent learners. Applied Mechanics and Materials, 135-136, 522–527 (2012)
51. Zhou, H., Zhao, X., Wang, X.: An effective ensemble pruning algorithm based on frequent patterns. Knowledge-Based Systems 56, 79–85 (2014)

Popularity Prediction of Tianya BBS Posts Based on User Behavior

Ge Li[1,2], Yue Hu[2], and Yanyu Yu[1,2]

[1] University of Science and Technology Beijing, Beijing, China
{lige,yuyanyu}@nelmail.iie.ac.cn
[2] Institute of Information Engineering, Chinese Academy of Sciences, Beijing, China
huyue@iie.ac.cn

Abstract. Predicting the popularity of online social networks information is an important task for studying the principle of the information diffusion. We here propose a popularity prediction model based on user behavior and historical information given by early popularity. Our approach is validated on datasets consisting of posts on Tianya BBS. Our experimental results show that the prediction accuracy is significantly improved with existing methods. We also analyze the influence of the temporal waveform of information diffusion for the linear prediction model.

Keywords: Social Networks, Tianya BBS, Popularity Prediction.

1 Introduction

Since the emergence of online social networks, Internet users are no longer just the consumers of network information, and they have become the producers. Users have brought unimaginable generation rate of information in online social networks. To solve the problem what information should be noticed, predicting the popularity of online content in online social networks has more and more attention.

Szabo and Huberman [1] proposed a method to predict the popularity of online content with linear regression method. They analyzed the popularity of YouTube videos and Digg stories and observed a high linear correlation between the log-transformed early and future popularities of online content up to a normally distributed noise. Based on that observation, they proposed a simple linear popularity prediction model, which was called Szabo and Huberman (S-H) model here. With this model, measuring access to given stories in Digg during the first two hours after posting to forecast their popularity 30 days ahead with a remarkable relative error of 10%, while YouTube videos were followed for 10 days to achieve the same relative error. Szabo and Huberman thought Digg stories quickly become outdated and YouTube videos are still found long after they are submitted to the portal. Therefore predictions were more accurate for which attention faded quickly. On the contrary, the content of the longer cycle will lead to larger statistical error.

L. Batten et al. (Eds.): ATIS 2014, CCIS 490, pp. 33–43, 2014.
© Springer-Verlag Berlin Heidelberg 2014

Pinto et al. [2] computing the number of views received per sampling interval (for example daily samplings) to predict the popularity of online content. Compared to the S-H model to predict views of YouTube videos, their models had significant reduction in relative squared errors, and larger reductions for videos that experience a high peak in popularity in their early days followed by a sharp decrease in popularity.

Bao et al. [3] analyzed the influence of structural characteristics for popularity prediction of short messages. They found that the popularity of content is well reflected by the structural diversity of the early adopters. Based on such a find, two approaches were proposed by incorporating the early popularity with the link density and the diffusion depth of early adopters.

Bandari et al. [4] predicted the popularity of news items on Twitter using features extracted from the content of news articles. They talked into account four features: the spectrum of the information, the category, subjectivity in the language and the named entities mentioned. Classifiers that they constructed had an overall accuracy of 84% on Twitter. This prediction method is suitable for short text information.

Online social network users tend to obtain and reply online content from their friends and other users who they focus on, so the diffusion of online social network information is under the influence of user behavior. There are differences of users' behavior, and these differences lead to the influence of different level on the popularity of online social network information. For example, news of the users who have a large number of fans is easier to be popular; the discussion among the users who are often active in online social networks makes information diffuse more. So establishing the prediction model of popularity of online social networking information should consider the influence of user behavior. We will use clustering algorithm to classifying users with user behavior as characteristics, then the classification results will apply to the popularity prediction of online social networking information.

In recent years, there has been a lot of research works in online social networks user behavior. Benevenut et al. [5] analyzed the user behavior in light of the clickstream data and the social graph. Their data analysis suggested insights into how users interact with each other in online social networks. Gyarmati et al. [6] presented a measurement framework to observe user behavior and addressed characterization of user behavior and usage patterns in online social networks. Maia et al. [7] divided the users into several categories with the user behavior as a characteristic parameter by clustering algorithm in online social networks, and they analyzed the influence of different user behavior feature to the user classification. These studies illustrate the importance of the user to research online social networks.

The social network data that we use is from Tianya BBS. It has almost 90 million registered users, and in the daily peak there are more than 1 million people at the same time on Tianya BBS. In 2013, FREE sector that is just one of hundreds of popular sector of Tianya BBS produced more than 1 million new posts. Users on Tianya BBS produce information by posting. Popularity of post can be represented by clicks and replies. The popularity prediction of Tianya BBS information is more challenging than that of other social network information. The first reason is that Tianya BBS is through the posts and users to build a network structure, unlike other social networks. There are complex connection relationship between Posts and users, so the BBS's structure can't simply be analyzed by a complex network model. Second, because the user can release any kinds of information format without Format limit and space constraints on Tianya BBS, such as the post that is only made of images and the long novel. Therefore using the method of semantic to analyze information of Tianya BBS is very difficult.

Users need to click a post to browse content of the post. There are many users browse posts that they should not browse only because of the striking title of posts. We don't think these posts affect the user. So we only consider the post replies without considering the post clicks, when we predict the popularity of posts. The popularity of online social networks information embodies in replies of Tianya BBS posts here. The more post replies, means that the higher the popularity of the post.

2   Popularity Prediction Models

In order to use the user behavior data to predict the popularity of social network, we first group users with similar behavior. Then we establish a new prediction method using the clustering centers that are taken though clustering users and the historical data that users reply posts.

2.1   Clustering User with Similar Behavior

There are differences behavioral characteristics between users on Tianya BBS. In the prediction of replies, consider each behavior of all the users is not realistic. So we first select some user behavior characteristics which are able to influence the spread of social network information. Then we group users according to their behavior characteristics for the convenience of processing user behavior.

On Tianya BBS every user has different behavior. We define our user feature vector as a vector of length eight, where each position contains information about the referred user. It is defined as follows: $u_j = \{f_1, f_2, f_3, f_4, f_5, f_6, f_7, f_8\}$ of user j. The user behavior characteristics we chose have some influence on the spread of information. Each user who is collected holds an individual feature vector. The eight features are detailed next.

1. **Number of Replies** (*f1*): Users' main activity is replying to posts on Tianya BBS. Through replying to posts, more users have the opportunity to browse these posts. So we chose this as one of user behavior characteristics. It could also indicate the potential of the user as a content consumer.
2. **Number of Followers** (*f2*): When some people are interesting in a user, they will follow the user. The more subscriptions made by the user, he is more famous. Users who are famous have influence on Tianya BBS. It also indicates the user potential as consumer.
3. **Number of Users Followed** (*f3*): The number of subscriptions received by the user. We considers each user as a channel. This is the number of different user information pages, or channels, a user has visited possibly when searching for posts.

It indicate the number of channels through which user can access to information. It also indicates the user potential as producer.

4. **Number of Logins** (f_4): this is how often the user logins in. The extent of users' activity also affects the social network information transmission.
5. **Number of Posts** (f_5): Users' another important activity is to write posts on Tianya BBS. These posts are the carriers of information. It could indicate the potential of the user as a producer.
6. **Age** (f_6): Each Tianya BBS user has also a timestamp relative to the time he performed his last login to the system. We consider as user age the time elapsed between the join date and the last login, or in other words, the amount of time that users had to perform all actions on Tianya BBS. New users and old users have different influence on the spread of social network information, so we think age is also one of user behavior we need to consider.
7. **Clustering coefficient** (f_7): This is a measure of the interconnection between the users and their neighbors. If user A subscribed to videos from user B and also to videos from user C, then there is a high probability of a subscription between users B and C.
8. **Reciprocity** (f_8): It indicates the probability of mutual subscriptions. The reciprocity of user i is the ratio $R_i = A/B$, where A is the number of reciprocal subscriptions user i has made and B represents all user i subscribers and subscriptions.

For obtaining "clustering coefficient" and "reciprocity", we need to calculate by users' and their neighbor's data. "Number of replies", "number of posts", "number of logins" and "age" contains attributes related to each individual user and "number of follows", "number of user follows", "clustering coefficient" and "reciprocity" holds attributes stemmed from the user social interactions.

We think these user behavior characteristics are all attributes that influence the spread of social network information on Tianya BBS. But for the other kinds social network other properties can be used, such as "number of retweet" on the weibo site. Our prediction model can still be used on these social networks. The reason we chose Tianya BBS to analyze is that it's difficult to use the method of semantic analysis and network structure to analyze complex structures and special form of the text of Tianya BBS. The method of user behavior is a good choice to analyze Tianya BBS.

In order to group users that share similar behavioral pattern we have used K-means as the clustering algorithm. K-means selects K points in space to be the initial guess of the K centroids. Remaining points are then allocated to the nearest centroid [8, 9]. The whole procedure is repeated until no points switches cluster assignment or a number of iterations is performed. We use the Clustering Identification Algorithm (CIA) to determine the value of K. An appropriate K value can make us more effectively get prediction results.

Algorithm 1 depicts our methodology. To help us define our stopping criteria, we can take any two centroid vector, for instance C_1 and C_2, and compute the difference between them as $d(C_1, C_2) = abs(\sum_{i=1}^{F}(C_1[i] - C_2[i])/F)$, where $abs(x)$ is the absolute value of x and F is the length of the vector, or the number of features. This difference measure ranges from 0 to 1. If d is below a certain threshold T we can argue that both vectors are very similar and then merge the users of the corresponding clusters into one single larger group. To be conservative, we use a threshold of $T = 10^{-3}$ and define our stopping criteria to be when a newly created cluster merges with an already merged one, for example, $(d\,(C_1, C2) < 10^{-3})$ AND $(d\,(C_2, C3) < 10^{-3})$.

Algorithm 1. Clustering Identification Algorithm

1: $K <= 2$;
2: **repeat**
3:　　$K <= (\,K + 1)$;
4:　　run K-means algorithm;
5:　　**for** (each cluster k returned by K-means) **do**
6:　　　　$C_k <=$ centroid of cluster k;
7:　　　　**if　then**
8:　　　　　　merge users from clusters k and x;
9:　　　　**end if**
10:　　**end for**
11: **until**
　;

After getting all of centroid vectors, we can classify new users. We define l_j as the category label of user j, that is:

$$l_j := \arg\min_i \left\| u_j - c_i \right\|^2$$

(1)

In this way, all the users can be divided into K classes.

2.2　Multivariate Linear Model Based on User Behavior (MLBU)

We establish multivariate linear model based on user behavior, because here is a high linear correlation between the early and future popularities of online content up to a normally distributed noise. Unlike other models, we consider the weight of User clustering results.

We define that the goal of our prediction models is to achieve the total number of replies $\hat{N}(v, t_r, t_t)$ predicted for post v up to day t_t based on data from the first t_r days($t_r < t_t$). The S-H model [1] uses the total number of replies of posts up to day t_r as input. We don't only consider these but also take into account the influence of different categories of users who reply the post. We can classify users who reply the post with Equation 1. After calculating all users' category, we think $x_i(v, t_r)$ is the number of replies of users whose category label l_j (of user j) is equal i in first t_r days. The vector $x_i(v, t_r)$ is defined as $X_k(v, t_r) = \big(x_1(v, t_r), x_2(v, t_r), \dots, x_k(v, t_r)\big)$ and we estimate the number of replies of the post v at t_t days as:

$$\hat{N}\left(v,t_r,t_t\right)=\Gamma_{\left(K,t_r,t_t\right)}\cdot X_K\left(v,t_r\right) \tag{2}$$

Where $\Gamma_{(K,t_r,t_t)} = (\gamma_1, \gamma_2, \dots, \gamma_K)$ is the vector of model parameters and depends only on K, t_r, and t_t.

We use the mean Relative Squared Error (mRSE) to evaluate the performance of the prediction models. Let $N(v,t_t)$ be the total number of replies post v receives up to day t_t ($N(v,t_t)$). For a collection C of posts, the mRSE is defined as the arithmetic mean of the Relative Squared Error values for all posts in C, that is:

$$mRSE = \frac{1}{|C|}\sum_{v\in C}\left(\frac{\hat{N}\left(v,t_r,t_t\right)}{N\left(v,t_t\right)}-1\right)^2 \tag{3}$$

Given a training set C, t_r and t_t, we can compute the optimal values for the elements of $\Gamma_{(K,t_r,t_t)}$ as the ones that minimize the mRSE on C, i.e.:

$$\arg\min\frac{1}{|C|}\sum_{v\in C}\left(\frac{\Gamma\left(K,t_r,t_t\right)\cdot X_K\left(v,t_r\right)}{N(v,t_t)}-1\right)^2 \tag{4}$$

We can solve this problem via gradient descent method. Then we can use our model predict the popularity of the posts. The aggregate results, in terms of mRSE, provided by our model should be always either equal or better than those generated by the S-H model. The complexity of our model is $O(nK^2)$.

2.3 The Influence of Temporal Waveform for the Linear Model

Reply of Posts on Tianya BBS has regular temporal waveform during life of the posts. Figure 1 shows two kinds of waveform: sudden waveform and continuous waveforms of hot posts reply. They also have a high linear correlation between the early and future popularities, but the correlations are different between them. The different will make linear models' error increased. So we hope to reduce the error through classify posts according temporal waveform of their replies.

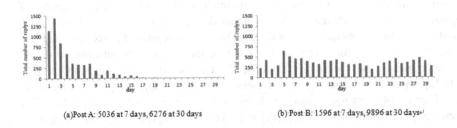

(a) Post A: 5036 at 7 days, 6276 at 30 days   (b) Post B: 1596 at 7 days, 9896 at 30 days

Fig. 1. Number of replies per day during the first 30 days of life of two Tianya BBS posts

Here we are using the K-SC (K-Spectral Centroid) method [10]. According to the temporal waveform of replies, posts are divided into two classes. We will show the detailed results and analysis of classification in section 3.3.

3   Experimental Results

3.1   Data Collection and User Clustering

We designed a Tianya BBS crawler to collect a sample from Tianya BBS based on a breadth-first search. This method starts with a set of users and adds other users who follow to the end of the list of available users [11]. The whole procedure is repeated until the crawler is manually stopped or the entire network component is exhausted. In this work, the users who reply the 10 hot posts of FREE sector constituted the initial set of users. For each user found in the search, we saved all information of the user including user behavior date such as the age, post, followers and so on.

We total collect 103,718 users' behavior data. We select eight features discussed in Section 2.1 of each user. Based on the aforementioned methodology, the yielded centroid vectors are displayed in table 1.

Table 1. Each Value of Ventroid Vectors, K=5

No.	Replies	Followers	Users followed	Logins	Posts	Age	Clustering Coefficient	Reciprocity
1	8410	18	7	882	615	1830	0.28	0.21
2	1007	1	1	127	1	546	0.09	0.15
3	1457	2	1	218	62	1351	0.32	0.18
4	2043	5	18	210	10	658	0.22	0.14
5	117	0	0	11	1	72	0.02	0.01

We collect 1,233 posts that are created in 2013 and replied over 1000 times. Using the above centroid vectors, we can get the category label of users who reply these posts. Then they were used as training set from which model parameters are learned.

3.2   Experimental Results of MLBU and S-H Model Results

Figure 2-a) shows mRSE values for both S-H models [1] and our MLBU models when predicting the popularity for a target date t_t equal to 30 days and various values of reference date t_r. If t_r is very small, there is too little information to get accurate prediction. So both models perform very similarly. When we use more historical data, mRSE will decrease rapidly. The mRSE produced by the MLBU and by the S-H models are less than 20%, if t_r is increased to 6 days. More importantly, Figure 2-a) shows that, outside these two extreme scenarios, the MLBU model leads to significant mRSE reductions over the S-H model, with gains in precision of 17.4%, on average.

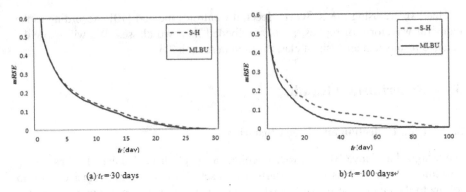

(a) $t_t = 30$ days   b) $t_t = 100$ days

Fig. 2. Model Prediction Errors (mRSE) as Function of Reference Date t_r for Various Target Dates t_t

For example, if we use $t_r = 15$ days, the mRSE produced by the ML and by the S-H models are 0.08223 and 0.0659, leading to an error reduction of 19.8%.

Figure 2-b) show similar patterns for results produced for $t_t = 100$. In the latter case, the reductions in mRSE values are even larger. For instance, if we use $t_r = 50$ to predict for $t_t = 100$, the mRSE produced by the MLBU and S-H models are 0.0206 and 0.0701, respectively, yielding a 60.4% error reduction on average.

We should determine the minimum number of daily samples so as to keep model errors below a given threshold, for the given target date t_t. For example, for $t_t=30$, we need to set t_r equal to at least 7 to keep the mRSE of our ML model below 20%.

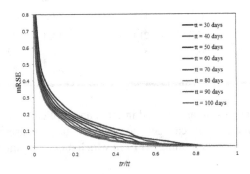

Fig. 3. Model Prediction Errors (mRSE) as Function of Fraction of History Monitored and Sampled

Figure 3 shows our model is sensitive to the choice of time, but its error is lower than other models. With the increase of t_t, model is more and more stable and error is lower.

According to the experimental results, we argue our prediction model is better than other prediction model ignoring the user behavior. So in the study of social network information transmission, we should pay more attention to the analysis of user behavior.

3.3   Experimental Results of the Influence of Temporal Waveform

In order to verify the influence of temporal waveform of the post replies for model prediction, we classify the post reply within 30 days (720 hours). According to the temporal waveform posts are divided into two classes. The result of Two types of waveform classification is shown in figure 4.

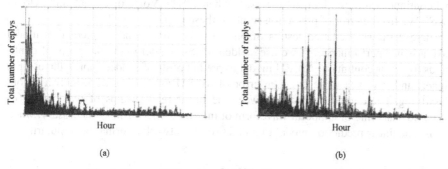

(a)   (b)

Fig. 4. Temporal Waveform of Two Classes Posts Replies

Table 2. Prediction Errors for MLBU Model, Sudden MLBU Model and Continuous MLBU Model for Posts of Two Kinds of Hot Topic (mRSE and 95% confidence intervals, t_r =7, t_t =30)

		Posts of the Sudden Topic		
Topic	Number of Posts	MLBU Model	sudden MLBU model	continuous MLBU model
the Judge in Shanghai	58	0.1821±0.0121	0.1762±0.0133	0.1812±0.0127
Urban inspector in Yan'an	102	0.1878±0.0064	0.1738±0.0062	0.1912±0.0067
Drink Driving in Tianshui	13	0.1952±0.0174	0.1827±0.0181	0.1878±0.0177
		Posts of the Sudden Topic		
Topic	Number of Posts	MLBU Model	sudden MLBU model	continuous MLBU model
Fangzhouzi vs. Hanhan	34	0.1872±0.0119	0.1814±0.0109	0.1681±0.0117
The Voice of China	26	0.1851±0.0091	0.1857±0.0093	0.1721±0.0089
Urban haze	128	0.1774±0.0044	0.1804±0.0035	0.1654±0.0038

Model Equations:

MLBU Model: $N(v, t_r, t_t) = 1.71x_1(v) + 2.21 \cdot x_2(v) + 2.14 \cdot x_3(v) + 2.09 \cdot x_4(v) + 1.32 \cdot x_5(v) + 1.23 \cdot x_6(v)$

Sudden MLBU model: $N(v, t_r, t_t) = 1.05 \cdot x_1(v) + 1.16 \cdot x_2(v) + 1.26 \cdot x_3(v) + 1.14 \cdot x_4(v) + 1.13 \cdot x_5(v) + 1.08 \cdot x_6(v)$

Continuous MLBU model: $N(v, t_r, t_t) = 1.81 \cdot x_1(v) + 2.02 \cdot x_2(v) + 2.74 \cdot x_3(v) + 3.09 \cdot x_4(v) + 2.59 \cdot x_5(v) + 1.36 \cdot x_6(v)$

The waveforms of figure 4-a fit the characteristics of sudden posts, and the waveform of figure 4-b fit the characteristics of continuous posts. We use two kinds of posts training our model respectively, then we get sudden MLBU model and continuous MLBU model.

We found posts of some hot topics on Tianya BBS in 2013.They are sudden topics: "the Judge in Shanghai", "Urban inspector in Yan'an", "Drink Driving in Tianshui" and continuous topics: "Fangzhouzi vs. Hanhan", "The Voice of China" and "Urban haze". We list the error of prediction result of these posts in table 2.

Table 2 shows Predicted results of posts by the corresponding prediction model have a better performance. If we use sudden MLSU model to predict posts of continuous topic (or continuous MLBU model to predict posts of sudden topic), the error is higher, and it's even more than the error of MLBU model that we establish before classifying. There are differences between the linear relationships of two classes of posts. So analyzing of temporal waveform of information diffusion is necessary, when we use the linear prediction model to predict social network information popularity.

4   Conclusions and Future Work

In order to predict popularity of Tianya BBS posts, we propose the new prediction model based on user behavior. Through the experiment the new model can get better results than the S - H model for the popularity prediction of social networking information. It shows that we should consider the influence of the user's behavior for social network information diffusion. Then we analyze the influence of the temporal waveform of replies for the linear prediction model.

Our finding provides a new perspective to understand the popularity prediction problem and is helpful to build accurate prediction models in the future. This method is not only suitable for BBS, also suitable for weibo and other online social network whose users have obvious behavior characteristic. According to the different online social network, we can select different user behavior characteristics, such as the number of '@' on the weibo, clustering coefficient and reciprocity on the online social community. We believe that more user behavior feature enables users clustering and popularity prediction of online social network information more accurately.

Acknowledgements. This work was supported by the National 973 Project (No. 2013CB329605).

References

1. Szabo, G., Huberman, B.: Predicting the popularity of online content. Communic of ACM 53(8) (2010)
2. Pinto, H., Almeida, J., Gonçalves, M.: Using early view patterns to predict the popularity of YouTube videos. In: Proc. WSDM (2013)
3. Bao, P., Shen, H., Huang, J., Cheng, X.: Popularity prediction in microblogging network: a case study on sinaweibo. In: WWW Companion, pp. 177–178 (2013)

4. Bandari, R., Asur, S., Huberman, B.A.: The pulseof news in social media: Forecasting popularity.CoRR, abs/1202.0332 (2012)
5. Benevenut, F., Rodrigues, T., Cha, M., Almeida, V.: Characterizing userbehavior in online social networks. In: Proc. of ACM SIGCOMM InternetMeasurement Conference. ACM (2009)
6. Gyarmati, L., Trinh, T.A.: Measuring User Behavior in Online Social Networks. IEEE-Network Magazine, Special Issue on Online Social Networks 24(5), 26–31 (2010)
7. Maia, M., Almeida, J., Almeida, V.: Identifyinguser behavior in online social networks. In: Proceedings of the 1st Workshop on Social Network Systems, pp. 1–6. ACM (2008)
8. Jain, A., Murty, M., Flynn, P.: Data Clustering: AReview. ACM Computing Surveys 31(3), 264–323 (1999)
9. Agichtein, E., Castillo, C., Donato, D., Gionis, A.: andG. Mishne. Finding High Quality Content in SocialMedia, with an Application to Community-BasedQuestion Answering. In: Proc. ACM Web Search andData Mining (WSDM), Stanford, CA, USA (February 2008)
10. Yang, J., Leskovec, J.: Patterns of temporal variation in online media. In: WSDM, pp. 177–186 (2011)
11. Lee, S.H., Kim, P.-J., Jeong, H.: Statistical Properties of Sampled Networks. Physical Review E 73, 016102 (2006)

Design and Implementation of Network User Behaviors Analysis Based on Hadoop for Big Data

Jianfeng Guan[1], Su Yao[2], Changqiao Xu[1], and Hongke Zhang[2]

[1] State Key Laboratory of Networking and Switching Technology
Beijing University of Posts and Telecommunications, Beijing, China, 100876
{jfguan,cqxu}@bupt.edu.cn
[2] National Engineering Laboratory for Next Generation Internet Interconnection Devices
Beijing Jiaotong University, Beijing, China, 100044
{13111027,hkzhang}@bupt.edu.cn

Abstract. The network user behaviors analysis under the big data environment is attractive to network security recently for that it can discover the abnormal user behaviors to prevent the potential threats. However, the user behaviors are dynamic which is difficult to capture the users' comprehensive behaviors in a single device by capturing or collecting the static dataset. More specially, the increase of the network users, network traffic and network services bring many challenges such as fast data collection, processing and storage. Therefore, we propose and implement a network user behaviors analysis system in this paper, which is based on the Hadoop distribution platform to capture the traffic and analyze the user behaviors in terms of the search keywords, user shopping trends, website posts and replies, and web visited history to acquire the uses' dynamic behaviors. To evaluate our system, we capture the packets in the campus networks, and the results show that our system can capture the users' long-term behaviors and acquire the user behaviors in detail.

Keywords: Big data, user behaviors analysis, Hadoop, search.

1 Introduction

The Network Behavior Analysis (NBA) is to monitor network for unusual behaviors, events or trends based on the network traffic statistic, which can be used to identify the potential security issues. While the user behaviors analysis aims to acquire the users' interests and hobbies in the Internet by capturing and analyzing the network traffic, visited logs, search keywords and so on. More recently, with the development of various online social networks, the user behavior analysis has attracted lots of attentions [1]. With the assist of the behaviors analysis, the network administrators can get the users' dynamic requirements and behaviors characters, and furthermore optimize the network management, Internet marketing [2], and service recommendation [3] and so on.

Currently, the network user behaviors can be acquired by analyzing the Web log, browsers history and network traffic [4]. The web log based method [5] cannot

L. Batten et al. (Eds.): ATIS 2014, CCIS 490, pp. 44–55, 2014.

acquire all users' network behaviors, and it only reflects a sequence of web pages accessing [6]. The browsers based method [7] needs to install the plugins in the browsers, and it can only be used to capture the users who have installed the related plugins in the clients. Therefore, it cannot reflect the all the users' behaviors. The network traffic based method captures all the packets in the given network which may include all the users' network behaviors information, and it can reflect users' multi-dimensional behaviors. However, most of traffic based methods only provide the simple traffic statistics and perform the protocol analysis below the application layer, which are difficult to discover the various applications information due to the limited hardware and software processing capacity. Therefore, it will take a long time to reassemble the TCP packets to acquire the application information, which cannot satisfy the current big data requirements [8] such as the large storage and fast processing.

In this paper, we propose and implement a distributed user behaviors analysis system to realize the network user behaviors analysis. The organization of this paper is shown as follows. Section 2 introduces the system components, Section 3 describes the function of each component, and Section 4 introduces the experiments and related results. Finally, Section 5 concludes this paper.

2   System Components

Fig.1 shows the system component structure of the proposed network user behaviors analysis system, which consists of the packet capture module, TCP reassemble

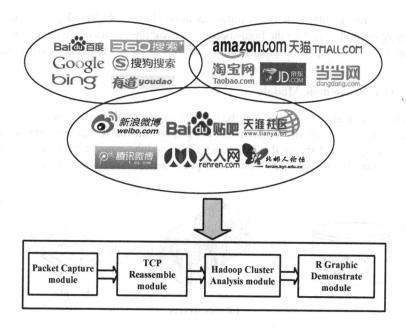

Fig. 1. Network user behaviors analysis system component

module, Hadoop cluster analysis module and R graphic demonstrate module. The proposed system can be deployed in the access networks to capture the various network applications information.

- **The packet capture module** clones all the traffic of the attached networks.
- **The TCP reassemble module** performs the coarse analysis, and it classifies the packets into the different sessions for further HTTP analysis. This module transfers the captured source files into the log files for the further analysis whose format is "Source IP @# Destination IP @# Source port @# Destination port @# host @# URL @# transfer address (refer) @# flag @# Post content @# flow length @# time". In which, the "@#" is the field separator, and "host" is the required web site host domain.
- **The Hadoop cluster analysis module** adopts the distributed Hadoop servers to deal with the TCP sessions in parallel to reduce the process time, and it performs the HTTP analysis to analyze the search keywords, user shopping tendency, website post and reply, website visited history.
- **The graphic demonstrate module** adopts the R language to show the graphic results.

3   System Functions Design

3.1   Packet Capture Module

Packet capture module is used for traffic monitor via the PF_RING [9] which is a zero-copy method to realize the high-speed packet capture by reducing the number of copy and CPU interrupt. It has many properties such as the device driver independent.

3.2   TCP Reassemble Module

Considering that HTTP packets may have TCP fragments that will result in packets disorder, our system adopts the Libnids [10] to perform the IP defragmentation and TCP assembly. Fig. 2 shows the TCP reassemble module, which abstracts the source IP, destination IP, source port, destination port, host IP address, URL, transfer IP,

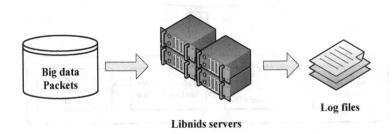

Fig. 2. TCP assembly module structure

Post content, traffic size, time information of the session, and stores them in the log files to realize the TCP reassembling.

3.3   Hadoop Cluster Analysis Module

Hadoop cluster analysis module consists of four parts involving the search keywords, shopping tendency, website post and reply, and website visited history to analyze the users' normal behaviors and abnormal behaviors for the subsequent network security management and other purposes. Fig. 3 shows its typical components. Besides, to improve the parallel computation speed, we can use the Spark [11], an open source in-memory distributed cluster system which is 100 times faster than Hadoop MapReduce in memory, or 10 times faster on disk.

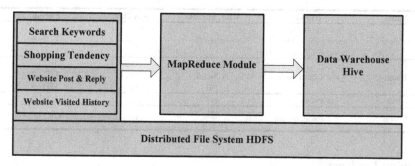

Fig. 3. Behavioral analysis module structure diagram

Search Keywords

Search engine is an important Internet service, and almost all Internet users adopt the "search-click" model to search what they want. In the user behaviors analysis, capturing or restoring the users' search keywords can locate the users' interests to optimize the network service and further find out the abnormal user.

Currently, these search keywords are generally transmitted through the HTTP GET method after being encoded and attached to the URL. Fig. 4 shows a typical URL encode format of "Baidu" search engine.

```
/s?ie=utf-
8&bs=dd&f=8&rsv_bp=1&rsv_spt=3&wd=%E6%B5%8B%E8%AF%95&rsv
_sug3=3&rsv_sug=0&rsv_sug1=2&rsv_sug4=150&inputT=4766
```

Fig. 4. The URL format of Baidu

In this example, the "wd=%E6%B5%8B%E8%AF%95" is the encoded search keyword, in which the "%E6%B5%8B%E8%AF%95" is the UTF-8 code of the Chinese character "Test". However, different search engines have different encode methods. To acquire the users' search keywords, we have to find out their encoding rules at first. After several tests, we summarize encoding rules of different search engines as shown in Tab. 1.

Based on these rules, it is easy to realize the keyword matching in MapReduce. In the stage of Map, it preprocesses the log file to reduce the incomplete records and match the HOST field to decode the search keywords. After acquired these keywords, it compare these keywords with the word segmentation repository [12] to find out the users' interests. In the end of this stage, it assigns the user ID as the key, and the keywords as the value for the Reduce stage. In the Reduce stage, it exports the User ID and its search keywords.

Table 1. Search engine keywords encode rules

Name	HOST	URL Format	Key flag	Encode
Google	www.google.com www.google.com.hk www.google.com.tw	/search?	q=	UTF-8
Baidu	www.baidu.com	/baidu? /s?word /s?	word= word= wd=	GB2312 UTF-8 UTF-8
360	www.so.com	/s?	q=	UTF-8
Sogou	www.sogou.com	/web? /sogou?	query=	GB2312

Shopping Tendency

The users shopping tendency analysis can provide the target AD and service recommendation. In term of the network security, it can be used to monitor the user's abnormal behaviors. For example, if a user buys some illegal or dangerous goods, it means this user may have harmful behavior in the future.

Similar to the search keyword analysis, currently most e-commerce websites provide the search service to inquire the target goods. Based on these input words, we can acquire the users' shopping tendency.

To do so, these websites adopt HTTP GET method to encapsulate the search words in the URL. For example, the Chinese character "爆炸" (English word is "explosive") in Taobao is ":/search?initiative_id=staobaoz_20130410&q=%D5%A8%D2%A9", and the "q=%D5%A8%D2%A9" is GB2312 encode of Chinese character "爆炸". After several tests, we summarize the encode rules of several e-commerce websites as shown in Table 2.

Table 2. The encode rules of e-commerce websites

Websites	HOST	URL Format	Key Flag	Encode
Taobao	s.taobao.com	/search?	q=	GB2312
Tmall	list.tmall.com	/search_product.htm? //search_product.htm?	q=	GB2312
JD	search.jd.com	/Search? /search?	keyword=	UTF-8 GB2312
Dangdang	search.dangdang.com	/?key	key=	GB2312
Amazon	www.amazon.cn	/s/	field-keywords=	UTF-8

The shopping tendency analysis is similar to that of the search keywords. In the Map stage, the user ID is the key, and the search words are the values. In the Reduce stage, the record (User ID, list (Shopping words)) is stored in the Hive for the future inquiry. After acquired these words, we can get the users' shopping tendency to capture their behaviors.

Website Post and Reply Analysis
Weibo, BBS and social networks are the important communication platforms. However, some lawbreakers use these platforms to spread rumors, and post some provocative information even some illegal information, which seriously affect the network security. Therefore, it is important to analyze the network users' post and reply information.

Table 3. The encode format of weibo services

Website	HOST	Format
Sina Weibo	weibo.com	text=UTF-8
Tencent Weibo	t.qq.com	content=UTF-8

Generally, the user's post and reply information are encapsulated in the HTTP POST method, and stored in the content field. Based on the Hadoop, we can abstract the content field, and decode them. In this paper, we mainly provide the Sina Weibo and Tencent Weibo encode format as shown in Table 3.

```
POST /aj/mblog/add?_wv=5&__rnd=1365600597848 HTTP/1.1\r\n
Host: weibo.com\r\n
Content-Length: 117\r\n
User-Agent: Mozilla/5.0 (Windows NT 6.1) AppleWebKit/535.11 (KHTML, like Gecko) Chrome/
    17.0.963.84 Safari/535.11 SE 2.X MetaSr 1.0\r\n
Content-Type: application/x-www-form-urlencoded\r\n
Accept-Encoding: gzip,deflate\r\n
text=%E5%A4%A7%E5%AE%B6%E5%A5%BD%E5%95%8A&pic_id=&rank=0&rankid=&_surl=&h
ottopicid=&location=home&module=stissue&_t=0
```

Fig. 5. The post format of Sina weibo

Table 4. The encapsulation formats of typical Chinese websites

Websites	HOST	Format
Baidu Tieba	tieba.baidu.com	content=UTF-8
Tianya	bbs.tianya.cn	content=UTF-8
Sina Weibo	weibo.com	content=UTF-8
Renren	status.renren.com gossIP.renren.com wpi.renren.com	c=UTF-8 body=UTF-8 <body>UTF-8<body>
Byr	bbs.byr.cn	content=UTF-8(content) subject=UTF-8(subject)
Zhixing	zhixing.bjtu.edu.cn	message=UTF-8

Fig. 5 shows an example of the post format of Sina weibo. We can get that the post content is stored in the HTTP POST method, which can be easily got. As for the reply, we mainly focus on the Baidu Tieba, Tianya, Sina weibo, Renren, Byr and Zhixing, and their data encapsulation formats are shown in table 4.

We take the Renren as an example to demonstrate the post content formation. We post "Hello, world 测试一下哈!" in Renren, and the capture information of this post is shown Fig. 6.

```
c=Hello%20world%20%E6%B5%8B%E8%AF%95%E4%B8%80%E4%B8%8B%20%E5%93%8
8%20%EF%BC%81%40%23&owner=235437623&rpLayer=0&source=15622345706&t=4&stype
=103&replyref=newsfeed&requestToken=1557220850&_rtk=28924c4c
```

Fig. 6. POST example of Renren

From the Fig. 6, we can find that the POST content adopts the HTTP and also defines the several fields and their values, which use the UTF-8 to encode. In our system, the string match and decode are finished in MapReduce. In the Map stage, it selects the content field which is not null, and then adopts the HOST to match the specific website, decodes and abstracts the POST content. In the Reduce stage, it reassembles the POST content and stores them in Hive.

Website Visited History

Website visited history analysis is to analyze the users' behaviors and demonstrate them via the graphic tools such as R language, which mainly contains the top k values, website category and ratio of the visited websites, the URL accessing frequency, and traffic analysis. Based on these analyses, we can acquire the uses' preferences, visited websites rank, visited websites category and traffic types.

4   Experimental Results Analysis

To evaluate our design, we implement and deploy our system in BUPT campus network to test its functions. Fig. 7 shows the experimental topology, which consists of Hadoop cluster servers to capture the packets and Libnids servers to perform the TCP reassembling, and the related configurations are shown in table 5 and table 6.

The Hadoop cluster consists of four machines, in which one of them is Namenode to perform the management function and the others are Datanode to capture the packet via PF_RING, and the hardware configurations are shown in table 6.

All operation systems in this topology adopt the Linux. More specifically, the Hadoop adopts the Ubuntu 12.04 and others adopt the Fedora 10.

Considering that the analysis procedure of website posts and reply is similar to the keywords analysis, we mainly show the search keywords, shopping tendency and website visited history in the following experimental results analysis.

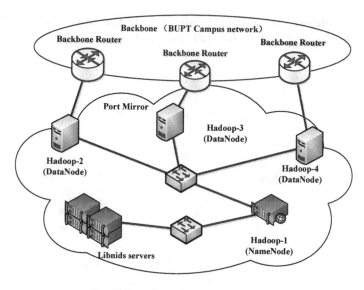

Fig. 7. Experimental test-bed topology

Table 5. Libnids hardware configuration

Name	Memory	Disk	CPU
Libnids1	2G	500G	Genuine Intel (R) CPU T1350 @ 1.86GHz
Libnids2	2G	500G	Intel(R) Core(TM)2 Duo CPU @ 2.93GHz
Libnids3	2G	500G	Genuine Intel (R) CPU T1350 @ 1.86GHz

Table 6. Hadoop hardware configuration

Name	Memory	Disk	CPU
Hadoop-1 (Namenode)	16G	500G	Intel(R) Xeon(R) CPU E5-2609@2.40GHz
Hadoop-2 (Datanode)	2G	250G	Genuine Intel (R) CPU T1350 @ 1.86GHz
Hadoop-3 (Datanode)	2G	250G	Genuine Intel (R) CPU T1350 @ 1.86GHz
Hadoop-4 (Datanode)	2G	250G	Genuine Intel (R) CPU T1350 @ 1.86GHz

4.1   Search Keywords

We use this system to acquire all search keywords, and perform the participle, deleting stop word, calculating the word frequency. Fig. 8 shows the words cloud plotted by the *R*.

From Fig. 8, we can find that during this stage the intern (Chinese word is "实习") is the center of the search keywords for that a lot of network users are looking for internship opportunities. Besides, written examination (Chinese word "笔试"), Matlab, Linux, Java are the high-frequency search keywords for that most network users of BUPT major in computer science and they are hunting for interviews. In addition, some IT companies such as Sina, Baidu (Chinese word are "新浪" and "百度", respectively) are also high-frequency words. From this words cloud, we can capture the overall network users search features. To perform the network management, our system can also define a management words list. If the user searches one of them, we can focus on this user and abstract all his search words to further analysis his behaviors.

Fig. 8. Search keywords cloud

4.2   Shopping Tendency

The shopping tendency is also abstracted by resolving the uses' search keywords in the e-commerce websites. Similarly, Fig. 9 shows the shopping tendency words cloud by capturing several typical e-commerce websites as shown in table 2.

Fig. 9. Users shopping tendency words cloud

From Fig. 9, we can observe that "adidas" (in form of "adidas", "三叶草", "阿迪达斯") is the center of the words cloud. Besides, there are lots of other words such as T-shirt (Chinese word is "衬衫"), shoes (Chinese word is "鞋"), and Computer (Chinese word is "笔记本")are also high-frequency words. In this analysis, we can get the whole network users shopping tendency during this stage. Besides, to observe the specific users' interests, we can get his shopping keywords history to track its dynamic interests. As for the security management, we can set a management word list as the filter to distinguish the abnormal users to prevent the potential threats.

4.3   Website Visited History

The website visited history includes many analyses. In this section, we demonstrate two results.

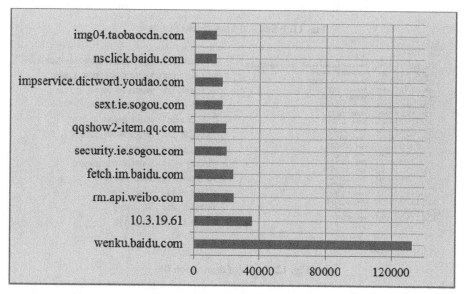

Fig. 10. Ranking of the visited websites

Fig. 10 shows the rank of the visited websites during this stage. We can observer that the "wenku.baidu.com is the most visited website, and the "10.3.19.61" is the internal network website. Besides, the "Weibo", "Sogou", "QQ" and "Taobao" are top visited websites.

As for the given website, we analyze two typical sites, Baidu and Sina. Fig. 11(a) shows the visited websites ranking of Baidu, and we can get that the "Wenku" is the most frequently visit content which is higher than others. Fig. 11(b) shows the detailed visited results of Sina. We can get that the Sina sport, Sina weibo and Sina login are in the top rank.

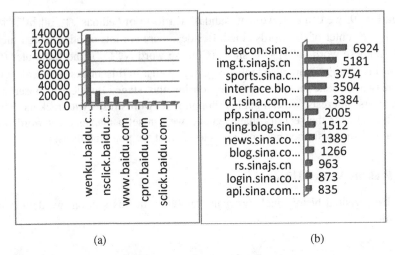

(a)   (b)

Fig. 11. Baidu and Sina visited results

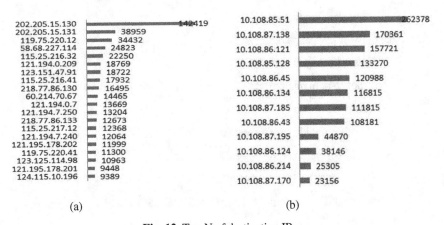

(a)   (b)

Fig. 12. Top N of destination IP

Fig. 12 (a) shows the ranking of the most visited IP destination, and we can get that 202.205.15.130/131 is higher than others. The number of click rank is shown in Fig.12 (b), in which the 10.108.85.51 is the most one which is higher than others. From these results, we can grasp the users' website preference to find out their behaviors characters.

5   Conclusions

In this paper, we proposed a network user behaviors analysis system based on the Hadoop platform, which mainly contains the packet capture modules, TCP reassembly module, Hadoop cluster analysis module and graphic demonstrate module. The Hadoop cluster analysis module is the kernel to acquire the users' behaviors from the search keywords, shopping tendency, post and reply, and website browser. Based on the captured packets in the campus network, we showed the analysis results, which show that this system can abstract the users' multidimensional behaviors. However, the current implementation of our system is an off-line analysis, while the future work is to provide the real-time analysis function.

Acknowledgement. Thanks for the Zengyong Hao's great work on the system test and analysis. This work was partially supported by the National Basic Research Program of China (973 Program) under Grant No. 2013CB329102, in part by the National Natural Science Foundation of China (NSFC) under Grant No. 61232017, 61372112 and 61003283, in part by the Beijing Natural Science Foundation (4142037), and the Natural Science Foundation of Jiangsu Province under Grant No. BK2011171.

References

1. Jin, L., Chen, Y., Wang, T., Hui, P., Vasilakos, A.V.: Understanding User Behavior in Online Social Networks: A Survey. IEEE Communications Magazine 51(9), 144–150 (2013)
2. Markendahl, J., Makitalo, O.: Analysis of Business Models and Market Players for Local Wireless Internet Access. In: Proceeding of 6th Conference on Telecommunication Techno-Economics, pp. 1–8. IEEE Press, Helsinki (2007)
3. Mo, Y., Chen, J., Xie, X., Luo, C., Yang, L.T.: Cloud-Based Mobile Multimedia Recommendation System With User Behavior Information. IEEE Systems Journal 8(1), 184–193 (2014)
4. Lancieri, L., Durand, N.: Internet User Behavior: Compared Study of the Access Traces and Application to the Discovery of Communities. IEEE Transactions on System, Man and Cybernetics – Part A: System and Humans 36(1), 208–219 (2006)
5. Tao, Y.-H., Hong, T.-P., Lin, W.-Y., Chiu, W.-Y.: A practical extension of web usage mining with intentional browsing data toward usage. Expert Syst. Appl. 36(2), 3937–3945 (2009)
6. Pablo Enrique Roman Asenjo, Web User Behavior Analysis, PHD thesis (2011)
7. Velayathan, G., Yamada, S.: Behavior Based Web Page Evaluation. In: Proceeding of 2006 IEEE/WIC/ACM International Conference on Web Intelligence and Intelligent Agent Technology Workshops, pp. 1317–1318. IEEE Press, Hong Kong (2007)
8. The best Internet data analysis solution, http://www.greenet.net.cn/en_us/a/solu/gov/
9. PF_RING^{TM}: High-speed packet capture, filtering and analysis, http://www.ntop.org/products/pf_ring/
10. Libnids, http://libnids.sourceforge.net/
11. Spark. Spark Homepage, http://spark-project.org/
12. Rwordseg, http://jliblog.com/app/rwordseg

The Research of Extraction Algorithm for Target Feature of Chest Bitmap

Tianshi Liu[1], Ruixiang Liu[1], Hongwei Wang[2], Liumei Zhang[1], and Cailing Wang[1]

[1] School of Computer Science, Xi'an Shiyou University, Xi'an, 710065, China
liutianshi@xsyu.edu.cn, 534610819@qq.com
[2] Engineering University of CAPF, Xi'an, 710086, China

Abstract. The chest bitmap is the most widely used in live-firing. The target surface information extraction is the chief question need to be solved for automatic target-scoring system. Therefore, this paper proposes a new low-complexity algorithm for target surface feature information extraction according to the characteristics of the chest ring image. Based on the pre-processing for image, background interference of the image is eliminated by using regional feature elimination algorithm. Besides, target's eye position is determined by employing gray two-way clipping projection, and all of the effective feature information of the target surface is extracted. The result of simulation shows that the target surface information extraction algorithm for chest bitmap is characterized by low-complexity, short time-consuming and high efficiency, and meets the real-time requirement.

Keywords: chest bitmap, target information, background subtraction, gray project.

1 Introduction

With the improvement of modern technology, automation has become the main developing trend of weapon equipment system. The extraction technology of target feature based on image processing is an important technology to realize the automatization of firing range. In order to improve the recognition ability and the accuracy of details of the targets with low contrast, real-time, fast and effective target image processing and feature information extraction become one of the key technologies of system performance[1-2].

At present there are two methods for extracting target feature: one is to use threshold segmentation to separate the target from background. Then region-labeling method is applied to locate the position of target. In the end the center of cross of the target is located by taking center of gravity and then calculated the position and radius of each ring of target image. Another method adopts template matching method to locate the target location firstly, then use taking center of gravity to locate the center of ten rings of the target and determine the position and radius of each ring[3-6].

Combining the above two methods, this paper proposes an algorithm of information extraction of target feature which is based on background subtraction of regional

L. Batten et al. (Eds.): ATIS 2014, CCIS 490, pp. 56–64, 2014.
© Springer-Verlag Berlin Heidelberg 2014

features, gray project and rings extraction, and has obtained good effect by using the algorithm to extract and simulate the chest bitmap.

2   Feature Information of Target

The target information of chest bitmap mainly includes ring information and invalid area information[7]. The ring information mainly contains location information of each ring from ring 10 to ring 5. The invalid region is mainly refers to the white background on the chest bitmap. Figure 1 is a standard chest bitmap, it is observed that: 1)the left and right of chest bitmap are symmetrical; 2)the rings from ring 10 to ring 6 are concentric circles; 3)the x coordinate of the center of ring 10 is symmetry of left side and right side; 4)the upper and lower part of the y coordinate are asymmetric; 5)there are some interferences such as "chest bitmap" and digits in Fig.1.

The information could be extracted from chest bitmap image after image processing is shown in Fig.2.

Fig. 1. The standard chest bitmap   **Fig. 2.** The feature information of target plane

In practical measurement, after using digital camera to collect images, the images include three parts: the valid area and invalid area in target paper and the background of firing range. The actual image is as shown in Fig.3.

Fig. 3. The practical picture of chest ring

This paper mainly processes images on the basis of Fig.3, thus picks up the useful information.

3   Target Surface Information Extraction

The information extraction of target feature mainly includes calculating the clout position of chest bitmap and extracting the rings of target. The collected images are 24-bit colored pictures in actual measurement. When target information is extracted, the collected color images need to be preprocessed. First the images are grayed. Then binarization is implemented on the gray images. At last the background is eliminated.

3.1   Image Gray Scaling

For the convenience of image processing and image information extraction in subsequent, the 24-bit colored pictures are transformed as the gradation pictures. The gray value of image can be gained by using formula as follows which is to calculate the R, G, B component of the image[8].

$$I=0.3B +0.59G +0.11R \tag{1}$$

3.2   Image Binarization

Processing the grayed images by binarization and setting the original gray image as $f(x, y)$. The binarized images is $g(x, y)$, τ is the threshold, the binarization process is as follows:

$$g(x, y) = \begin{cases} 1, f(x, y) \geq \tau; \\ 0, f(x, y) < \tau; \end{cases} \tag{2}$$

3.3   Background Elimination

After binarization, the background information in the image needs to be eliminated. According to the sources of background noise, the background information of firing range is mainly distributed in both side of images and the background is continuous, which is continuous black area in a binary image. By using the prior knowledge of the background noise above, this paper proposes a method of background elimination based on regional characteristics.

For background information in the image, the realization of elimination method based on region feature which uses traversal. Starting from the left side, due to the starting position is the typical background region which is manifested as black, set it as white. Sequentially, until the connected domain of pixels is white region, at this time the black background on the left side will be eliminated as white. Similarly, the same operation is implemented on the right side. The algorithm flow chart is shown in Fig.4.

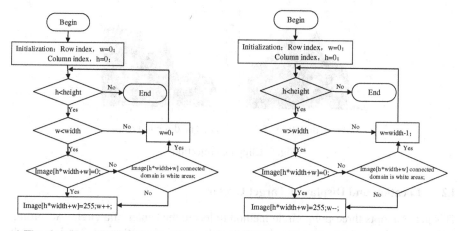

a) The algorithm of left background removal b) The algorithm of right background removal

Fig. 4. The flowchart of eliminate background algorithm

4   The Information Extraction of Ring in Target Image

4.1   Gray Projection Determine Target Area

It can be seen from the chest bitmap image (Fig.3) that the most parts of pixel distribution of image are dark-gray target and white background, of which the color is obviously different and distributed evenly. Based on this feature gray projection method can be used to extract the target surface area. Gray clipping projection method maps the image into independent one-dimensional waveform in x direction and y direction according to the formula as follows. Through one-dimensional waveform, it is easy to find the boundary of the target surface in each direction.

$$G(i) = \sum_j G(i, j) \tag{3}$$

$$G(j) = \sum_i G(i, j) \tag{4}$$

In the above formula, G(i) and G(j) represent the sum of all pixel gray value of the image in i column and j line. $G(i, j)$ is the pixel gray value of (i, j) in the image. Projections in the x direction and y direction are shown in Fig.5, (a) represent the projection of image in x direction and (b) represent the projection in y direction.

The coordinates of the center of ring 10 can be calculated accurately by using clipping projection, then use three-point circle to realize accurate extraction for the center. Finally calculate the information of the other rings through the coordinate of the center.

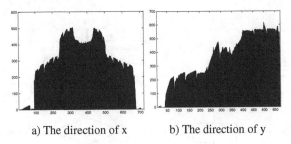

a) The direction of x   b) The direction of y

Fig. 5. Clipping projection

4.2   Location and Display of Target Center

This paper adopts three-point circle method to locate the center of a circle. According to the principle of plane geometry, it can only draw one circle through 3 points which are not in a straight line, and the perpendicular bisectors of any two unparallel strings on the circumference of a circle intersect at the center. The three-point circle method uses the property of plane geometry to get the center coordinates.

The basic principle of circle center location is the inverse transformation of that the three points are in one circle. Assuming that select 3 points $A(x_A, y_A)$, $B(x_B, y_B)$, $C(x_C, y_C)$ on the edge of bullet holes, the radius is r, the coordinates of the center of the circle is $O(x_O, y_O)$, the equations can be listed as shown in Fig.6.

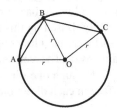

Fig. 6. The Schematics of ascertaining a circle with three points

$$\begin{cases} (x_A - x_O)^2 + (y_A - y_O)^2 = r^2 \\ (x_B - x_O)^2 + (y_B - y_O)^2 = r^2 \\ (x_C - x_O)^2 + (y_C - y_O)^2 = r^2 \end{cases} \tag{5}$$

Solving the equations, the coordinates of the center of the circle $O(x_O, y_O)$ can be expressed as:
Assuming that

$$M = (y_A - y_C)(x_A^2 - x_B^2 + y_A^2 - y_c^2) \tag{6}$$

$$N = (y_A - y_B)(x_A^2 - x_C^2 + y_A^2 - y_c^2) \tag{7}$$

$$P = (x_A - x_B)(x_A^2 - x_C^2 + y_A^2 - y_c^2) \tag{8}$$

$$Q = (x_A - x_B)(x_A^2 - x_B^2 + y_A^2 - y_B^2) \tag{9}$$

We can get:

$$\left\{\begin{array}{l} x_o = \dfrac{M-N}{2(y_A-y_C)(x_A-x_B)-2(y_A-y_B)(x_A-x_C)} \\[3mm] y_o = \dfrac{P-Q}{2(y_A-y_C)(x_A-x_B)-2(y_A-y_B)(x_A-x_C)} \\[3mm] r = \sqrt{(x_A-x_o)^2-(y_A-y_o)^2} \end{array}\right\} \qquad (10)$$

4.3   The Information Extraction of Each Ring on Target

The radius and the coordinates of bull's-eye of ring 10 has been got. We can draw the horizontal axis X and longitudinal axis Y which the origin is the top left corner of the image, and draw a straight line that parallel to the Y axis through $O(x_o, y_o)$, which has an intersection point with ring 9 to ring 5 respectively.

By determining the coordinates of intersection point to get the radius of each circle, the algorithm takes the following steps.

- Refining processing. The width of loops in binarization image is several pixels. At this time, we can't accurately get the coordinates of intersection point, but can get the circle image of single pixel by using the refined processing.
- Assuming that the intersection of straight line 1 and X axis is $A(x_0, 0)$, the intersections of each loop are $a_4(x_4, y_4)$, $a_3(x_3, y_3)$, $a_2(x_2, y_2)$, $a_1(x_1, y_1)$ separately.
- The radius of loops can be calculated according to the coordinates of known intersections.

The expression of outer loop of ring 10 is:

$$(x_i - x_0)^2 + (y_i - y_0)^2 = r_{10}^2 \qquad (11)$$

The radius of outer loop of ring 9 is:

$$r_9 = \left[(x_1 - x_0)^2 + (y_1 - y_0)^2\right]^{1/2} \qquad (12)$$

The radius of outer loop of ring 8 is:

$$r_8 = \left[(x_2 - x_0)^2 + (y_2 - y_0)^2\right]^{1/2} \qquad (13)$$

The radius of outer loop of ring 7 is:

$$r_7 = \left[(x_3 - x_0)^2 + (y_3 - y_0)^2\right]^{1/2} \qquad (14)$$

The radius of outer loop of ring 6 is:

$$r_6 = \left[(x_4 - x_0)^2 + (y_4 - y_0)^2\right]^{1/2} \qquad (15)$$

Thus, the accurate information of chest bitmap can be obtained from the bull's-eye and the radius of each ring.

5   Algorithm Implementation and Experimental Analysis

The software simulation of information extraction algorithm of target feature is made in the environment of matlab2009a, Windows xp sp3, 2GB memory and 500GB hard disk. The process of algorithm implementation is shown in Fig.7.

The collected chest bitmap images are grayed, the result is shown in Fig.8.

The binarization is implemented on the grayed image and the result is shown in Fig.9.

And then background noise is removed, as shown in Fig.10.

For the convenience of comparison, each ring curve after extraction is displayed in the original image as shown in Fig.11.

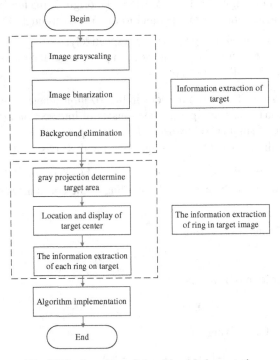

Fig. 7. The flowchart of algorithm implementation

We can get the complete information of ring 10 to ring 8 from the rings extraction result of target image, but other rings are not a complete circle. So the valid area and invalid area of ring 7 to ring 5 need to be separated. Thus the repeated operations of dilation and erosion for binarization image are used to extract the valid area. The extracted result is shown in Fig.12.

With the result of valid area, we can easily draw the location of the ring 7 to ring 5.

Fig. 8. The target plane of greyed

Fig. 9. The target plane of binary

Fig. 10. The target plane of eliminated background

Fig. 11. The result of extracting rings for target plane

Fig. 12. The valid region

The proposed algorithm takes 0.00547s that runs on the platform, it fully proves that the algorithm has the advantages of low algorithm complexity, time saving and high efficiency when extracts information of chest bitmap, and can satisfy the real-time requirements. The algorithm is easy to transplant and implemented on hardware platform, and provide technical support for weapon equipment automation based on the chest bitmap.

6   Conclusion

This paper makes pre-processing on images, and projection for the images along the horizontal and vertical directions, resulting with a target area. It uses three-point circle to locate the center of a circle, and determines the bull's-eye and the radius of ring 10. It calculates the radius of each ring according to known information. Based on the Matlab platform, the target surface information extraction algorithm for chest bitmap proposed in this paper is verified with low-complexity, short time-consuming and high efficiency, and meets the real-time requirement.

Acknowledgment. This study was supported by national project of 973 No.2012JM8037, National Natural Science Foundation No.41301382 and Natural Science Foundation Project of Shaanxi Province of China No.2012JM8037.

References

1. Gao, D., Li, S., Lin, K., Zhou, D.: Adaptive fast algorithm design of digital image processing based on BZX-1 system. Computer Engineering 30(08), 149–150+161 (2004)
2. Guo, C., Li, T.: Direct video acquisition and displaying by DSP. Acta Electronica Sinica 23(3), 119–120 (1995)
3. Xu, S., Li, Z.: The study on bridge recognition in natural scene[J]. Journal of Zhejian University 29(3), 275–281 (1995)
4. Zhang, X., Sun, W., Han, G., Wang, Y.: An automatic recognition algorithm for bullet holes. Optics and Precision Engineering 13(06), 747–753 (2005)
5. He, D.: Digital Image Processing. Xidian University Press, Xi'an (2003)
6. Zhu, G., Guo, Z.: Intelligent image recognition and tracking. Journal of Beijing Institude of technology 15(2), 218–222 (1995)
7. Chen, H.: Study of automatic scoring system for shooting sports based on image processing. Nanjing University of Aeronautics and Astronautics (2005)
8. Zhou, J., Peng, F.: A method of selective image graying[J]. Computer Engineering 32(20), 198–200 (2006)

A Method for Detecting Trojan Based on Hidden Network Traffic Analysis

Zhiwen Chen, Yizheng Tao, and Gongliang Li

Institute of Computer Application, China Academy of Engineering Physics,
No.64, Mianshan Road, Mianyang, Sichuan, P.R. China
prikey@sina.com, {taoyz,ligl}@icaep.cn

Abstract. With the development of Trojan horse detection technology, the survivability of the Trojan hidden in the space of operating systems becomes more and more weak. As a result, more kernel hidden and hardware hidden techniques have been proposed and applied to the design of new Trojans. Because of the complexity and diversity of kernel hiding technologies and the emergence of hardware Trojans, detection becomes more and more difficult. We propose a black-box model to simplify the communication processing system of a computer. The modules of complex communication processing in the kernel of the operating system and the hardware are reduced to a black box with two end points. Hidden traffic can be easily extracted regardless of the Trojan hidden technologies. After this, a special-Trojan detection system based on the extraction of the hidden traffic is present. The experimental result has demonstrated the usage of the traffic extract model.

Keywords: Trojan horse detection, Hidden network traffic, Black-box, Network sensor, Host sensor.

1 Introduction

Trojan, or Trojan horse is a type of malicious code that is designed to control the target machine secretly. There is no doubt that Trojans bring more serious threat to information security today. Data leakage is the most common and serious harm of Trojans, since data have become an important asset of many companies and very important in terms of personal privacy. They also have great impact on national security. How to detect the Trojans is essential to protect sensitive data in many areas.

The main research areas for Trojan detection include host-based methods which analyze the behavior or signature of application, and network-based methods which analyze the behavior or signature of network communication [1-6]. With both types of the methods, signature-matching methods are only applicable to detection of known Trojans. A minor version change of the known Trojans will make these detection methods fail. Some Trojans can even generate self variations to avoid signature detection [4-6]. On the other hand, behavior analysis methods also appear to be inadequate with the development of the Trojan hidden technology. Especially, with the advent of hardware Trojans [5-6], traditional host-based detection methods are powerless.

L. Batten et al. (Eds.): ATIS 2014, CCIS 490, pp. 65–72, 2014.
© Springer-Verlag Berlin Heidelberg 2014

Hence, we will not directly study on the signature matching or behavior analysis approaches to detect Trojans. Instead, we focus on the Trojan hidden characteristics of communication, and propose an efficient and simple method for detecting hidden network traffic. A Trojan horse detection system is then developed to detect the special Trojans, which try to hide their communication under the user mode of operation system.

The rest of the paper is structured as follows. In section 2, we present our key idea for extracting hidden traffic based on a black-box model of the communication processing system. In Section 3, a special-Trojan detection system based on the hidden traffic analysis is proposed. The experimental results is presented in Section 4, and the conclusion is drawn in section 5.

2   Model

In this session, we present a simplified black-box model of a computer system for analyzing Trojan hidden communications. A hidden communication detection method is then proposed based on the model.

2.1   Computer Communication System

Before discussing the black-box model, refinement of a model of computer communication system must first be mentioned to explain the complexity of Trojan communication hiding technology and to illustrate the need for simplified model of the system.

In Windows operating system, for example, receiving or sending an application's data must be processed through the multiple layers as shown in Fig. 1. These layers include the Application, Socket API and SPI layers in the user space, and layers of TDI, NDIS, NIC Driver, Bus Driver and NIC in the kernel space.   Some of the layers can be further broken down into a number of layers [7].

Each layer is described as follows [7]:

- Applications: Application that interfaces with Windows Sockets for network services.
- Socket API: The Windows Sockets interface (Ws2_32.dll).
- SPI: The Windows Sockets service provider interface.
- TDI: The Transport Driver Interface (TDI) defines a kernel-mode network interface that is exposed at the upper edge of all transport protocol stacks.
- NDIS: The Network Driver Interface Specification (NDIS) library abstracts the network hardware from network drivers.
- NIC Driver: Driver for network interface card.
- Bus Driver: Driver for data bus. A bus driver drives an individual I/O bus device and provides per-slot functionality that is device-independent. Bus drivers also detect and report child devices that are connected to the bus.
- NIC: The network interface card.

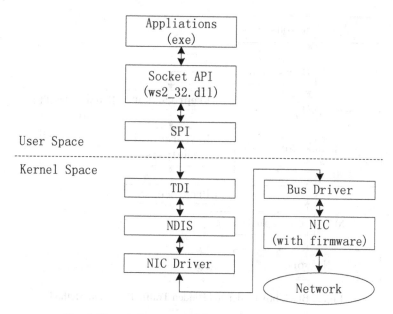

Fig. 1. The windows cmmunication processing system

2.2   Black-Box Model of Computer System

As mentioned earlier, computer communication system is a multi-layer processing system consisting of a number of loosely coupled modules. In this tiered system, each layer may become the Trojan hidden places. With the development of Trojan horse detection technology, the survivability [8] of the Trojan hidden in user space of the operating system becomes more and more weak. As a result, increasing kernel hidden and hardware hidden techniques have been proposed and applied to the design and development of new Trojans. Because of the complexity and diversity of kernel hiding technology and the emergence of hardware Trojans, detection becomes more and more difficult.

Our main approach is to extract information on hidden communication data stream. For this purpose, we propose a black-box model to simplify the computer communication processing system mentioned earlier (see Fig. 1), as shown in Fig. 2, complex communication processing modules in the kernel of the operating system and the hardware are reduced to a black box with two end points. One end point is service access point (SAP) and the other is network access point (NAP).

The SAP is an user space communication access point. How to select the point depends on the actual implementation. We select the socket API as a SAP. The socket API is implemented as a Dynamic libraries that be called by all of the normal applications. Therefore, it is easier to achieve a test access point to implement bypass monitoring for all the user applications.

The NAP is the bottom of the computer communications interface, in this model referring to the NIC.

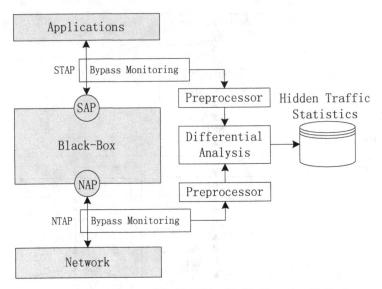

Fig. 2. Black-box model and Hidden Traffic Detection Method

2.3   Hidden Network Traffic Detection

Based on the black-box model, two test access points are placed to implement bypass monitoring. One is the socket test access point (STAP), which is placed between applications and SAP. The other one is network access test point (NTAP), which is placed in the network where the communication data of the black box have to pass through. The STAP is a software module implemented as a socket API wrapper; while the NTAP can be implemented through a switch port mirroring or special TAP hardware directly accessing the network cable. The communication data between applications and SAP pass through the STAP directly, and the data between NAP and Network also pass through the NTAP directly. Afterwards both STAP and NTAP record the summarize info of the data flow and output the message through a bypass monitoring interface. Because we do not concern the payload of the packet, so the original recording info of STAP is normalized into a 7-tuple represented as Sp as follows:

Sp = (time, transPro, srcIP, srcPort, dstIP, dstPort, payloadLen)

Where time is the time when this packet was recorded and transPro is the identification of transport layer protocol (udp or tcp, or null for the lower protocol). srcIP is the soure IP address of the paket. srcPort is source port. dstIP is the destination IP address. dstPort is the destination port. payloadLen is the length of the application data payload.

The NTAP recording info is an 8-tuple represented as Np as follows:

Np = (time, validFlag, transPro, srcIP, srcPort, dstIP, dstPort, payloadLen)

Where the validFlag is used to identify the availability, with value limited in valid, bad, or repeat. The other elements of Np are the same as Sp.

Typically, a packet produces a Sp tuple and a Np tuple. In order to reduce the amount of data recorded, the Sp and Np tuples are submitted to the PreProcess module. The PreProcess module merges the data and reduces the amount of data recorded through statistical analysis.

The PreProcess module for Sp uses a new 11-tuple represented as Sps to store the original statistical result as follows:

Sps = (starTime, endTime, transPro, smallIP, smallPort, bigIP, bigPort, upPacets, upBytes, downPacets, downBytes)

Where the starTime is the time of the firs packet in this statistical tuple, and the endTime is the time of the last packet. Here, we do not use the "src " or "dst" identification. Instead the "small" and "big" are used. The PreProcessor compare the srcPort and dstPort first. If they are equal, the comparison of srcIP and dstIP continues. If srcPort is less than dstPort. The value of (smallIP, smallPort) is set as (srcIP, srcPort) and (bigIP,bigPort) set as the value of (dstIP, dstPort). Otherwise, if srcPort is large than dstPort, the value of (smallIP, smallPort) is set as (dstIP, dstPort), and (bigIP,bigPort) set as the value of (srcIP, srcPort).Similarly, if the srcPort is equal to dstPort, by comparing srcIP with dstIP, the value of "small" and "big" can also be set. After identifying the "small" and "big" value, "up" is defined as the packet transmission direction from smallIP to bigIP, and "down" means that the packet is transmitted from bigIP to smallIP. In this way, we do not care the sessions' restructuring problem and are able to match the statistical tuple efectively when achieving a new Sp tuple. The other element of Sps can be easily understood from the name. Therefore no details are provided here.

The PreProcess module for Np uses a new 12-tuple represented as Nps. It is used to store the original statistical result as follows:

Nps = (starTime, endTime, validFlag, transPro, smallIP, smallPort, bigIP, bigPort, upPacets, upBytes, downPacets, downBytes)

Where "small" and "big", "up" and "down" is the same as the elements in Sps.

After the preprocess, Sps and Nps are compared by the Differential Analysis module to calculate the differences, the calculation has a few basic rules: (1) tuples which has the same (smallIP, smallPort, bigIP, bigPort) and a close starTime in Sps and Nps are compared; (2) if the number of Packets of Sps is larger than the Nps, the tuple will be tagged as not available. It may mean the network is unavailable when the application tries to call communication API; (3) if the sum value of packets or bytes of Sps tuple is less than the value of Nps tuple, a hidden info will be recorded; (4) if a tuple of Nps cannot match a Sps tuple for comparison, while the smallIP host or bigIP host has a host STAP, then Hidden traffic will be recorded directly. (5) if a tuple of Nps cannot match a Sps tuple for comparison, and both of the smallIP host and bigIP host have not a STAP, then it will be tagged as unavailable.

However, the above approach to obtaining the original hidden traffic statistics is a ideal model. There are three problems need attention before the model being able to be used in a Trojan Detection System: (1) The hidden traffic recorded may be legitimate. Some examples are some legitimate ICMP or ARP traffic; (2) The payloadLen of Np tuple may have to go through a preprocess to meet some special protocol, such as VPN protocol. Otherwise it will cause false result; (3) due to the existence of network transmission error and network retransmission, NTAP must be able to distinguish these packets and set the value of validFlag correctly. Otherwise it may lead to errors in calculation.

3   Special-Trojan Detection System

As shown in Fig. 3, we design a special-Trojan detection system based on the hidden traffic analysis. The system is composed of network sensor, host sensor and analysis center.

The network sensor service captures the NTAP and the Nps original statistic, and the host sensor service captures the STAP and Sps statistic. After the analysis center implements the extraction of the hidden traffic, a Trojan Detection module uses the expert rules to analyze the hidden traffic and detect the special-trojan. Due to the time limitation, we only create one rule currently, and the result is ignored when validFlag is not equal to valid. The data are also ignored when tranPro is unavailable, and when there is no match with the Sps. Some thresholds are also set up. These include a hidden-packets threshold for both upPacets and downPacets as Hp, a hidden-bytes threshold for both upBytes and downBytes as Hb, and a hidden-packet ratio threshold Hr. Note that Hr is the ratio of larger value and the other value between upPacets and downPackets. If the corresponding value is large than all the threshold at the same time, an alarm is generated. It will be decide that the smallIP is the host that has been implanted a Trojan if the upBytes statistic is large than the downBytes. Otherwise, the bigIP is the host that has been implanted a Trojan.

The network sensor is implemented based on the snort IDS[9]. The module function of network sensor is described as follows:

- TAP: A test access point device to access the network cable directly and achieve the packet info through bypass monitoring.
- Network Traffic Capture: It captures the packet from TAP monitoring port.
- Data Preprocessor: The data packet state analysis and classification. Its function includes dealing with the protocol encapsulation to obtain the length of the application data payload, and then outputting the Np tuple.
- Traffic Statistics: It implements the Np statistic and output the Nps before summit the output to the Analysis Center component.

The host sensor component is implemented based on a ws2_32.dll wrapper. The module function is described as follows:

- Socket API Wrapper: It implements the interfaces of the ws2_32.dll, and replaced it to service the applications.
- Application Traffic Capture: It outputs the Sp tuple to the Traffic Statistic module.
- Traffic Statistics: It implements the Sp statistic and output the Sps before submit the output before submitting the output to the Analysis Center component.

The analysis center component is a service that collects the data from network sensor and host sensor, implements the function of hidden traffic extraction algorithm, and then analyze the hidden traffic based on expert rules to detect the special Trojans.

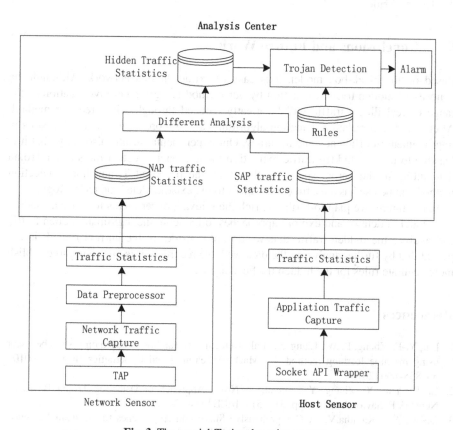

Fig. 3. The special-Trojan detection system

4   Experimental Results and Analysis

We has implemented a prototype system recently, and deployed it on an internal development experimental network environment for data collection and testing. During the test, we run a simulation Trojan that hides in the kernel space as a driver and use the port reuse technology to communication with the controller. After recording five days' data, we stop the system.

According to the experimental result, the communication of the simulation Trojan caused positive alarms as expected. In addition, we also got a few false alarms, which was caused by a file share service in our experimental environment after careful analysis. Because the file share services are run on the kernel space of the operating system, the STAP doesn't collect the packet data, which cause all the communication data being seen as hidden traffic. Finally, we analyzed the hidden traffic extract by our system statistically, and found that the proportion of the hidden packet is 3.6%. However, most of them are ARP, or ICMP, or retransmit packets, which do not match the detection rule.

5   Conclusions and Future Work

Based on the black-box model, it is easy to extract hidden network. Although the majority of hidden traffic extraction by our method is legitimate, investigation of the range of real illegal traffic will be greatly reduced through this screening method. After this, the correlation detection algorithm can be more targeted, which results in improvement of efficiency and accuracy. Our experimental results also show that it is feasible to use our hidden traffic extraction mode model to detect the special-Trojan that hiding in the kernel space. In this case, the proposed Trojan horse detection method can be used as a useful complement to the existing detection technology.

In the future, we plan to further enrich the relevant experiments to test our method and model in details, and explore approaches to reducing the legitimate hidden traffic and analyze the hidden traffic that we do not consider in the current rule. It is expected that by further analyzing the data we have recorded, it is promising to establish more accurate rules for the hidden traffic analysis.

References

1. Liu, Y.-F., Zhang, L.-W., Liang, J., et al.: Detecting Trojan horses based on system behavior using machine learning method. In: Machine Learning and Cybernetics (ICMLC 2010), pp. 855–860 (2010)
2. Li, S., Yun, X., Zhang, Y.Z., et al.: A Novel Approach of Detecting Trojan Based on Network Behavior Analysis, pp. 513–518. IEEE Press (2012)
3. Deepa, A.J., Kavitha.V.: A Comprehensive Survey on Approaches to Intrusion Detection System. In: International Conference on Modeling Optimisation and Computing 2012, pp. 2064–2069. Elsevier Ltd. (2012)
4. Xiang, B., Hao, Y.-J., Zhang, Y., et al.: A Novel Anti-Trojan Approach using Behavioral Analysis. In: Apperceiving Computing and Intelligence Analysis, ICACIA 2008, pp. 311–314 (2008)
5. Fu, D., Zhou, S., Cao, C.: A Windows Rootkit Detection Method Based on Cross-View. In: The International Conference on E-Product, E-Service and E-Entertainment (ICEEE 2010), pp. 1–3 (2010)
6. Wang, X., Tehranipoor, M., Plusquellic, J.: Detecting Malicious Inclusions in Secure Hardware: Challenges and Solutions. In: 1st IEEE International Workshop on Hardware-Oriented Security and Trust (HOST), pp. 15–19 (2008)
7. MSDN, http://msdn.microsoft.com/zh-cn/
8. Kalyoncu, H., Sankur, B.: Estimation of survivability of communication networks. Electronics Letters 28(19), 473–480 (1992)
9. Snort, http://www.snort.org

A Survey on Encrypted Traffic Classification

Zigang Cao[1,2], Gang Xiong[2,*], Yong Zhao[2], Zhenzhen Li[2], and Li Guo[2]

[1] Beijing University of Posts and Telecommunications, Beijing, China
[2] Institute of Information Engineering, Chinese Academy of Sciences, Beijing, China
xionggang@iie.ac.cn

Abstract. With the widespread use of encryption techniques in network applications, encrypted network traffic has recently become a great challenge for network management. Studies on encrypted traffic classification not only help to improve the network service quality, but also assist in enhancing network security. In this paper, we first introduce the basic information of encrypted traffic classification, emphasizing the influences of encryption on current classification methodology. Then, we summarize the challenges and recent advances in encrypted traffic classification research. Finally, the paper is ended with some conclusions.

Keywords: traffic classification, encrypted traffic, statistical classification, fine-grained, behavior based.

1 Introduction

Network traffic classification is the keystone of network management, network planning and network flow model researching. The emergence of new applications using encryption techniques has resulted in a boom in encrypted traffic, bringing new challenges to the traffic classification field. The increase in encrypted traffic results from the following aspects:

- Peer to Peer (P2P) applications, since 2005, have been trying to break the restrictions of Internet Service Providers (ISPs), by using encryption and protocol obfuscation techniques [1-3].
- Internet users are paying more attention to their online security and privacy. Security Socket Layer (SSL), Virtual Private Network (VPN), and Secure Shell (SSH) are widely exploited to ensure network security. Anonymous communications (e.g. Onion Routing [4]) are used to enhance privacy preserving.
- With the fast growth in computing capability of general devices, even a personal computer or mobile devices can easily run complicated encryption and decryption calculation, which provides essential conditions for applications using encryption.

As is known to us, the main purpose of traffic classification is quality of service (QoS). The challenges encrypted traffic brings for traffic classification are in the following aspects, which call for further advances.

---

* Corresponding author.

L. Batten et al. (Eds.): ATIS 2014, CCIS 490, pp. 73–81, 2014.
© Springer-Verlag Berlin Heidelberg 2014

- First, it is difficult to achieve accurate and real-time identification of encrypted network applications, such as P2P downloading and online video, to fulfill the QoS requirements.
- Second, enterprise information security is challenged by encrypted channels. Malwares such as botnets, Trojans and advanced persistent threat (APT) [5] are using encrypted techniques to bypass firewall and intrusion detection system (IDS), so they can transmit confidential information to the outside network.
- Third, fine-grained user network behavior management requires accurate classification of encrypted traffic. In most companies and organizations, playing games, watch videos, and P2P downloading are forbidden during working hours. However, some employees try to break the rules by using encrypted tunnels. So it is necessary to know what applications are running inside encrypted tunnels.

Encrypted traffic classification can provide technical support for QoS, network behavior management, as well as the detection and forensics analysis of cybercrime. Some recent survey works in traffic classification are [6,7,8,9]. However, to the best of our knowledge, these survey works are not specially focused on the encrypted traffic problems. Thus, some important and unique challenges in encrypted traffic classification are not discussed, such as the definitions of encrypted traffic, and the different classification requirements. Therefore, it is essential to survey recent works and pinpoint the key problems, which may promote further research in the field.

The rest of this paper is organized as follows. Section 2 introduces the foundation of encrypted traffic, including encrypted traffic categories, classification requirements, classification methodology and challenges. In section 3, recent advances in encrypted traffic classification are reviewed. Finally, Section 4 concludes the paper.

2   Encrypted Traffic Classification Foundation

2.1   Scope and Classification Requirements

In a broad sense, encrypted network traffic should include traffic which has been transformed or generated by an encryption algorithm. While in practice, encrypted traffic mainly refers to the traffic in which the real content to be transferred is encrypted. However, if one uses plaintext HTTP protocol to download an encrypted file, the traffic cannot be taken as encrypted since the protocol itself is not encrypted.

To the best of our knowledge, encrypted traffic categories studied publicly are as follows: SSH, VPN, SSL, encrypted P2P, encrypted voice over Internet Protocol (VoIP), and encrypted traffic by certain anonymity tools (e.g. Tor [10] and JAP [11]). It should be noted that there may be a cross between two types. For instance, SSL VPN traffic can be grouped into both SSL and VPN. Another example is Skype, which belongs to both encrypted P2P and encrypted VoIP.

As for the classification requirements, encrypted traffic has the natural fine-grained classification. Encrypted traffic often has tunnels inside, which further carry several different applications, so not only encrypted traffic need to be identified, but also the applications running in the encrypted tunnels need to be classified, too. This is why encrypted traffic classification is much more difficult.

2.2 Classification Methodology

The important premise of classification is that there are features for different applications which can be used to distinguish each other. In our opinion, the essential difference between the classification of encrypted traffic and unencrypted traffic is that the classification methods change as available useful features alter due to the encryption. What the encryption process changes in network communications can be summarized as follows. First, the content inside the IP packets changes from plaintext to ciphertext. Second, the statistics of the payload is changed after encryption, namely randomness or entropy. Third, changes are also in the statistical properties of packet level and flow level, such as packet length, intervals and flow numbers. It is just these changes that greatly challenge the current classification methods.

Port-based method is based on the feature that certain application services use IANA assigned port numbers [12]. This method suffers from the following shortcomings. First, P2P applications use random or dynamic port numbers. Second, common service ports may be used by other services, such as malwares. Third, there are port numbers besides the assigned. Fourth, it is coarse-grained. Finally, port numbers can be hidden by transport layer or IP packet encryption.

Payload based method generally refers to the deep packet inspection DPI [13] technique, which uses static application signatures in the payload to identify protocols. Finamore A et al [14] proposed another payload based method named stochastic packet inspection (SPI) which makes use of statistical properties of payload in packets. DPI is greatly damaged by encryption since the plaintext signatures turn invisible. However, it can be used in coarse classification for certain encrypted traffic such as SSL. As for SPI, it has the fine-grained classification ability in theory since its features are generally specific for application-layer protocols. However, statistical payload properties it relies on will be greatly changed after encryption. It can be useful when the encryption is partial and structured.

Statistical classification mainly refers to the methods based on statistical properties of traffic, in which machine learning is the most common one. The statistics used can be roughly divided into packet level and flow level. The former includes packet length, packet intervals and directions et al, and the latter contains the count and ratio of the upstream and downloading in bytes and packets, the duration of flow, ratio of different types of packets, etc. Though encryption changes the statistics of packet and flow, there are often strong correlations between the unencrypted traffic and original encrypted one. This is the main reason why statistical protocol identification is useful.

Behavior based classification is to analyze the behavioral characteristics of different types of applications from the host perspective, which mainly depends on the connection patterns, so the classification results are usually a series of coarse-grained classes, such as P2P and web. It is not enough due to the following reasons. Firstly, it is coarse-grained. Secondly, it can hardly work in case of transport layer encryption. Thirdly, network environment such as the use of network address translation (NAT)

[15] and asymmetric routing can affect its performance due to incomplete connection information.

To sum up, port based method can be auxiliary. Besides the lack of general fine-grained classification ability, payload based methods have a problem of privacy invasion. Statistical classification and host behavior based classification do not rely on content signatures, and both of them are robust to most application layer encryption. That is why they are the mainstream methods for in the field today.

2.3 Challenges in Encrypted Traffic Classification

Though there are many works, several challenges in this field have not been overcome yet. The main challenges are summarized as follows.

Fine-Grained Classification of Encrypted Traffic Is a Tough Task

It is far from enough to tell the encrypted traffic from the unencrypted, since what the real world need is to distinguish the tunneled application layer protocols to fulfill the network management. So the question is that can encrypted traffic be fine-grained classified in real world by port-based, payload based, statistical properties based, or behavior based method, as well as combinations of different methods.

Problems in Large-Scale Datasets Generation and Labeling Are Still to Be Solved

Datasets used in research generally come from three sources, i.e. public datasets, self-generated ones, and shared ones. Lack of payload information and ground truth is very common in public datasets and shared ones, so some researchers have to rely on port number for labeling [16], causing the benchmark inaccurate. An obvious problem of self-generated data sets is that the amount of data is too small.

As for the labeling, the most common ways are based on port number and DPI, so the accuracy is not trustworthy. Moreover, to meet the fine-grained requirements of encrypted traffic, it is essential to know what is running inside the encrypted tunnels, which makes the problem worse. Therefore, how to obtain accurate benchmark is a great challenge.

Overcoming Countermeasures against Traffic Analysis Is a Long-Term Fight

Since statistical classification is the most commonly used method for encrypted traffic, the adversaries have been developing new countermeasures. A confrontational encryption technique called protocol obfuscation [1] or traffic morph [17] has been developed, which is designed to fight against statistical methods by camouflaging one protocol to look like the target one or normal traffic in statistical properties. Experiment results in related works [17,18] showed that their methods were effective to beat statistical methods. Recently, Dyer K P et al [19] proposed a method called format transforming encryption to mimic any protocol format that can be denoted by a regular expression no matter what the input is. It is a universal framework for bypassing payload based classification.

3   Recent Advances in Encrypted Traffic Classification

First, classification explorations for accurate and fine-grained encrypted traffic classification are introduced in Section 3.1 to 3.3. Finally, advances in traffic analysis countermeasures and solutions are summarized in Section 3.4.

3.1   Accurate Classification Explorations

From *comparison* works in [20, 21], a rough conclusion may be that C4.5 and multi-objective genetic algorithm (MOGA) are two better choices in SSH encrypted traffic classification. Works in [22,23,24] showed that proper combinations of different techniques could overcome already well-performing stand-alone ones.

Exploration of new methods is always a direct path to effective solutions. Bacquet C et al [25] applied genetic programming to encrypt traffic classification. They used an extended MOGA in feature selection and cluster count optimization for K-Means, resulting in that the detection rate got an increase of 2% to 5%, while the FPR did not increased significantly. Xie G et.al [26] used subspace clustering to make the new classifier learn to *identify each application separately* just using its own relevant features instead of distinguishing one application from another using the unified feature sets. The approach showed very high accuracy on five traces from different ISPs, and was adaptable to change.

3.2   Multi-phased Fine-Grained Classification

Since fine-grained classification becomes the general need in real world, it is a common idea to achieve the goal by *multi-phased classification*, in which different tasks are finished respectively. A two-phased method [27] was used to classify SSH tunnel traffic, in which the SSH traffic was identified firstly, and then the statistical attributes such as average packet length et al were used to classify the applications inside the tunnel. Adami D et.al [28] proposed a joint signature-based and statistical approach called Skype-Hunter to detect and classify Skype signaling and data flows in real time. Korczynski M et.al [29] presented a three-phase method for classifying SSL encrypted Skype service TCP flows based on statistical protocol identification, which distinguished voice calls, skypeOut, video conferencing, chat, file upload and download in different phases. In [30], fine-grained classification was done by hierarchical multi-staged classification using multiple different classifiers.

To sum up, a possible general rule for encrypted traffic classification can be a multi-step process. The first phase is to identify certain encrypted traffic, and the left thing to do is fine-grainedly classifying the inner services.

3.3   Behavior Based Fine-Grained Classification

Behavior based methods are one of the common solutions to encrypted traffic classification, which is especially useful for identifying P2P applications. Behaviors here can be roughly divided into host behavior and application behavior. Host based behaviors are coarse behaviors for a class of similar applications, so the classification results are coarse-grained, such as in [31,32,33]. This type of behavior is robust for encryption, application update, and new protocols, so it may play an important role in real-time coarse-grained classification of the backbone network traffic.

Application behavior based methods relying on periodic application operations, communication mode inside the certain network, et al can be useful for fine-grained classification. Schatzmann D et.al [34] exploited host and protocol correlations, as well as periodic behavior features to detect encrypted webmail out of HTTPS traffic by Netflow data. In [35], the count of packets and bytes exchanged among peers during small time-windows were relied on for fine-grained classification of P2P-TV traffic. Xiong G et.al [36] proposed a real-time detection method for encrypted P2P traffic based on host behavior association. Based on some priori knowledge, P2P connections were identified by the communication mode between peers, peer and server, and so on. However, priori knowledge is needed and DNS traffic has to be inspected for correlation analysis. In [37], the behavior of an SSL-encrypted application, i.e. the possible SSL message type sequences, was modeled by a first-order homogeneous Markov chain and used in fine-grained application classification.

Though it seems reasonable that application behavior based approach is useful for fine-grained classification, the fact may be that only a small set of encrypted application traffic can be classified by the method. The performance of application behavior based method for encrypted traffic is still to be explored.

3.4   Countermeasures of Statistical Traffic Analysis

The countermeasures for traffic analysis of encrypted traffic are mostly against statistical classification. As is mentioned above, Wright C et.al [17] proposed a method to morph one class of traffic to look like another class in packet size distribution, which used convex optimization techniques to modify the packets real-time. SkypeMorph [18] was able to disguise the traffic from Tor clients to the bridges of Tor network as Skype video traffic, both in packet size and packet intervals, as well as the behaviors. Meanwhile, the official site of Tor provided its encryption proxy called OBFSProxy [38], claiming that the Tor traffic can be obfuscated as traffic of another protocol, such as regular HTTP, with multi-protocol supported. Similar statistical packet features masking work can be seen in [39, 40].

On the contrary, Dyer K et al [41] provided a comprehensive analysis of traffic analysis countermeasures in HTTP traffic over encrypted tunnels and showed that nine known countermeasures were vulnerable to simple attacks which exploited coarse features of traffic. In [42], It was clearly pointed out that the protocol mimicry in [18, 39] et al were not good enough, and the partial imitation could be easily identified by several passive and active methods.

In a word, protocol imitation is widely used by anonymity tools, malwares (such as P2P botnet) and attackers today to resist traffic classification techniques. It can be predicted that more anti-classification techniques will appear in future, and current classification methods much evolve to confront the coming challenges.

4   Summary and Conclusions

Encrypted traffic classification is one of the most challenging problems in traffic classification field. In this paper, we exhibit the landscape of encrypted traffic classification comprehensively. Firstly, the necessity of encrypted traffic classification is introduced. Then, the basis of encrypted traffic is summarized, followed by the classification methodology and challenges. After that, recent advances and the focuses are reviewed. We believe our work can benefit researchers in the field. In our opinion, main challenges in the field are:

- How to build large-scale datasets of encrypted traffic with accurate fine-grained ground truth is a huge burden.
- With a large number of applications using encryption techniques, how to fine-grainedly classify the traffic of a wide variety of different encryption applications is another challenge.
- How to tackle the countermeasures against statistical classification and payload-based identification is a difficult issue in future.

From the current practice, no single method is good enough. A possible practical solution to fine-grained classification may be a multiple layer classification framework composed of two or more methods. Moreover, better performance can be achieved if data related constraints are considered as in [43]. A conclusion in encrypted traffic classification is that fine-grained classification is both an essential need and a promising direction. Besides, we believe that encrypted traffic classification will benefit network forensics in future.

Acknowledgements. This work is supported by the National Science and Technology Support Program under Grant No. 2012BAH46B02 and 2012BAH45B01; the National High Technology Research and Development Program (863 Program) of China under Grant No. 2011AA010703; and the Strategic Priority Research Program of the Chinese Academy of Sciences under Grant No. XDA06030200.

References

1. eMule-Project.net - Protocol Obfuscation,
   http://www.emule-project.net/home/perl/help.cgi?l=1&rm=show_topic&topic_id=848
2. BitTorrent protocol encryption-Wikipedia,
   http://en.wikipedia.org/wiki/BitTorrent_protocol_encryption
3. Help for Skype: Does Skype use encryption,
   https://support.skype.com/en/faq/FA31/does-skype-use-encryption?frompage=search&q=encryption
4. Goldschlag, D., Reed, M., Syverson, P.: Onion routing. Communications of the ACM 42(2), 39–41 (1999)
5. Tankard, C.: Advanced Persistent threats and how to monitor and deter them. Network Security 2011(8), 16–19 (2011)

6. Valenti, S., Rossi, D., Dainotti, A., Pescapè, A., Finamore, A., Mellia, M.: Reviewing traffic classification. In: Biersack, E., Callegari, C., Matijasevic, M., et al. (eds.) Data Traffic Monitoring and Analysis. LNCS, vol. 7754, pp. 123–147. Springer, Heidelberg (2013)
7. Dainotti, A., Pescape, A., Claffy, K.: Issues and future directions in traffic classification. IEEE Network 26(1), 35–40 (2012)
8. Hu, B., Shen, Y.: Machine learning based network traffic classification: A Survey. Journal of Information and Computational Science 9(11), 3161–3170 (2012)
9. Nguyen, T., Armitage, G.: A survey of techniques for internet traffic classification using machine learning. IEEE Communications Surveys and Tutorials 10(4), 56–76 (2008)
10. Tor Project, https://www.torproject.org/
11. JAP – ANONYMITY & PRIVACY, http://anon.inf.tu-dresden.de/index_en.html
12. Service Name and Transport Protocol Port Number Registry, http://www.iana.org/assignments/service-names-port-numbers
13. Dubrawsky, I.: Firewall evolution - deep packet inspection. Infocus (July 2003), http://www.symantec.com/connect/articles/firewall-evolution-deep-packet-inspection
14. Finamore, A., Mellia, M., Meo, M., et al.: Kiss: Stochastic packet inspection. In: The First International Workshop on Traffic Monitoring and Analysis, pp. 117–125 (2009)
15. Tsirtsis, G.: Network address translation-protocol translation (NAT-PT). RFC 2766, IETF (2000)
16. Alshammari, R., Zincir-Heywood, A.N.: A flow based approach for SSH traffic detection. In: IEEE International Conference on Systems, Man and Cybernetics, pp. 296–301 (2007)
17. Wright, C., Coulls, S., Monrose, F.: Traffic morphing: an efficient defense against statistical traffic analysis. In: The 14th Annual Network and Distributed Systems Symposium (2009)
18. Mohajeri, M.H., Li, B., Derakhshani, M., et al.: Skypemorph: protocol obfuscation for tor bridges. In: 2012 ACM Conference on Computer and Communications Security, pp. 97–108 (2012)
19. Dyer, K.P., Coull, S.E., Ristenpart, T., et al.: Protocol misidentification made easy with format-transforming encryption. In: 2013 ACM SIGSAC Conference on Computer & Communications Security, pp. 61–72 (2013)
20. Alshammari, R., Zincir-Heywood, A.: Machine learning based encrypted traffic classification: identifying SSH and skype. In: the 2009 IEEE Symposium on Computation Intelligence in Security and Defense Applications, pp. 1–8 (2009)
21. Bacquet, C., Gumus, K., Tizer, D., Zincir-Heywood, A., Heywood, M.: A comparison of unsupervised learning techniques for encrypted traffic identification. Journal of Information Assurance and Security 5, 464–472 (2010)
22. Bar - Yanai, R., Langberg, M., Peleg, D., Roditty, L.: Realtime classification for encrypted traffic. In: Festa, P., et al. (eds.) SEA 2010. LNCS, vol. 6049, pp. 373–385. Springer, Heidelberg (2010)
23. Dainotti, A., Pescapé, A., Sansone, C.: Early classification of network traffic through multi-classification. In: Domingo-Pascual, J., Shavitt, Y., Uhlig, S. (eds.) TMA 2011. LNCS, vol. 6613, pp. 122–135. Springer, Heidelberg (2011)
24. Jaber, M., Cascella, R.G., Barakat, C.: Using host profiling to refine statistical application identification. In: The 2012 IEEE INFOCOM, pp. 2746–2750 (2012)
25. Bacquet, C., Zincir-Heywood, A., Heywood, M.: Genetic optimization and hierarchical clustering applied to encrypted traffic identification. In: IEEE Symposium on Computational Intelligence on Cyber Security, pp. 194–201 (2011)

26. Xie, G., Iliofotou, M., Keralapura, R., et al.: SubFlow: towards practical flow-level traffic classification. In: IEEE INFOCOM, pp. 2541–2545 (2012)
27. Hirvonen, M., Sailio, M.: Two-phased method for identifying ssh encrypted application flows. In: The 7th International Conference on Wireless Communications and Mobile Computing (IWCMC), pp. 1033–1038 (2011)
28. Adami, D., Callegari, C., Giordano, S., et al.: Skype-Hunter: A real-time system for the detection and classification of Skype traffic. International Journal of Communication Systems 25(3), 386–403 (2012)
29. Korczynski, M., Duda, A.: Classifying service flows in the encrypted skype traffic. In: 2012 IEEE International Conference on Communications (ICC), pp. 1064–1068 (2012)
30. Grimaudo, L., Mellia, M., Baralis, E.: Hierarchical learning for fine grained internet traffic classification. In: The 8th International Wireless Communications and Mobile Computing Conference (IWCMC), pp. 463–468 (2012)
31. Karagiannis, T., Papagiannaki, K., Faloutsos, M.: BLINC: multilevel traffic classification in the dark. ACM SIGCOMM Computer Communication Review 35(4), 229–240 (2005)
32. Li, B., Ma, M., Jin, Z.: A VoIP traffic identification scheme based on host and flow behavior analysis. Journal of Network and Systems Management 19(1), 111–129 (2011)
33. Hurley, J., Garcia-Palacios, E., Sezer, S.: Host-based P2P flow identification and use in real-time. ACM Transactions on the Web (TWEB) 5(2), 7 (2011)
34. Schatzmann, D., Mühlbauer, W., Spyropoulos, T., et al.: Digging into HTTPS: flow-based classification of webmail traffic. In: 10th ACM SIGCOMM Conference on Internet Measurement, pp. 322–327 (2010)
35. Bermolen, P., Mellia, M., Meo, M., et al.: Abacus: Accurate behavioral classification of P2P-TV traffic. Computer Networks 55(6), 1394–1411 (2011)
36. Xiong, G., Huang, W., Zhao, Y., Song, M., Li, Z., Guo, L.: Real-time detection of encrypted thunder traffic based on trustworthy behavior association. In: Yuan, Y., Wu, X., Lu, Y. (eds.) ISCTCS 2012. CCIS, vol. 320, pp. 132–139. Springer, Heidelberg (2013)
37. Korczynski, M., Duda, A.: Markov chain fingerprinting to classify encrypted traffic. In: 2014 IEEE INFOCOM, pp. 781–789 (2014)
38. Tor Project: obfsproxy, https://www.torproject.org/projects/obfsproxy.html
39. Weinberg, Z., Wang, J., Yegneswaran, V., et al.: StegoTorus: a camouflage proxy for the Tor anonymity system. In: The 2012 ACM Conference on Computer and Communications Security, pp. 109–120 (2012)
40. Iacovazzi, A., Baiocchi, A.: From ideality to practicability in statistical packet features masking. In: The 8th International Wireless Communications and Mobile Computing Conference (IWCMC), pp. 456–462 (2012)
41. Dyer, K., Coull, S., Ristenpart, T., Shrimpton, T.: Peek-a-boo, i still see you: why efficient traffic analysis countermeasures fail. In: The 2012 IEEE Symposium on Security and Privacy, pp. 332–346 (2012)
42. Houmansadr, A., Brubaker, C., Shmatikov, V.: The parrot is dead: observing unobservable network communications. In: 2013 IEEE Symposium on Security and Privacy (SP), pp. 65–79 (2013)
43. Wang, Y., Xiang, Y., Zhang, J., et al.: Internet traffic clustering with constraints. In: The 8th International Wireless Communications and Mobile Computing Conference (IWCMC), pp. 619–624 (2012)

An Approach to Detect the Internet Water Army via Dirichlet Process Mixture Model Based GSP Algorithm

Dan Li[1,*], Qian Li[2], Yue Hu[2], Wenjia Niu[2], Jianlong Tan[2], and Li Guo[2]

[1] University of Science and Technology Beijing,
No.30, Xueyuan Road, Haidian District, Beijing, 100083, China
danli@nelmail.iie.ac.cn
[2] Institute of Information Engineering,
Chinese Academy of Sciences,
No.89Minzhuang Road, Beijing, 100093, China
{liqian,niuwenjia,tanjiantong,guoli}@iie.ac.cn

Abstract. The Internet Water Army (IWA) brings a great threat on cyber security. How to accurately recognize the IWA has become a challenging research issue. Most work exploits the behavioral analysis to distinguish IWA and non-IWA. These approaches are mainly divided into categories: direct compute method and training learning method. The direct calculation method mainly relies on crawler, and makes multidimensional eigenvector to detect IWA. Nevertheless, it did not consider the behavior rules based on the time sequence, and just determine the user behavior by feather vector, so the results are not very accurate. The recognition rate also needs to be improved. The second method mainly relies on cluster approaches. However, cluster approaches require predetermined the number of clustering, which will directly lead to the model over fitting and owe fitting because of inadequate unit number. In this paper we propose a sequential pattern approach based on DPMM for IWA identification. Firstly, we analyze the user behavior of potential IWA and get a feature vector of user behavior. Secondly, we use DPMM to get effective and accurate clustering results. Finally, we use the sequential pattern mining algorithms to detect navy accounts. Our clustering results with datasets come from Tianya forum show a very ideal consequence.

Keywords: Internet Water Army, DPMM, Sequential Pattern Mining Algorithm, GSP.

1 Introduction

With the rapid development of social network, security problems have become more and more prominent, which comes from the internet water army (IWA) is the most common. They are employed by public relationship companies. According to the relevant institutions survey, the number of pushing hands who are engaging in

---

* Corresponding author.

L. Batten et al. (Eds.): ATIS 2014, CCIS 490, pp. 82–95, 2014.

online marketing activities has reached millions. They make money by posting comments and articles on different online communities and websites. However, the behavior of IWA has broken the law. Since the laws and supervision mechanisms for Internet marketing are still not mature in China, it is possible to spread wrong and malicious information. This behavior will lead to malicious network culture infiltration, even endanger national security. So, it is necessary to design ways to help common online users and administrators quickly detect potential IWA.

Detecting IWA is not an independent research subject, and will be a relatively complex multidisciplinary comprehensive research. Now domestic and foreign scholars mainly focus on machine learning and data mining. The research can be divided into two categories, one kind is content-based analysis, and another kind is behavior-based analysis. From posting content itself, the content-based analysis distinguishes normal and abnormal by statistical language features, and then find IWA. While behavior-based analysis distinguishes normal and abnormal by the modeling analyzes registration behavior, social behavior, forwarding and comments etc, and then find IWA.

The behavior-based analysis mostly relies on the crawler technology crawl user registration behavior, social behavior, forward behavior, comments behavior and so on, and then carve multidimensional eigenvector. However, content-based analysis mainly rely on post content. Most of analysis has good understanding ability for regular machine posting, and language of senior IWA has usually higher concealment and changing in the fight, it is difficult to extracts the rumors and fraud in a time and effective manner through the evolution of high-level semantics, so this way cannot timely catch up the rhythm of IWA evolution without strong support of behavior analysis. So we can find IWA behavioral regularities by comparing multidimensional eigenvector, and work out identify plans. This way fundamentally improved IWA recognition rate, and contribute to the rapid progress of research on IWA recognition.

We can find the behavior-based analysis is the most common way by related work. This way has greatly improved than the based on post content analysis in the recognition speed and accuracy. However, on the one hand behavior-based analysis depends on the selection of features to a large extent. It is no clear conclusion that which behavior characteristics of IWA are relatively effective. It is not enough that we just rely on features to analyze the user behavior. On the other hand multidimensional eigenvector does not also consider the time sequence that is the more correct to analyze user behavior. In conclusion, we establish feature vector based on time sequence, and then excavate user behavior to use sequential pattern mining algorithm [7]. Sequential pattern mining algorithm is the first applied in IWA detection, and is applied to analyze user behavior. For example, the customer purchasing behavior, DNA sequence analysis and so on.

The sequential pattern algorithm needs clustering algorithm to accomplish cluster, such as K-means, CURE, KNN, and Neural Networks and so on. However, these approaches require pre-determined the number of clustering or mixers, the models will appear over fitting or under fitting because of inadequate unit number. Therefore, it is critical that how to choose the right number of clusters for cluster analysis, while which also decides how to select model in the pattern classification. For above problems, we adopt Dirichlet Process Mixture Model (DPMM), DPMM is nonparametric clustering method, and has strong flexibility and robustness. DPMM do not need to specify the category number in advance, but according to the observation data automatically calculate the required number, and DPMM allow new category to create in probability way when new data emerge. When we calculate a posteriori probability of DPMM, due to the posterior probability can't be calculated directly, so we use Gibbs sampling method to sample repeatedly and update the model parameters. Gibbs sampling method produces a Markov Chain which can achieve steady state after a sufficient number of samples.

We can get better result of clustering through DPMM, then we use GSP algorithm to analyze every category, and get satisfied condition of sequential patterns. Every sequential pattern indicates one user's behavior patterns over a period of time. Through analyzing user behavior, we can detect IWA. We make the following contributions.

- We collect real data from Tianya, a Chinese famous internet forum, in which we believe there are many hidden IWA.
- We analyze the user behavior of potential IWA and get a feature vector of user behavior, and we describe user behavior to use it.
- We use DPMM to cluster without allocating number of cluster, and the result of cluster get more effective and more accurate comparing to other clustering algorithms.
- We use the sequential pattern mining algorithms [9] to detect IWA on the basis of result with cluster.

The rest of the paper is organized as follows. We identify several key features about user behavior in Section 2. Section 3 describes DPMM cluster algorithm. In Section 4, we present the sequential pattern mining algorithms to detect account of IWA. In Section 5, we present the experiment. Related work is discussed in Section 6. We conclude the paper in Section 7.

2   Water Account Feature Vector

In a social network, a user contains a lot of information, such as user name, password, registration time, logins, recent login time, browsing history, posting record Replies record, circle of friends, browsing history, login IP records, and so on. It is obviously different between the normal users and the navy in some information, for example, the user name of normal users usually have a specific meaning, so the user name length is generally between 4-12 English characters, and the navy in order simple, often use the user name one or two English characters. Normal users have corresponding circle of friends in the forum, form a small social network, and IWA only for the purpose of posting hardly exists circle.

According to the study, the patent proposes network forum user behavior history multi-attribute Description Framework, vectors for the user to describe the historical behavior, so as to quantify the behavior of said user history and DPMM clustering analysis foundation. We describe user historical behavior to use vectors. Network forum user history description framework as shown in Table 1.

Table 1. Network forum user history behavior description framework

Attribute Name	Explanation
UserName	This is userID
ReplyPostNumber	This is number of replying post
FansNumber	This is number of fans
ConsiderNumber	This is attention number
ActiveDays	This is active days of users

3   DPMM Clustering Algorithm

3.1   DPMM

As distributed on distribution, Dirichlet process is generated by the Dirichlet distribution, which is a Dirichlet distribution extension on continuous space. As usual, Dirichlet process is expressed as[4]:

$$G \sim DP(\alpha, G_0) \tag{1}$$

Where G_0 is the based distribution; α is ($\alpha > 0$) the concentration parameter and represents the approximation degree between G and G_0; G represents a random distribution which is generated based on the based distribution and concentration parameter. As α increase, G is closer to G_0. Supposing that $\eta_1, \ldots, \eta_n$ are independent random observed variables which obey G distribution.

$\eta_1^*, \ldots, \eta_k^*$ are different observed values, so the forecast conditional distribution of new random observed variable η_{n+1} is that [1]:

$$p(\eta_{n+1} = \eta^* | \eta_1, \ldots, \eta_n, \alpha_0, H_0) = \frac{1}{n+\alpha_0} \sum_{k=1}^{K} N_k \, \delta(\eta^*, \eta_k^*) + \frac{\alpha_0}{n+\alpha_0} H_0(\eta^*) \tag{2}$$

Where N_k is the number of variables which are equal to η_k^* in the sequence of $\eta_1, \ldots, \eta_n$.

From (2) formula, we can see that Dirichlet process has a good performance of clustering property [1],which gathers those data that has the same value as a class. While if the two data are not equal, regardless of how much similar between them, they can't achieve clustering by using the Dirchlet process, which greatly limits its application. So that we introduce the Dirchlet process mixture model [15,16].

X={x₁,…,xₙ}is a data collection to be clustered [4], N represents the number of samples in this collection, x_i={x_{i1},x_{i2},…,x_{iG}} is the i-th sample, x_{ig} is the g-th eigenvalue of the i-th sample, and each sample is independent. Based on the limited model clustering algorithm, X is consisted by K normal mixture models (K has been known). In order to solve K, we define a hidden variable s={s_1,…,s_N}, s_i∈{1,2,…,K} represents the cluster label of samples, s_i=k shows that the i-th sample belongs to the k-th type after clustering analysis. The p(·) is the distribution of each component in this model, and every complies with different distribution parameters θ_k, θ_k={μ_k,σ_k^2}, μ_k represents the average value of the k-th component of the model, σ_k^2 represents the variance. As the posteriori estimate of clustering, π_k is the mixing coefficient of k-th component in the model, and π_k≥0, k={1,2,…,k}, and $\sum_{k=1}^{k} \pi_k = 1$ .Supposing that θ={π_1,π_2,…,π_k;θ_1,θ_2,…,θ_k}, θ represents each unknown parameter in the finite mixture model, so that we build a finite normal mixture model, as shown in (3):

$$p(x_i|\theta) = \sum_{k=1}^{K} \pi_k \, p(x_i|\theta_k), p(x_i|\theta_k) = N(x_i; \mu_k, \sigma_k^2) \tag{3}$$

Supposing that θ={π_1,π_2,…,π_k;θ_1,θ_2,…,θ_k}, θ represents each unknown parameter in the unlimited hybrid model. Because the number of clusters k is unknown, we assume that it is the approaching infinity in the unlimited hybrid model. Based on high-dimensional data, this paper proposes the Dirchelet unlimited hybrid model, as shown in (4):

$$x_i \sim p(x_i|\theta_{s_i})(i = 1,2, … , N), \theta_i \sim G, G \sim DP(\alpha, G_0) \tag{4}$$

The digraph of Dirichlet process mixture model [17,18] is shown in Figure 1[11,14]. In all digraphs, open circles represent variables, the shaded circle represents an observable variable, rounded rectangles represent parameters or basic distribution, the rectangular box represents the iteration loop and the lower right corner of digital represents the number of cycles.

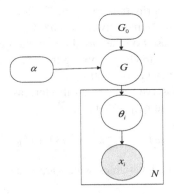

Fig. 1. The Dirichlet process mixture model

Data clustering and distributed parameter estimation can be achieved by using of the Dirchlet process mixture model. In the Dirchlet process mixture model, there are two methods to achieve data clustering analysis: one has been developed in recent years, which takes advantage of variational inference for approximate calculation of the probability distribution of the data in order to achieve clustering analysis or distributed parameter estimation [11,12]. And the other utilizes the Gibbs sampling algorithm to estimate the data clustering result by cycle sampling [13].

Currently, nonparametric Bayesian model is mainly using Gibbs sampling algorithm which looks the Dirichlet process as a prior distribution. This method has a better feasibility than the variational inference and generally it doesn't need to make approximations only need to do loop sampling for a series of conditional probability distribution. The calculation speed of variational inference is fast, but it is difficult to get an effective variational inference algorithm. Therefore, this patent mainly adopts the Gibbs sampling algorithm.

3.2   The Sampling of Dirichlet Process Mixture Model

Data collection obeys Dirichlet process mixture model which is $X=\{x_1,...,x_N\}$. Since the observed data is commutative which is conditionally independent [6], we can regardless the order when the observed data is being on a cluster analysis. The propose of cluster analysis is to obtain a cluster tag of each data s_i promise: when the superscript or subscript of variable has a symbol "\" in the text, for instance $S_{\backslash i}$ indicates that corresponding to subscript variables are removed from the set of variables. This is to say that $S_{\backslash i}$ is a dataset which is composed by the remaining data that is got after removing s_i from the $s=\{s_1,...,s_N\}$. Given that other data indicating factors $S_{\backslash i}$ have been given, we can obtain the conditional distribution of s_i based on the Bayesian formula:

$$p\big(s_i|x_1,...,x_N,S_{\backslash i},\lambda,\alpha_0\big) \propto p\big(s_i|S_{\backslash i},\alpha_0\big)p\big(x_i|s_1,...,s_N,X_{\backslash i},\lambda\big) \tag{5}$$

Where the right-hand can be expressed by CRP of the Dirchlet process. Because each observation can be exchangeable, we can think the i-th observation data as the last observation. If $S_{\backslash i}$ has contained K categories and the number of observations is $N_k^{\backslash i}$ in each category, the first is:

$$z_i|Z_{\backslash i},\alpha \sim \sum_k^K \frac{N_k^{\backslash i}}{N-1+\alpha}\delta\,(z_i,k) + \frac{\alpha}{N-1+\alpha}\delta(z_i,\bar{k})$$

If the indicating factor of i-th observation is the $s_i=k$, then

$$p\big(x_i|s_i=k,X_{\backslash i},\lambda\big) = p\big(x_i|\{x_i|s_j=k,j\neq i\},\lambda\big) = \frac{\int_\theta f(x_i|\theta)\prod_{s_j=k,j\neq i}f(x_j|\theta)g(\theta|\gamma)\,d\theta}{\int_\theta \prod_{s_j=k,j\neq i}f(x_j|\theta)g(\theta|\lambda)\,d\theta} \tag{6}$$

If $s_i = \bar{k}$ is a new category, then

$$p\big(x_i|s_i=\bar{k},X_{\backslash i},\lambda\big) = p(x_i|\lambda) = \int_\theta p(x_i|\theta)g(\theta|\lambda)\,d\theta \tag{7}$$

Therefore,

$$p(s_i|x_i, \dots, x_N, S_{\backslash i}, \lambda, \alpha) \propto$$

$$\sum_k^K \frac{N_k^{\backslash i}}{N-1+\alpha} \times P(x_i|\{x_j|s_j = k, j \neq i\}, \lambda)\delta(s_i, k) + \frac{\alpha}{N-1+\alpha} \int_\theta p(x_i|\theta)g(\theta|\lambda)\,d\theta\delta(s_i, \bar{k}) \tag{8}$$

The sampling algorithm Gibbs of Dirichlet process mixture model can be derived by using of (6) ~ (8). In this algorithm, $S^{(t)}$ can describe the classification results of the observation data in the t-th loop sampling, and $K^{(t)}$ represents the number of clusters. After entering the (t-1)-th sampling results: $S^{(t-1)}$, $K^{(t-1)}$, $\alpha^{(t-1)}$, we can be sampled in accordance with the following procedure [14]:

(a) Making the N observations ordered randomly, $\sigma(i), i=1,\dots,N$.
(b) Assigning $\alpha = \alpha^{(t-1)}$ and $S = S^{(t-1)}$. And $i \in (\sigma(1),\dots,\sigma(n))$, then the S_i is sampled.
   (i) Existing K clusters, the likelihood estimation of each observational data is calculated for every cluster:

$$f_k(x_i) = p(x_i|s_i = \bar{k}, X_{\backslash i}, \lambda) \text{ and } f_{\bar{k}}(x_i) = p(x_i|s_i = \bar{k}, X_{\backslash i}, \lambda) \tag{9}$$

   (ii) S_i is sampled according to the following distribution:

$$p(s_i|x_1, \dots, x_N, S_{\backslash i}, \lambda, \alpha) \sim \frac{1}{s_i}(\sum_k^K N_k^{\backslash i} f_k(x_i)\delta(s_i, k) + \alpha f_{\bar{k}}(x_i)\delta(s_i, \bar{k})) \tag{10}$$

Among $s_i = \sum_k^K f_k(x_i) + \alpha f_{\bar{k}}(x_i)$, and N\i k denotes the amount of the data that has been already in the k-th type. If $S_i = \bar{k}$ then add 1.

(c) Checking the amount of data observations in each class, if the total number of someone is zero, this class will be removed and the total number of clusters K minus 1.
(d) If the initial parameter is sampled in the $\alpha \sim \Gamma(a, b)$, the parameters are updated according to the following formula:

$$\alpha^{(t)} \sim p(\alpha|K, N, a, b) \tag{11}$$

The above procedure is commonly used algorithms Collapsed Gibbs sampling algorithm, removing the unwanted variables integral, only our concern variables are sampled. We can use CRP to describe this algorithm: According to the formula (8), a customer is selected randomly and assigned to one dining table. If the customer chooses a new table, then we add a table in the restaurant and the number of table plus one. After all customers are totally assigned, if some dining tables aren't selected we remove them out from restaurant and the number of table minus the corresponding number.

4   Determining IWA Accounts by Using the Sequential Pattern Mining Algorithms

We can get a better clustering effect through Dirichlet process mixture model but not distinguish which belongs to navy accounts. So we have to find a effective method to distinguish those navy accounts. In this patent, we find the most frequent transaction sequence of each class by using the sequential pattern mining algorithms, and distinguish the navy account from each sequence of user actions.

4.1   Sequential Pattern Mining Module Processes

The sequential pattern mining is to find all sequences satisfy the minimum support under a certain condition which has a given a sequence in the database and the minimum support degree min_sup. Every of those sequences is called to a sequence mode. Where support degree is the proportion of sequence S in the sequence database DT.

The process of sequential pattern mining module is as follows[5]:

1   Sort all sequences by the key word which contains user identify and time behavior,and then the transaction set of user behavior data is converted to a sequence database D.
2   Scan D, and then find out the frequent item sets according to the given minimum support degree min_sup, and cast light upon some recognizable simple symbols, such as letters or consecutive numbers.
3   Each sequence of D is converted into the frequent items format which is included in the D and represented by mapping symbols.
    Process:
    If (the sequence of D contains the given frequent item) Then
        Transform this sequence.
    Else make the frequent item be symbolic
    Endif
4   To accomplish the sequential pattern mining, we adopt appropriate mining algorithm to those data which has done the conversion process.
5   Mode optimization.
    Process: Mode optimization is mainly doing some dealings to a series of sequential pattern which are generated through the sequential pattern mining, which contains deleting those unvalued sequence mode, generalizing, consolidation and classification sequence mode. After optimization, the ultimately retained mode is the desired sequence.

4.2   The Description of Social Network User Behavior Patterns

The final class is marked as $I_k(1<=k<=K)$, which is obtained by the social network clustering. And $I_K=\{i_1,i_2,...,i_n\}$ denotes each class collection of user behavior.The item $i_j(1<=j<=n)$ is the various functional applications about the using of social network users. Suppose X as the user behavior affairs and marked as <ID, U_ID, s,

time>.Where ID is the transaction identification number , U_ID denotes user identification number, s represents a collection of social applications which is applied by users in some special time and is called for transaction set; time represents the time when transaction occurs(it may be a moment, someday, one week and so on). The sequence S= <s_1, s_2,..., s_n> represents a transaction set sequence which is applied to social applications by users. All transactions have the same user identification number U_ID and are arranged in chronological order. By transforming users browsing behavior transaction data, we record and merger those which has the same U_ID, and then arrange them in chronological order. Finally, we get the transaction set sequence and then obtain a sequence database. Sequential pattern mining can be achieved in this sequence database. The task of social network users behavior sequence pattern mining is to find out the most interested frequent transaction sequence from the social affairs sequence used by users.

4.3   The Sequential Pattern Mining Algorithm

Selecting the GSP algorithm to complete the mining process, the core of this algorithm is that we search through the drill and generate and detect the candidate set to achieve the sequential pattern mining, based on the property what all non-empty set of frequent sets are frequent. The GSP algorithm follows the main course:

Input: according to the frequent item set conversion sequence database, getting the minimum support min_sup.
Output: The collection of sequence mode
1   L_1 is the maximum value in sequences set;
2   For (k = 2;$L_k \neq 1$;k ++) DO BEGIN
3   Ck= GSPgenerate(L_k-1);
4   For each sequences in the database DT DO
5   Increment the count of all candidates in C_k that are contained in s;
6   End For
7   L_k = Candidates in C_k with minimum support;
8   End For;
9   Return $\cup_k L_k$;

Assigning the threshold of minimum support min_sup and scanning the sequence database, we get a frequent item set and make it mapping simultaneously. Using the above algorithm, we can obtain the sequence pattern which satisfies the conditions for each category. By analyzing each category sequence pattern, we can find some like listening songs and uploading photos; some is keen on interacting with others, and only one of those types devote their mind to post. When you observe the content of those posts in a certain period of time, you will find that all contents is on a same topic. By comparing each category sequence pattern, we can get those users' behaviors for each category and then can determine which category is navy account.

5   Experiment

5.1   Setting Up

We get 3019 user information from Tianya forum by using web crawlers. The information contains 5 behavior related dimensions which including username, the number of replying post, the number of fans, the number of attention, active days. Then we try to cluster directly by DPMM. Building a DPMM is to do cluster analysis for above dataset, and model parameters are estimated by MCMC Gibbs sampling analysis. Through the parameter α which is constantly updated by the MCMC Gibbs sample, we can estimate the final potential cluster number of above datasets. Finally, we use GSP algorithm to obtain useful sequence, and analyze sequence to get user behavior. In this way, we can detect IWA well.

5.2   Result

We get four categories after 430 times of MCMC Gibbs sampling, and this result is fully corresponding to the model parameter of simulated datasets. The figure 2 is clustering histogram. Experimental results show that when DPMM is used for cluster analysis, it can automatically calculate the required number of categories according to the observation data so that doesn't need to pre-assign the number of categories. At the same time, it allows to generate a new category by way of probability when a new data appears. It can be seen, the clustering algorithm of DPMM has good clustering effect, strong flexibility and robustness.

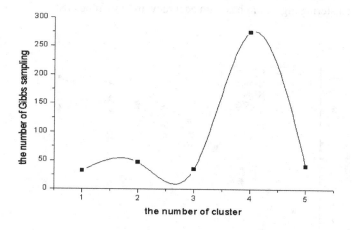

Fig. 2. Cluster Histogram

We conducted sequential pattern mining for each class, and identify users frequent transaction sequence pattern. We use GSP algorithm to process data through the frequent sequences conversion. Through analysis with compare, we find that only one class gets frequent sequences at support more than 80%. The result is shown in Table 2. Including 01 represent users post articles, 02 represent user comment posts, 05 represent exit the forum. Reflecting sequence pattern: more than 80% of users will quit forum after comment; more than 80% of users will quit forum after posting. We find that the post or the message is about a certain topic by look at the content of the post or the message. So this class is IWA.

Table 2. Mining results of meeting support

Number	Frequent sequence
1	<02,05>
2	<01,05>

5.3   Performance Comparison

In Figure 3, we design the experiment to show cluster accuracy with different number of data. The dataset has 2000 data. Every time we add 200 data to calculate accuracy of four kind algorithms. With the increase of data, four kind of clustering algorithm showed a trend of growth. However, DPMM always has an averagely better accuracy than other clustering algorithm. In Figure 4, we design the experiment to show the cluster cost with different cluster accuracy. We determined that we should take an accuracy of 85% to 90% as a threshold to get time cost of four kind algorithms. We can see the time cost of four kind algorithms when achieve the accuracy goal from figure. We can also observe that the time cost of DPMM algorithm is much lower than other three kinds of clustering algorithms. From the above, the DPMM clustering algorithm has high accuracy and low time cost.

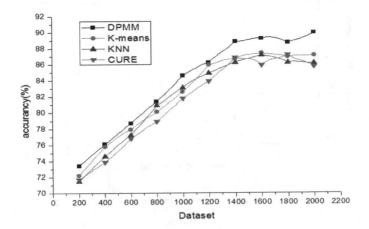

Fig. 3. Cluster Accuracy

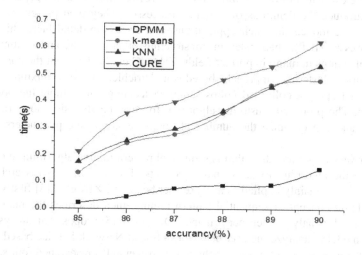

Fig. 4. Cluster Cost

6   Conclusions

This paper proposes a DPMM based on GSP algorithm for IWA identification. We found that DPMM can accelerate the user data pre-process when the data set is complex and large. And that the GSP algorithm also can efficiently analyze user behavior. We believe that this research still runs its beginning stage, and in the future, we will put more study and discussion on how to control the balance point between computing cost and identification accuracy.

7   Related Work

In this paper, we focus on detecting water account. We use DPMM [3,4,6,1,7]to cluster of no classified sample data collection, Cluster analysisis done by Gibbs sampling algorithm, repeated sampling and update the model parameters from the conditional distribution ,estimated clustering results. When clustering effect is more obvious, we get the behavior sequence for each class with equential pattern mining algorithm [5,8,9,10]. Through analyzing user behavior sequence, we will get the user behavior and well distinguish Internet water army. To the best of our knowledge, this paper is the first to detect TWA on using DPMM.

Some of previous work about DPMM is similar to ours. Researchers have done plenty of work in this area to design better cluster mechanisms. Xu et al.[3] introduces the origin and development of Dirichlet process, and the methods for model calculating. This paper also demonstrates how to use this model to solve natural language processing task. Zhang et al.[4] built a Dirichlet process infinite mixture model to cluster high dimensional data. All parameters, including the number of potential clusters were estimated through Gibbs sampling MCMC method in this paper. ZHOU et al.[6] introduce the denitions of Dirichlet processes. They then present Dirichlet process mixture models and their applications, and discuss in detail hierarchical Dirichlet processes(HDP), their roles in constructing other models, and examples of related applications in many important fields. ZHANG et al.[1] present the concept of nonparametric clustering approach based on Dirichlet process mixture model (DPMM), and apply a collapsed Gibbs sampling technique to sample the posterior distribution. The proposed clustering algorithm follows the Bayesian nonparametric framework and can optimize the number of components and the parameters of the model.

Another very important algorithm is sequential pattern mining algorithm in our paper, we use the algorithm to detect navy accounts. The algorithm is researched by many people, and mainly applied to analyze user behavior. XIA et al.[8] firstly introduces the basic concept of sequential pattern mining, then describes the main algorithms and finally analyzes their performance. Ding et al. [5] proposed an analysis and prediction model to analyze the user behavior in Social Network Service based on the sequence characteristics of SNS user behavior. LIAN et al.[9] researched four sequential patterns mining algorithms namely AprioriAll, GSP, FreeSpan, Prefixspan, and studied their characters. They also pointed out the conditions in which each algorithm was applied. CHEN et al.[10] provided a review of the research of sequential pattern mining. Firstly, introduced the background and context. Secondly, summarized the general methods of sequence pattern mining, introduced and analyzed the most representative algorithm to provide a basis for improving old algorithms or developing new effective ones. Finally, discussed some future research trends on this area.

Acknowledgements. This work was partially supported by the National 973 Project (No. 2013CB329605) and the National Natural Science Foundation of China (NO.61103158),The Strategic Priority Research Program of the Chinese Academy of Science Grant (XDA06030200),the National High-Tech Research and Development Plan 863 of China (Grant NO.2011AA010703),the Securing CyberSpaces Research Cluster of Deakin University.

References

1. Zhang, Y.: Data Clustering via Nonparametric Bayesian Modelsm. Journal of Ningbo University (NSEE) 26(4), 24–28 (2013)
2. Chen, C., Wu, K., Srinivasan, V., et al.: Battling the internet water army: Detection of hidden paid posters. In: Proceedings of the 2013 IEEE/ACM International Conference on Advances in Social Networks Analysis and Mining, pp. 116–120. ACM (2013)
3. Xu, Q., Zhou, J., Chen, J.: Dirichlet Process and Its Applications in Natural Language Processing. Journal of Chinese Information Processing 23(5), 25–32 (2009)
4. Zhang, L., Liu, H.: A clustering method based on Dirichlet process mixture model. Journal of Chian University of Mining Technology 41(1), 159–163 (2012)
5. Ding, Z., Song, W., Li, J.: User Behavior An alysis in Social Network Service Based on Sequential Pattern. Journal of Moder Information 33(3), 56–60 (2013)

6. Zhou, J., Wang, F., Zeng, D.: Hierarchical Dirichlet Processes and Their Applications. Acta Automatica Sinica 37(4), 389–407 (2011)

7. Mei, S., Wang, F., Zhou, S.: Dirichlet process mixture model, extensions and applications. Chin. Sci. Bull. (Chin Ver.) 57(34), 3243–3257 (2012)

8. Xia, M., Wang, X., Sun, Y., Jin, T.: Research on Sequential Pattern Mining Algorithms. Computer Technology and Development 16(4), 4–6 (2006)

9. Lu, F., Zhang, W.: Research on the Characters of Four Sequential Patterns Mining Algorithms. Journal of Wuhan University of Technology 28(2), 57–60 (2006)

10. Chen, Z., Yang, B., Song, W., Song, Z.: Survey of sequential pattern mining. Application Research of Computers 25(7), 1960–1963 (2008)

11. Teh, Y.W., Jordan, M.I., Beal, M.J., et al.: Hierarchical dirichlet processes. Journal of the American Statistical Association 101(476), 1566–1581 (2006)

12. Wang, C., Blei, D.M.: Variational inference for the nested Chinese restaurant process. In: Proceedings of the 23rd Annual Conference on Neural Information Processing Systems, Canada, pp. 1990–1998 (2009)

13. Casella, G., George, E.I.: Explaining the Gibbs sampler. The American Statistician 46(3), 167–174 (2009)

14. Sudderth, E.B.: Graphical Models for Visual Object Recognition and Tracking [Ph. D. dissertation], Department of Electrical Engineering and Computer Science, USA (2006)

15. Escobar, M.D., West, M., West, M.: Bayesian density estimation and inference using mixtures. Journal of the AmericanStatistical Association 90(430), 577–588 (1995)

16. Antoniak, C.E.: Mixtures of Dirichlet processes with applications to Bayesian nonparametric problems. The Annals of Statistics 2(6), 1152–1174 (1974)

17. Hjort, N.L., Holmes, C., Muller, P., Walker, S.G.: Bayesian Nonparametrics. Cambridge University Press, Cambridge (2010)

18. Koller, D., Friedman, N.: Probabilistic Graphical Models:Principles and Techniques. The MIT Press, Massachusetts (2009)

19. MacQueen, J.: Some Methods for Classification and Analysis of Multivariate Observations. In: Proceedings of the fifth Berkeley Symposium on Mathematical Statistics and Probability, vol. 1(14), pp. 281–297 (1967)

20. Ester, M., Kriecel, H.P., Aander, J., et al.: A density-based algorithm for discovering clusters in large spatial database with noise. In: Proceedings of the 2nd International Conference on Knowledge Discovering and Data Mining, Portland, pp. 226–231 (1996)

21. Sheikholeslami, G., Chattrerjee, S., Zhang, A.: WaveCluster:A Multi-Resolution Clustering Approach for Very Large Apatial Databases. In: Proceedings of the 24th VLDB Conference, New York, USA, pp. 428–439 (1998)

Modeling and Analysis of Network Survivability under Attack Propagation

Su Yao[1,2], Jianfeng Guan[3], Shuwei Ding[2], Hongke Zhang[1], and Fei Song[1]

[1] School of Electronics and Information Engineering,
Beijing Jiaotong University, Beijing, China
{13111027,hkzhang,fsong}@bjtu.edu.cn
[2] China Aero-Polytechnology Establishment, Beijing, China
bjtuyaosu@163.com
[3] Insisute of Network Technology,
Beijing University of Posts and Telecommunications, Beijing, China
jfguan@bupt.edu.cn

Abstract. Survivability of networks has emerged as a fundamental concern for network design and operation. The network physical infrastructures are vulnerable to correlated faults from the natural disasters and malicious attack. Particularly, malicious attacks attract more attention rather than natural disasters recently. This paper investigates network survivability in the presence of network attack propagation. Especially, a continuous-time Markov chain model is used to characterize the network survivability performance during the transient period that starts from the attack occurrence, in the subsequent attack propagation, and until the network has been full recovery. On the basis of the model, we compare two different schemes with the transient reward measures. Furthermore, network survivability of each scheme is exemplified for four propagation and repair strategies. The numerical results indicate the scheme with immunized state is more survivable than the scheme without immunized state, which is not only helpful to the survivability of network design but also useful to choose the suitable repair strategies.

Keywords: Network survivability, Attack propagation, Markov chain.

1 Introduction

In the past decade, Internet has become the most critical infrastructures of our society. As a result, the survivability of network is the key factor of the network security, which can be defined as the ability of the network continually delivering the required data when facing natural events and human threats [1].

Due to natural events (hurricane, earthquake) and human threats (worm virus, DDoS attack), disaster and network attack propagation has a significant impact on the network communication. Over the year, network attack has become a much more serious threat to the survivability of Internet. According to the recent Security Report 2013[2], compiled by network security firm NSFOCUS, which details network attack

L. Batten et al. (Eds.): ATIS 2014, CCIS 490, pp. 96–108, 2014.

trends and methodologies during the past year. In each hour, there are about 27.9 network attacks all over the world and most of the attacks (91.1 percent) lasted less than 30 minutes.

The definitions, metrics and quantification methods of network survivability have been studied over the decades in paper [3],[4],[5]. As a fundamental property, network design and operation is need to consider. In paper [3], a framework is proposed to seek ways to improve the survivability of current networks. It requires an understanding of dynamical network recovery behaviors under failure patterns. In paper [4],[5],[6], different mathematical models have been proposed, to analyze the impact of disasters on the network as well as for estimating the benefits of network survivability. In paper [7], a Markov model is applied to characterize the network survivability in the presence of static disastrous failures and repairs, which considers a static disastrous event that destroy telephone access network. In paper [8], the authors make extensive study of modeling and analyzing disaster propagation. However, their model is limited in the area of disaster propagation.

Therefore, up till now little is known about the network survivability in the propagation of network attack. Similarly, the propagation can be typically modeled via Markov theory. In this paper, we will still use the Markova model to characterize the survivability in the presence of network attack, which considers a static event that destroys all network components in one area.

2   Model Description

To quantify the meaning of survivability, we use the definition given by ANSI T1A1.2 committee [9], the attributes are shown in Fig.1, which gives a clear illustration of the properties of survivability. The X-axis of the figure indicates time while the Y-axis indicates the survivability performance. In this paper, we characterize the network survivability under the network attack propagation based on the ANSI T1A1.2 framework.

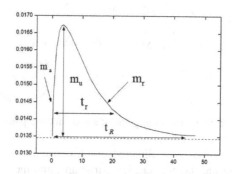

Fig. 1. Illustration of survivability (adapted from [6])

It is well known, Internet is composed of many core networks and access networks. Given an access network, we can easily derive its topology. A node in the topology presents a subnet in the access networks. Let random variable $X_i(t)$ denote the state of a node i at the discrete time t. Then we have

$$X_i(t) = \begin{cases} Hea., healthy \begin{cases} Sus., susceptible, \\ Im\,m., immunizied, \end{cases} \\ Inf., inf\,ected. \end{cases} \quad (1)$$

The state transition graph of node i has been shown in Fig. 2. As shown in the graph, when node i is at the susceptible state, it can either transmits to the infected state (the infection probability is presented by $\lambda(t)$) or the immunized state (the re-cover probability is presented by $\mu(t)$). However, when the node is in the infected state, it can only transits to the immunized state with the recovery state $\mu(t)$. Then the node will stay in the immunized state. Moreover, no matter which state the node is at, it may transit to the immunized state at last.

To evaluate and analyze the survivability of a network system subject to an attack, which consisted of a time sequence of single events, a quantitative assessment model is highly needed. It starts by an initial attack on a subnet of access network and spreads to another subnet, and the next. The propagation continues in a cascade-like manner to other subnets. Such phenomena is called network attack propagation. Different from the disaster propagation, network attack propagation can be originated from the internal network, and may have more state. In the following, we develop a model of network system, particularly for network attack, where the propagation can be across geographical areas.

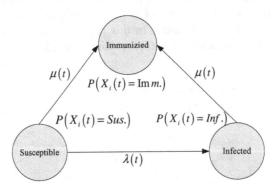

Fig. 2. State transition graph of a node in the topology

A network can be viewed as a directed graph consisting of nodes and directed edges. The nodes represent the network infrastructures and the directed edges denote the directions of transition. The network is vulnerable to all sorts of disaster, which may start on some network nodes and propagate to other node during the random time. The disaster propagation can be considered as a stochastic process, the states of which represent the states of available nodes along with the transition.

Suppose the number of nodes in the network system is n. We consider an attack event, which occurs on theses nodes in successive steps. Without loss of generality, we assume the attack initially occurred in node 1. Then the attack propagates from the affected node to another within a random time period. The propagation is assumed to have ╱ memory less ╱ property: the probability of attack events spreading from one given node to another depends only on the current system state but not on the history of the system. This assumption is justified in many cases since the propagation speed and direction of disaster are determined by the local conditions of the terrain or of the surrounding ambient. The affected node can be repaired (or replaced by a new one) in a random period. Moreover, all times of the propagation and repair are exponentially distributed.

In order to model the propagation, suppose a network be modeled as a directed graph consisting of nodes and directed edges. A node may be a sub-network. The directions of possible propagation among different nodes can be denoted by the directed edges. In this paper, we investigate the performance of the network after the network attack occurred, in the subsequent attack propagation and until the network is fully repaired. It is assumed the above transient period can be evolved as a continuous-time stochastic process with a set of phases.

Let $\{X, t>0\}$ with finite state space $S= \{1, 2..., N\}$ denote the above phased recovery process of a network system. Consider an access network composed of n subnet for different subareas. The network attack propagated through the whole network. Then, the state of the network system at any time t can be completely described by the collection of the state of each subnet. Here, a n-dimensional vector

$$X(t) = \left(X_1(t), X_2(t),...X_n(t)\right), t \geq 0 \tag{2}$$

Where for each subnet $k \in \{1,2,...,n\}$, $X_k(t)$ denotes the state of subnet k at time t. There is three kinds of state which the subnet k may stay at. First, when the network attack did not occur until time t, the state of the k-th subnet goes to "1". Secondly, if the k-th subnet has suffered an attack at the time t, the state will change from "1" to "0". Thirdly, we will have $X_k(t)=1'$ in the case when the k-th subnet has been repaired or recovered at time t. To be specified, the third state $X_k(t)=1'$ is quite different from the first normal state $X_k(t)=1$. The reason goes to the third state is an immunized state which cannot be attacked by the same method or virus.

$$X_k(t) = \begin{cases} 1, & \textit{when the attack not occured} \\ 0, & \textit{when the attack occured} \\ 1', & \textit{when the subnet have been repaired} \end{cases} \tag{3}$$

With the above assumptions, the transient process $X(t)$ can be mathematically modeled as a continuous-time Markov chain (CTMC) with state space as:

$$\Omega = \left\{ (X_1, X_2,..., X_n), X_1, X_2,..., X_n \in (0,1,1') \right\} \tag{4}$$

The state space Ω consists of total $N = 3^n$ states. The process $X(t)$ starts from the state $(0,1,...,1)$ and finishes in the absorbing state $(1\checkmark,1\checkmark,...,1\checkmark)$, which indicates all the subnets in the access network are working and immunized.

In brief, the model can be summarized as the following:

- The state of each subnet of network system at time t lies within the set $\{0,1,1\checkmark\}$.
- At the initial time $t=0$, an attack affects the first subnet and the network system is in the state $(0,1,...,1)$.
- The attack propagates from the subnet k-1 to subnet k according to Poisson processes with damage rate λ_k.
- An attack can occur on only one subnet at a time.
- Each subnet has a specific repair process which is all the terminal can be repaired at once and the repair rate of subnet k is exponentially distributed with mean value μ_k.
- Subnet are not repaired before all the terminals in the subnet are affected.
- The damage or repair propagation transits only determined by the current state, not on the path until reaching the current state.

With the above assumptions, the phased recovery process is mathematically modeled as a temporally homogeneous continuous-time Markov chain (CTMC) on the state space S. For each $t \geq 0$ and $i \in S$, define the probabilities

$$\pi_i(t) = \Pr\{X(t) = i\} \tag{5}$$

Suppose

$$\pi(t) = [\pi_1(t), \pi_2(t), ..., \pi_N(t)] \tag{6}$$

denote a row vector of transient state probabilities of $X(t)$. When the system is in state $i \in S$, let Υ_i be a reward rate. Defined over the states of CTMC, the reward rates vector associated with the state is expressed as follows:

$$\Upsilon = [\Upsilon_1, \Upsilon_2, ..., \Upsilon_N] \tag{7}$$

Using this model, different measures can be defined. Since we cannot predict the exact system state during the restoration period, we will study the expected value of the performance from the functioning of network systems. In our model, the performance is considered as reward. The network survivability performance at time t is measured by the expected instantaneous reward $E[M(t)]$ as follows:

$$E[M(t)] = \sum_{i \in \Omega} \gamma_i \pi_i(t) \tag{8}$$

Here, the reward rate can be many types, such as economic return vector or cost vector in business continuity planning. Suppose the system states are ordered so that in states $1, 2, ...,k$ $(k < N)$ the system has fault propagation and in states $k+1, k+2, ..., N$

the system is only in restoration phase. Then, the transition rate matrix $P=[p_{ij}]$ of the process $\{X(t),t\geq0\}$ can be written in partitioned form as

$$P=\begin{pmatrix} p_{11} & \cdots & p_{1k} & \cdots & p_{1N} \\ \vdots & \ddots & \vdots & \ddots & \vdots \\ p_{k1} & \cdots & p_{kk} & \cdots & p_{kN} \\ \vdots & \ddots & \vdots & \ddots & \vdots \\ p_{N1} & \cdots & p_{Nk} & \cdots & p_{NN} \end{pmatrix} \tag{9}$$

Where p_{ij} denotes the rate of transition from state i to state j.

Generally, a row vector of transient state probabilities of   at time t can be defined as:

$$\pi(t)=\{\pi_i(t),i\in\Omega\} \tag{10}$$

With P, the dynamic behavior of the CTMC can be described by the Kolmogorov differential-difference equation:

$$\frac{d\pi(t)}{dt}=\pi(t)P \tag{11}$$

3   Attack Scenario Evaluation

To illustrate the performance of the model discussed above, an infrastructure network attack scenario is proposed in this section.

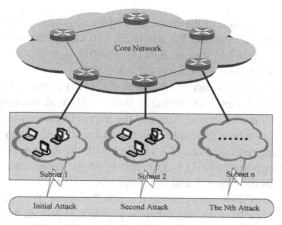

Fig. 3. Attack scenario composed by core network and access network

Suppose an infrastructure of network system deployed in a certain geographical area. The network system is composed by core network and access network. The access network consists of a set of subnets with one access route accessed into the core network. For the sake of simplicity, the analysis is started with a network having $n=2$ subnets as shown in Fig. 3. Consider the average number of users in the two subnets are N_1 and N_2, respectively. At the beginning, assume an attack occurs in subnet 1 and damages subnet 1. Then it propagates its effect to subnet 2 in successive steps.

To demonstrate the use of the proposed model in survivability analysis, we consider two strategies:

- Scheme 1: The subnet which has been infected but with immunized ability.

- Scheme 2: The subnet which has been infected but without immunized ability.

Scheme 1. In this case, suppose the repair rate of subnet i is μ_i. Fig. 4 show the 9-state transition diagram of the CTMC model of network example. As a result, the transition matrix is of size 9*9 and the initial probability vector is $R=(1,0,0,0,0,0,0,0,0)$.

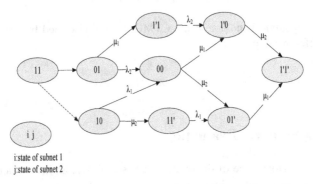

Fig. 4. State-transition-rate diagram of survivability model in repair scheme 1

We define the state space of the chain as $S=\{S_0,...,S_\theta\}$ $(\theta=3^2-1)$ and describe each transient state by a double as (X_1, X_2), where $X_i \in \{0,1,1'\}$ refers to the state of subnet i, $i=1,2$. The set of possible state is: $S_0=(11)$, $S_1=(01)$, $S_2=(10)$, $S_3=(1 \diagup 1)$, $S_4=(00)$, $S_5=(11 \diagup)$, $S_6=(1 \diagup 0)$, $S_7=(01 \diagup)$, $S_8=(1 \diagup 1 \diagup)$.

Given a network attack occurs and damages the subnet 1, the all the users in subnet 1 disconnect to the Internet Thus the initial state is (01).With the damage rate λ_2, the initial state can be transited to state (0,0) and the impact of the network attack propagation from subnet 1 to subnet 2 should be taken into account. Also with the repair rate μ_1, the CTMC can jump into the state $(1 \diagup 1)$. Then with the damage rate λ_2, the state of network will change from $(1 \diagup 1)$ to $(1 \diagup 0)$.It is on the same case, when the attack occurs and damages the subnet 2, and the initial state is (10).

On state (0,0), the CTMC may jump to two possible states: With the repair rate μ_1, it may jump to state $(1 \diagup 0)$ if the first subnet is repaired. However, when the repair rate is μ_2, it may jump to state $(01 \diagup)$ if the subnet 2 is repaired.

No matter the subnet is stay at $(1 \diagup 0)$ or $(01 \diagup)$, with different repair rate, the CTMC will jump into the absorbing state $(1 \diagup 1 \diagup)$ at last .The frequency of initial event is not considered in our survivability model.

In our model, the row vector of transient state probabilities at time t can be denoted as

$$\pi(t) = \left[\pi_{(0\,0)}(t)...\pi_{(X_1,X_2)}(t)...\pi_{(1',1')}(t) \right] \tag{12}$$

As depicted in Fig.4, the infinitesimal generator matrix for this CTMC is defined as P. Thus, by the Kolmogorov differential-difference equation the dynamic behavior of the CTMC can be described in the matrix form

$$\frac{d\pi(t)}{dt} = \pi(t)\Pi \tag{13}$$

$$\Pi = \begin{pmatrix} 0 & 0 & 0 & 0 & 0 & 0 & 0 & 0 & 0 \\ 0 & -\mu_1-\lambda_2 & 0 & \mu_1 & \lambda_2 & 0 & 0 & 0 & 0 \\ 0 & 0 & -\mu_2-\lambda_1 & 0 & \lambda_1 & \mu_2 & 0 & 0 & 0 \\ 0 & 0 & 0 & -\lambda_2 & 0 & 0 & \lambda_2 & 0 & 0 \\ 0 & 0 & 0 & 0 & -\mu_1-\mu_2 & 0 & \mu_1 & \mu_2 & 0 \\ 0 & 0 & 0 & 0 & 0 & -\lambda_1 & 0 & \lambda_1 & 0 \\ 0 & 0 & 0 & 0 & 0 & 0 & -\mu_2 & 0 & \mu_2 \\ 0 & 0 & 0 & 0 & 0 & 0 & 0 & -\mu_1 & \mu_1 \\ 0 & 0 & 0 & 0 & 0 & 0 & 0 & 0 & 0 \end{pmatrix} \tag{14}$$

Here, by the convolution integration approach [12], they can be obtained in a closed-form. What to solve for is the transient probability that the system is in each state i at time t, which is denoted by $\pi_i(t), i = 0,...,8$.

$$\pi_1(t) = -e^{-(\lambda_2+\mu_1)t} \tag{15}$$

Inserting Eq. (15) into Eq. (13) we can derive

$$\pi_2(t) = 0 \tag{16}$$

Continuing by induction, then we have

$$\pi_3(t) = e^{-\lambda_2 t}(1 - e^{-\mu_1 t}) \tag{17}$$

$$\pi_4(t) = \frac{\lambda_2 e^{-\mu_1 t}}{\mu_2 - \lambda_2}(e^{-\lambda_2 t} - e^{-\mu_2 t}) \tag{18}$$

$$\pi_5(t) = 0 \tag{19}$$

$$\pi_6(t) = \frac{\lambda_2 e^{-\lambda_2 t}}{\mu_2 - \lambda_2}e^{-\mu_1 t}e^{-\mu_2 t}(e^{\mu_2 t} - e^{\lambda_2 t})(e^{\mu_1 t} - 1) \tag{20}$$

$$\pi_7(t) = \frac{e^{-\mu_1 t}}{\mu_2 - \lambda_2}\left(\mu_2\left(1 - e^{-\lambda_2 t}\right) + \lambda_2\left(e^{-\mu_2 t} - 1\right)\right) \tag{21}$$

$$\pi_0(t) = 0 \tag{22}$$

$$\pi_8(t) = 1 - \pi_0(t) - \pi_1(t) - \pi_2(t) - \pi_3(t) - \pi_4(t) - \pi_5(t) - \pi_6(t) - \pi_7(t) \tag{23}$$

Scheme 2. Similar to scheme 1, the set of all possible states in this situation is:S_0= *(11)*, S_1= *(10)*, S_2= *(01)*, S_3= *(00)*. Accordingly, the transition diagram of the CTMC has the reduced 4-state as illustrated in Fig.5.

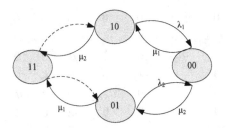

Fig. 5. State-transition-rate diagram of survivability model in repair scheme 2

The transition matrix of it takes the form

$$\Lambda = \begin{pmatrix} -\lambda_1 & 0 & \lambda_1 & 0 \\ 0 & -\lambda_2 & \lambda_2 & 0 \\ \mu_1 & \mu_2 & -\mu_1-\mu_2 & 0 \\ 0 & 0 & 0 & 0 \end{pmatrix} \tag{24}$$

According to the convolution approach, the transient probability $\pi_i(t), i = 0,...,3$,which indicates each state k at time t of the system, can be obtained in a closed-form by the convolution approanch.

$$\frac{d\pi_1(t)}{dt} = -\lambda_1\pi_1(t) + \mu_1\pi_3(t) \tag{25}$$

$$\frac{d\pi_2(t)}{dt} = -\lambda_1\pi_2(t) + \mu_2\pi_3(t) \tag{26}$$

$$\frac{d\pi_3(t)}{dt} = \lambda_1\pi_1(t) + \lambda_1\pi_2(t) - (\mu_1 + \mu_2)\pi_3(t) \tag{27}$$

$$\pi_0(t) = 1 - \pi_1(t) - \pi_2(t) - \pi_3(t) \tag{28}$$

4   Numerical Analysis

In this section, numerical results of the survivability model and analysis established in the previous sections are given. To illustrate the applicability of proposed methodology, we use the network system with the worm propagation to evaluate the survivability. First, we set the model parameters and then compare different model solving schemes. Finally, the implications of our numerical results will be discussed.

Here, the performance metric under consideration is a normalized measurement, defined as the fraction of users affected by outage to service. This fraction is used as the reward rate in (8). Thus, the expected instantaneous reward rate $E[M(t)]$ describes the impact of users of the system at time t.

Given the number of the users of each subnet N_1 and N_2, as defined, the reward rate for each state is easily found. For example, the reward rate of scheme 1 are respectively: $\gamma_0=1$, $\gamma_1=\dfrac{N_2}{N_1+N_2}$, $\gamma_2=\dfrac{N_1}{N_1+N_2}$, $\gamma_3=1$, $\gamma_4=0$ $\gamma_5=1$, $\gamma_6=\dfrac{N_1}{N_1+N_2}$, $\gamma_7=\dfrac{N_2}{N_1+N_2}$, $\gamma_8=1$.

First, we investigate the effect of network survivability performance under different propagation and repair rates. Then, we compare reward rate of scheme 2 with scheme 1.

Consider a subnet is composed of 255 hosts at most, we set the proper parameters. As shown in Table I, for two subnets, we assume $N_1=150$, $N_2=200$. For the setting of propagation and repair rates, we refer the data from [10]. It is acceptable, the network attack repair rate is less than two order of magnitude than propagation rates, and the units of repair time of a subnet is hours.

Table 1. Parameter setting

Parameter	Type	Values
λ_1 / λ_2	Slow Propagation	1.00hours^{-1}
	Fast Propagation	3.00hours^{-1}
μ_1	Slow Repair	0.04hours^{-1}
	Fast Repair	0.12hours^{-1}
μ_2	Slow Repair	0.08hours^{-1}
	Fast Repair	0.24hours^{-1}

According the parameter setting from Table 1, we use different propagation and repair rate values to examine the impact of them on network survivability. No matter propagation rates or repair rates, we set the high rates is three times of low rates. The results are summarized in Fig. 6, where the chosen repair strategy is scheme 1. Suppose the scenario in which the fault propagates slowly and repairs fast. In the scenario, the fraction of active users is high (roughly 0.5, 4 hours after the failure) and will reach 0.95 at last. In the contrast, if the fault propagates fast and repairs slowly, the fraction of active users is low (roughly 0.2, 4 hours after the failure) and may reach 0.7 in the end. From the figure, we can easily get if the repair rate is the same, it will have the same active users at last. However, different fault propagation rate will have the effect on the active users. If the fault propagation is faster, it will have lower fraction users in the beginning.

The plus-marked lines cross each other at time $t \approx 2$ (fast repair) or $t \approx 4$ (slow repair). It can be concluded, before the cross time, the fault propagation rates have more effect on the service performance than repair rates. And the higher repair rates will have the short recovery speed. However, if we account for longer periods of time, the higher repair rates yield more benefits and will have higher fraction of active users.

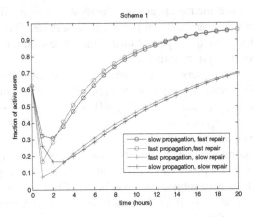

Fig. 6. Survivability impact of different propagation and repair strategies in scheme 1

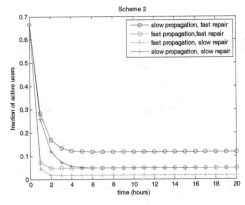

Fig. 7. Survivability impact of different propagation and repair strategies in scheme 2

For a given fault propagation rate, plot is helpful to determine the proper value of repair rates required to achieve a certain network survivability. In the following, we compare the different repair schemes. Figure 7 gives us another repair strategy which the subnet is without immunized state. As depicted in the figure, no matter the repair rates are, it will have almost the same low fraction of active users in the end. If we account for longer periods of time, it will have the situation as before. Different from scheme 1, scheme 2 will have low fraction of active users once the network attack propagation, and can never recover to the high fraction as before. Therefore, compared to scheme 1, scheme 2 have lower reward rate and bad network survivability. The reason goes to the subnet with immunized function can keep the system more stable and recover to the normal state more easily.

5   Conclusion and Future Work

The CTMC analytical model proposed in this paper enable us to quantify the survivability of infrastructure-based subnet which incorporates the correlated fault by network attack propagation. This paper use an attack scenario to illustrate the applicability of our model. Especially, we compare two different schemes with transient reward measures which can describe the network survivability of our model. Furthermore, plots have been presented to study the impact of different propagation and repair strategies on network survivability.

Future work is considered in several direction. It is may not be true in real scenario the propagation time in our model has been assume to be exponentially distributed for simplicity. In addition, more general models, such as semi-Markov mode and phase-type model could be used. The location of access network which play an important role in network survivability are not considered in our model. While our model is an approximation of the real network attack propagation, we will extend the system state by adding the dormant state of subnet which is also a kind of infected node. We shall extend the current study to make out model more accurate in describing such behavior of the network attack propagation.

Acknowledgement. This work was partially supported by the National Basic Research Program of China (973 Program) under Grant No. 2013CB329101, in part by the National Natural Science Foundation of China (NSFC) under Grant No. 61232017, 61372112 and 61003283.

References

1. Habib, M.F., Tornatore, M., Dikbiyik, F., Mukherjee, B.: Disaster survivability in optical communication networks. Computer Communications 36(6), 630–644 (2013)
2. NSFOCUS Security Report (2013),
   http://en.nsfocus.com/2014/SecurityReport/165.html
3. Zolfaghari, A., Kaudel, F.: Framework for network survivability performance. IEEE Journal on Selected Areas in Communication 12(1), 46–51 (1994)
4. Dharmaraja, S., Jindal, V., Varshney, U.: Reliability and survivability analysis for umts networks: An analytical approach. IEEE Transactions on Network andService Management 5(3), 132–142 (2008)
5. Jindal, V., Dharmaraja, S., Kishor, S.: Analytical survivability model for fault tolerant cellular networks supporting multiple services. In: IEEE International Symposium on Performance Evaluation of Computerand Telecommunication Systems, pp. 505–512 (2006)
6. Heegaard, P.E., Trivedi, K.S.: Network survivability modeling. Computer Network 53, 1215–1234 (2009)

7. Liu, Y., Mendiratta, V., Trivedi, K.S.: Survivability analysis of telephone access network. In: 15th International Symposium on Software Reliability Engineering, pp. 367–377 (2004)
8. Xie, L., Heegaard, P.E.: Network Survivability under Disaster Propagation:Modeling and Analysis. In: IEEE Wireless Communications and Networking Conference (2013)
9. ANSI T1A1.2 Working Group on Network Survivability Performance,Technical Report on Enhanced Network Survivability Performance, No. 68 (2001)
10. Wen, S., Zhou, W., Zhang, J., et al.: Modeling propagation dynamics of social network worms. IEEE Transactions on Parallel and Distributed Systems 24, 1633–1643 (2013)

A Scalable Approach for Vulnerability Discovery Based on Security Patches

Hongzhe Li, Hyuckmin Kwon, Jonghoon Kwon, and Heejo Lee*

Dept. of Computer Science and Engineering, Korea University
{hongzhe,chasm,signalnine,heejo}@korea.ac.kr

Abstract. Software vulnerability has long been considered an important threat to the system safety. A vulnerability often gets reproduced due to the frequent code reuse by programmers. Security patches are often not propagated to all code clones, however they could be leveraged to discover unknown vulnerabilities. Static auditing approaches are frequently proposed to scan code for security flaws, unfortunately, they often generate too many false positives. While dynamic execution analysis can precisely report vulnerabilities, they are in effective in path exploration which limits them to scale to large programs. In this paper, we propose a scalable approach to discover vulnerabilities in real world programs based on released security patches. We use a fast and scalable syntax-based way to find code clones and then, we verify the code clones using concolic testing to dramatically decrease the false positives. Besides, we mitigate the path explosion problem by backward data tracing in concolic execution. We conducted experiments with real world open source projects (Linux Ubuntu OS distributions and program packages) and we reported 7 real vulnerabilities out of 63 code clones found in Ubuntu 14.04 LTS. In one step further, we have confirmed more code clone vulnerabilities in various versions of programs including Apache and Rsyslog. Meanwhile, we also tested the effectiveness of vulnerability verification with test cases from Juliet Test Suite. The result showed that our verification method achieved 98% accuracy with 0 false positives.

1   Introduction

Programmers often make code reuse when they develop their software. These code reuses are considered to be code clones which refer to the same or similar code fragments in source code files. This usually causes the propagation of vulnerabilities when a piece of vulnerable code get reproduced. We call this kind of vulnerability as "code clone vulnerability."

Security patches are released to fix vulnerabilities. However, a patch of certain vulnerability often fails to propagate to code clones at other locations which, very possibly, present latent code clone vulnerability. Once a security patch is released,

---

* This research was supported by the MSIP(The Ministry of Science, ICT and Future Planning), Korea and Microsoft Research, under IT/SW Creative research program supervised by the NIPA(National IT Industry Promotion Agency)(H0503-13-1038).

L. Batten et al. (Eds.): ATIS 2014, CCIS 490, pp. 109–122, 2014.

attackers could leverage patch information to dig out 0-day vulnerabilities and make great damage to systems. Thus, there is an urgent need to detect them in an effective and efficient way.

For a long time, software testing has been actively researched to detect security vulnerabilities. Static code analysis [17] [6] [7] has been proposed to discover vulnerabilities by analyzing source code or binary. The large coverage of code and the access to the internal structures makes this approach very efficient to find potential warnings of vulnerabilities. However, they often approximate or even ignore runtime conditions, which makes them suffer from high false positives.

Dynamic analysis monitors program execution to discover security flaws [1] [2]. These tools detect software vulnerabilities by generating input test cases and monitoring its run-time behavior. Although dynamic analysis reduces false alarms, it requires the generation of actual bug triggering test inputs which often make us cannot find critical security flaws in a reasonable time. Moreover, the coverage of the huge inputs space is either too much time costly or just impractical to achieve. Symbolic execution [4] has been widely proposed to detect vulnerabilities. However, as branches in programs increase, program paths increase exponentially. These approaches are either ineffective in path exploration or do not scale well to large programs.

In order to gain both preciseness and scalability in vulnerability discovery, we propose an approach which takes advantages of both static and dynamic analysis to discover code clone vulnerability based on released security patches. We first detect code clones in target source code by doing syntax-based pattern matching in a scalable and efficient way. Second, we analyze the security sensitive data in code clones and perform backward input tracing to instrument the program source and prepare the testing object. Finally, we verify code clones to report real vulnerabilities using concolic(CONCrete + symbOLIC) testing [8] [11] which dramatically reduces false positives. We have conducted our experiments with real world open source projects such as Ubuntu OS distributions. In the results, there are 7 real vulnerabilities reported out of 63 code clones found in Ubuntu 14.04 LTS(recent release by then) within 7 hours to process nearly 260K source files. In one step further, we have found more code clones and confirmed more vulnerabilities in different versions of program packages. Meanwhile, we have also tested our vulnerability verification phase of our mechanism with test cases from Juliet Test Suite. The result shows that our verification method achieves 98% accuracy with no false positive and the average verification speed is 0.24s.

Our contributions could be described like this:

–**Combination of static and dynamic analysis**. We have developed a novel mechanism which combines the advantage of static and dynamic analysis to detect code clone vulnerability. Our mechanism suggests that the code clone vulnerability detection is scalable and with low false positives.

–**Backward data tracing**. The backward data tracing enables our approach perform concolic testing to do verification in a way that mitigates the path explosion problem in conventional concolic execution approaches.

2   Related work

Previous researchers have proposed different approaches for static source code auditing. Some of them focus on detecting code clones [9] [10]. Deckard [10] and Deja vu [9] first parse the program to produce an abstract syntax tree(AST) to represent the source program and then use the vector as a fingerprint for ASTs. Similarity comparison is done among fingerprinting vectors. These approaches require a very robust parser for the programming language and they are not efficient and scalable enough in real large source code pools according to Redebug [3]. Even though it can handle subtle code changes which may help them to find more code clones, this approach may suffer from high false positive rate.

Redebug [3] tokenizes the source code into n-tokens and uses feature hash function to hash n-tokens. The code clone detection is performed by membership checking in bloom filter which stores the hash value of n-tokens. It is very practical and can scale very well in real world usage in terms of code clone detection. However, due to a lack of automatic verification mechanism, most of un-patched code clones they reported are turned out not to be real vulnerabilities which gives them a super high false positive rate in terms of vulnerability detection.

Based on the shortness of the above discussion, we are looking into an automatic and efficient way to do vulnerability verification. Symbolic execution has been proposed to do program path verification and has shown good performance in detecting some vulnerabilities [12]. Concolic testing [8] [11] was proposed later to improve symbolic execution in order to make it more practical in real world programs. KLEE [11] was developed to automatically generate high-coverage test cases and to discover deep bugs and security vulnerabilities in a variety of complex code. CREST-BV [8] has shown a better performance than KLEE in branch coverage and the speed of test case generation. Nonetheless, the branch coverage rate of CREST-BV was still below 25% with baseline testing strategy and below 70% with the special designed testing strategy [8] which means, for some vulnerabilities, it is either impossible or too much time consuming to report them out. The greatest challenge for these approaches is the scalability problem. They still could not handle the path explosion problem properly. Moreover, when detecting software bugs or vulnerabilities, they usually consider each normal statement(such as memory copy, buffer access, arithmetic operations and etc) as a potential bug. This makes the concolic testing very time and resource wasting due to a huge input searching space, since only very small portion of the potential bugs turn out to be real security vulnerabilities in real world programs.

In our mechanism, we do vulnerability verification using concolic testing after a scalable process of code clone detection which reduces false positives. We also propose backward data tracing to assist concolic testing so as to mitigate the path explosion problem.

3   Proposed Mechanism

Discovery of vulnerabilities in a program is a key process to the development and management of secure systems. Security patches are released to fix already

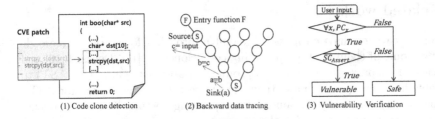

Fig. 1. General overview of our approach

found security flaws and vulnerabilities. However, not all the patches are well adopted and applied in all related programs. In a common case, released security patches are often not propagated to all vulnerable programs due to the heavy usage of the same piece of vulnerable code. To make things worse, attackers often find more critical vulnerabilities based on the information learned from released security patches. As security researchers, we had better move ahead of attackers to identify those vulnerabilities related to un-patched code clones. In this paper, we call these vulnerabilities as code clone vulnerabilities.

Before we go into detail of our approach, the general process is illustrated in figure 1. We are first trying to find code clones by doing static syntax-based pattern matching in a scalable and efficient way and then we perform backward data tracing to prepare testing object. At last, we verify the code clones to report real code clone vulnerability using concolic testing in a way that mitigates the path explosion problem in conventional concolic testing domain which helps us dramatically reduce false alarms in terms of vulnerability detection.

3.1   Finding Code Clones

Code clones could be described like this: if a same piece of vulnerable code occurs in any other locations or programs released. We call them as un-patched code clones. Figure 2 shows the concept and possible scenarios of code clones(e.g., CC@SP@S means code clone vulnerability at same program,at same location). In figure 3, we could see that in some cases, after patch release, the vulnerability may not be patched until several versions later or the same vulnerability reoccurs in the later program versions. This, if leveraged by attackers, may cause serious damages to our systems.

In order to find accurate code clones in an efficient and scalable way, we would first like to make our detection engine scale well to large code bases such OS distributions. Second, we want to report code clones with minimum false positives. By doing this way, we will find more precise code clones which will greatly help us to identify real code clone vulnerability later. The main steps of our code clone detection phase are as follows.

Normalization of each file. We do normalization by removing all non-ASCII character, redundant whitespaces, converting all characters to lower cases and braces.

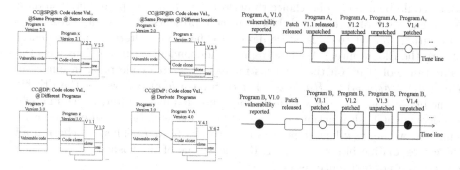

Fig. 2. Code clone vulnerability

Fig. 3. Code clone vulnerability in the same program but different versions

Tokenization of each file. After normalization, each file is tokenized by each line. We define each line as one 't' (token).

N-tokens. We slide a window of n length over the tokenized file. Each n-tokens are considered a basic unit to compare. We define this basic unit as u. Figure 4 shows a 4-token window sliding.

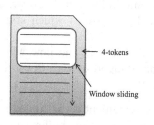

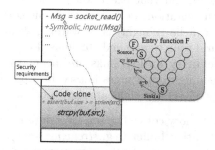

Fig. 4. Window sliding of 4-tokens

Fig. 5. Instrumentation of program source

Hence a file $f(t_1, t_2, t_3, ..., t_l)$ could be represented as $f(u_1, u_2, u_3, ..., u_x)$, where $x = l - n$ (l is the number of lines in a certain file).

Checking definition for code clones. We extract original buggy code from a security patch basically by removing lines prefixed by '+' and adding lines prefixed by '-'. Then we regard this original piece of buggy code as a single file called f_v. A code clone is reported when f_v is contained in any file f from target source code pool. Then, how can we define this containment? From the above steps, we get a N-token set for each file and we define this n-token set for each file as $S = \{u_1, u_2, u_3, ..., u_x\}$. We say f_v is contained in f when $S_v \subseteq S$.

Fast membership checking. Since, in practice, there are tons of files that we need to deal with. So, to do membership checking in an extremely fast way is really necessary. Bloom filter [13] is well known as fast membership checking which could be a very good choice to perform our task. Suppose there is a data set S, eg, a set of n-tokens. A bloom filter represents set S as a vector of m bits initially all set to 0. To store data into the bloom filter(add an element x of S to the Bloom filter), We first apply k independent hash functions with the value range of [1,m] on the n-tokens for files in source code pool, in our case, $Hash(u_1), Hash(u_2), ..., Hash(u_x)$. For each hash $h(x) = i$, we set the i'th bit of the bit vector to 1. To check the membership in a bloom filter, we again apply k independent hash functions on the target n-tokens data set. In our scenario, similarly, we apply k hash functions on n-tokens from f_v. Then we check if all the corresponding bits are set to 1. If at least one of the hashed bits is 0, then we return a non-existence result.

3.2 Preparing Testing Source Object

In order to reduce the input search space of the whole program, we propose backward sensitive data tracing to make a testing source object. The preparing of testing source object is considered to be a preprocess for our concolic testing. It is done by backward source code analyzing and program source instrumentation. The stage mainly contains 2 steps: 1) make assertions 2)make symbolic inputs.

Assertions are to be made to set up security constraints before the potential vulnerable statements and symbolic input are used to generate different test cases for different execution paths. Before we expain how to actually do the instrumentation, we talk about some concepts and definition. In software, data flow can be thought as in water flow in aqueduct systems which starts from natural sources and ends to sinks [14].

Security sinks: Sinks are meant to be the points in the flow where data depending from sources is used in a potentially dangerous way. Several typical types of security sinks are shown below.

- Memory copy: The sensitive data is used as argument to be copied in a destination buffer (e.g.,*strcpy,memcpy*). When destination buffer cannot hold the sensitive data, serious security problems may occur like buffer overflow.
- Memory allocation: Memory allocation: The sensitive data is used as argument in memory allocation functions (e.g., *malloc,alloca*) and it usually causes insufficient memory allocation.
- Format string: The sensitive data is used improperly as argument in format functions (e.g., *printf, sprintf*). Attacker can take use of this vulnerability to take control of the system.
- Arithmetic operations: The arithmetic operations may cause integer overflow, underflow or divided by zero problems.

Sources: *Sources* are to be considered starting points where un-trusted input data is taken by a program.

Sensitive data: Sensitive data are considered to be data depending on *Sources* which are used in the *security sinks*.

Security Constraints(SC): Security constraints are clearly high-level security requirements. E.g., the length of the string copied to a buffer must not

Table 1. Security requirements for security-sensitive functions

Security-critical func.	Security requirement
strcpy(dst,src)	dst.space > src.strlen
strncpy(dst,src,n)	(dst.space $\geq$ n) $\wedge$ (n $\geq$ 0)
strcat(dst,src)	dst.space > dst.strln + src.strlen
printf(format, ...)	# formats = # parameters-1

exceed the capacity of the buffer. We need to define security requirements for statements like security-sensitive function parameters, memory access, integer arithmetic and etc(See Table 1).

Backward sensitive data tracing: We first identify *security sinks* and *sensitive data* in the code clone source. Then, we backwardly trace the *source* from the *sensitive data* to find the related input location. Afterwards, we instrument the program source to make assertions based on security requirements right before the security sink and replace the input statement with symbolic values. We could see this process from Figure 5.

Until now, we could prepare a testing source object logically from the program input to the potential vulnerable sinks. This testing source object is usually a small part of the whole program source which helps us to release the burden of our next stage.

3.3   Code Clone Verification using Concolic Testing

Symbolic execution and concolic execution have been widely used in software testing and some have shown good practical impact, such as KLEE [11], CUTE [1] and DART [5]. However, they suffer from path explosion problem which makes them cannot scale well to large real world programs. H.Li et al [15] has proposed variable backward slicing to analyze a program. This approach helps us to concentrate on those paths only related to sensitive sinks which dramatically reduce the number of paths to analyze. However, pure static symbolic execution does not give us enough support on real world programs. Driven by the above concerns, we are trying to apply concolic testing in our code clone verification phase to help the verification of code clone vulnerabilities. The general principle of the verification is to find an input which satisfy all the program constraints(PCs) but violate the security constraints(SCs) as shown in figure 1. The concept of PC and SC could be find in H.Li et at [15]. In our scenario, we focus on the paths related to code clones rather than the countless number of paths in the whole program which could help us to mitigate the path explosion problem to a large extent. Our approach for concolic testing to verify code clones mainly follows a general concolic testing procedure [8](*Instrumentation,Concrete execution,Obtain a symbolic path formula,Select the next input values, Iterates back to execution*). However, the difference is that we are trying to generate an input to execute the vulnerable branch instead of trying to generate inputs to traverse every possible paths of the program. Our approach for concolic testing is target branch oriented rather than branch coverage oriented. Hence, we are more time

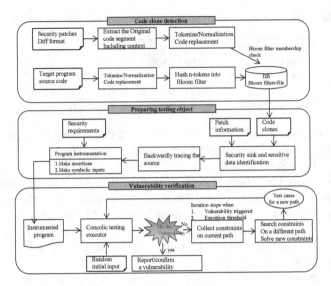

Fig. 6. The mechanism architecture

cost efficient when doing concolic testing. The detailed process is described in Figure 6.

In Figure 6, we can also see the detail mechanism architecture. Our mechanism consists of 3 phases: **Code clone detection, Preparation of testing source object** and **Vulnerability verification**. Our mechanism is used to discover un-patched code clone vulnerabilities in real world projects. We choose CREST-BV [9] as a basic concolic execution engine because of its good performance in test case generation speed. In the next part, we are going to talk about the implementation and experimental results.

4   Experimental Results

4.1   Implementation

Environment setup: We performed all experiments to discover code clone vulnerabilities on a desktop machine running Linux ubuntu 12.04 LTS (3.2 GHz Intel Core i7 CPU, 8GB memory, 512GB hard drive).

Dataset: For the security patches, we collected 106 security patches from 28 CVE [16] patch files (e.g., CVE-2010-0405.patch) related to Linux programs released from 2010 to 2014. We mainly collected patches related to buffer overflows and integer overflows because these are most common types of vulnerabilities. Table 2 shows the number of CVE patch files we collected on yearly base.

For the target testing programs, we collected the source of Linux Ubuntu 14.04 OS distribution to test our mechanism. Based on the results, in one step further, we again collected various versions of linux packages in which code clones vulnerabilities have been found in the previous test such as Rsyslog and Apache

Table 2. Yearly distribution of collected CVE patches

CVE patches	2010	2011	2012	2013	2014
Buffer overflow	0	1	2	6	4
Integer overflow	1	0	2	0	7
Buffer cased by IOS	0	0	3	1	0
Other	0	1	0	0	0
Total			28		

Table 3. Code clone detection results

Target	CVE patches	Target src pool	# of files	# of reported code clones	Execution time
Src pool-1	CVE patch pool (2010-2014, for C code)	Ubuntu 14.04 OS distribution	259346	63	24812.5 sec (7 hours)
Src pool-2	CVE patch pool (2010-2014, for C code)	Httpd-2.2.23 to 2.4.6	7820	14	738.6 sec (12.31 min)
Src pool-3	CVE patch pool (2010-2014, for C code)	Rsyslog-5.8.13 to 8.2.1	1692	7	274.7 sec (4.57 min)

trying to find more vulnerabilities in different program versions. What's more, in order to prove the efficiency of our vulnerability verification phase statistically, we collected 100 test cases from Juliet Test Suite. Juliet Test Suite is created by US National Security Agency's (NSA) Center for Assured Software which has been widely used to test the effectiveness of vulnerability detection tools.

4.2 Experimental Results

We have conducted our experiments with different target source pools.

Target source pool-1. Linux Ubuntu 14.04(latest version) OS distribution

We have found over 63 code clones in Linux Ubuntu 14.04(latest version) OS distribution. Table 3 shows the number of files processed and the execution time in detecting code clones

Our processing time is nearly 7 hours which means this experiment could be conducted in daily base. Among the 63 code clones, we have reported 7 real world vulnerabilities. Table 4 shows the detail information of the real vulnerabilities that we verified.

Table 4. Code clone vulnerabilities reported

program	CVE patch	Location of the vulnerability
Cmake-2.8.12.2	CVE-2010-0405.patch	/Utilities/cmbzip2/decompress.c:381
Firefox-28.0+build2	CVE-2010-0405.patch	/modules/libbz2/src/decompress.c:381
Thunderbird-24.4.0+build1	CVE-2010-0405.patch	/plugins/pmrfc3164sd/pmrfc3164sd.c:381
rsyslog-7.4.4	CVE-2011-3200.patch	/plugins/pmrfc3164sd/pmrfc3164sd.c:272
gegl-0.2.0	CVE-2012-4433.patch	/operations/external/ppm-load.c:87
linux-3.13(Linux kernel)	CVE-2014-2581.patch	/net/ipv4/ping.c:250
httpd-2.4.7(Apache)	CVE-2011-3368.patch	/server/protocol.c:625

In terms of vulnerability detection, our approach reported no false positives which is a huge improvement over other code clone detection approaches [3] [9] [10] without automatic verification.

Target source pool-2 and 3. Source packages of different program versions(Rsyslog and Apache).

Based on the result of the previous experiment, we are trying to look into different versions of the affected programs to see code clone vulnerability in different program versions. We collected different versions(released after the publication time of the security patch) of Rsyslog and Apache and used them as target source code pool-2 and source code pool-3 respectively. For the Apache case, we collected 11 different versions from 2.2.23 to 2.4.6. Our mechanism processed totally 7820 source files (3642170 code of lines) in nearly 12.3 minutes. As a result, we have found 10 code clones and confirmed all of the 10 code clones to be actually vulnerable. We could see the detail from Table 3 and Table 5.

Table 5. Code clone vulnerabilities reported with source pool-2 (Apache)

Version	# LOC	# of reported code clones	# of vulnerability found/verified	# of false positives
Httpd-2.2.23	350145	1	1	0
Httpd-2.2.24	350256	1	1	0
Httpd-2.3.6	209369	1	1	0
Httpd-2.3.8	210564	1	1	0
Httpd-2.3.11-beta	219427	1	1	0
Httpd-2.3.15-beta	226497	0	0	0
Httpd-2.4.1	223050	1	1	0
Httpd-2.4.2	223265	1	1	0
Httpd-2.4.3	223921	1	1	0
Httpd-2.4.4	226000	1	1	0
Httpd-2.4.6	233330	1	1	0

Actually, these code clones are detected from CVE-2011-3368.patch. From the result, we could see that after the release time of the CVE-2011-3368.patch, the Apache2 developers didn't actually fix the vulnerability in the later release versions. For some reason, it was fixed in Httpd-2.3.15-beta and then, the same vulnerability occurred again in the later release versions. This case corresponds to the code clone type–CC@SP@S as we have talked about in 3.1.

Similarly, we also collected different versions of Rsyslog and reported 7 affected versions. Table 3 and Table 6 showed the results.

Our mechanism processed totally 1692 source files(656708 code of lines) in nearly 4.57 minutes. These reported code clones are related to CVE-2011-3200.patch. After the release time of this security patch, the developing team fixed this vulnerability originally in the source file /syslogd.c. However, from the version Rsyslog-5.8.13, this code clone vulnerability re-occurred in another file /pmrfc3164sd.c due to the careless code re-use by developers. This case corresponds to the code clone

Table 6. Code clone vulnerabilities reported with source pool-3 (Rsyslog)

Version	# LOC	# of reported code clones	# of vulnerability found/verified	# of false positives
Rsyslog-5.8.13	78937	1	1	0
Rsyslog-5.10.0	78259	1	1	0
Rsyslog-5.10.1	77811	1	1	0
Rsyslog-6.6.0	92448	1	1	0
Rsyslog-7.4.0	105324	1	1	0
Rsyslog-7.6.3	111218	1	1	0
Rsyslog-8.2.1	112711	1	1	0

```
CVE-2011-3200.patch: Rsyslog Buffer overflow
      i = 0;
  - while(lenMsg > 0 && *p2parse != ':' && *p2parse != ' ' && i < CONF_TAG_MAXSIZE) {
  + while(lenMsg > 0 && *p2parse != ':' && *p2parse != ' '&&  i < CONF_TAG_MAXSIZE - 2) {
        bufParseTAG[i++] = *p2parse++;
        --lenMsg;
      }
```

```
Code clone vulnerabiltiy: rsyslog-7.4.0/plugins/pmrfc3164sd/pmrfc3164sd.c
1    static rsRetVal parse(msg_t *pMsg)
2    {
3        uchar *p2parse;
4        [...]
5            i = 0;
6            while(lenMsg>0&& *p2parse!= ':' && *p2parse!=' '&& i < CONF_TAG_MAXSIZE){
7                bufParseTAG[i++] = *p2parse++;
8                --lenMsg;
9            }
10           if(lenMsg > 0 && *p2parse == ':') {
11               ++p2parse;
12               --lenMsg;
13               bufParseTAG[i++] = ':';
14           }
15
16           bufParseTAG[i] = '\0';
17           MsgSetTAG(pMsg, bufParseTAG, i);
18       }
19       [...]
20       CHKmalloc(pBuf = MALLOC(sizeof(uchar) * (lenMsg + 1)));
```

Fig. 7. Code clone vulnerability from Rsyslog.

type–CC@SP@D(see 3.1) and Figure 7 shows the code clone vulnerability in Rsyslog-7.4.0 .

Comparison with conventional concolic testing: As we mentioned before, we apply backward sensitive data tracing to assist concolic testing for our verification. We have compared our approach with CREST [18]. We have used Rsyslog-7.4.0 for our testing target. Both approaches have generated a triggering input and successfully verified CVE-2011-3200(see Figure 7) vulnerability in Rsyslog. However, Figure 8 has shown a performance comparison in terms of *number of branches covered* and *number functions reached* when the triggering input has been generated.

As we can see, in order to generate a triggering input for the vulnerability, our approach(concolic testing with backward tracing) has reduced the number of covered branches from 344 to 59 and has reduced the number of reached functions from 48 to 9. What's more, our approach only spent 1.2 secs to trigger

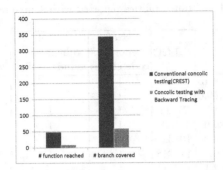

Fig. 8. The comparison with conventional concolic testing

this vulnerability while CREST took 24 mins. This indicates that, with backward data tracing, we can dramatically reduce the number of paths to traverse and decrease the input searching space which mitigates the path explosion problem.

4.3   Evaluations of Vulnerability Verification Phase

In order to prove the efficiency of our vulnerability verification phase, we collected 100 test cases from Juliet Test Suite. For every test case, there are "good" functions and "bad" functions which provides the ground truth for our evaluation. Our 100 test cases consist of different vulnerable types(see Table 7) and there are totally 250 spot to verify(100 bad functions and 150 good functions). We could see the results from Table 8.

Table 7. Distribution of test cases number

Vulnerability type	Number of test cases
Stack-based buffer overflow	25
Heap-based buffer overflow	25
Integer overflow	25
Format string	25

Table 8. Evaluation metrics of vulnerability verification on Juliet Test Suite test cases

	True	False
Positive	95	0
Negative	150	5

As we can see, our verification system generates no false positive and we got the verification accuracy of 98%. We also measured the average verification time needed to verify each test case, average verification time = 0.24s. This proves that our system has good verification accuracy and time cost effective.

5   conclusion

In this paper, we have developed a novel mechanism which combines the advantage of static and dynamic analysis to detect code clone vulnerability. Our mechanism suggests a good performance for code clone vulnerability. What's more, by tracing the input from the sensitive data in code clones and preparing the testing source object, our approach performs concolic testing to do verification in a way that mitigates the path explosion problem. We conducted several experiments with different target source pools. The results showed our approach could find real world vulnerabilities with extremely low false positive rate within reasonable amount of time.

However, there are several concerns as well. First of all, some CVE patches patch in header files whose information is not enough to identify sensitive sinks. Sometimes, several patches contribute to one vulnerability case. This also makes us confused when we do verifications. Finally, due to the limitation of branch coverage of the concolic testing, we will have some false negatives in verification phase. In future research, we will look into classification of security patches and study about the searching strategy of concolic testing for higher branch coverage.

References

1. Sen, K., Marinov, D., Agha, G.: Cute: a concolic unit testing engine for C. In: ACM SIGSOFT International Symposium on Foundations of Software Engineering, pp. 263–272 (2005)
2. Haugh, E., Bishop, M.: Testing c programs for buffer overflow vulnerabilities. In: Network and Distributed System Security Symposium, pp. 123–130 (2003)
3. Jang, J., Agrawal, A., Brumley, D.: ReDeBug: finding unpatched code clones in entire os distributions. In: IEEE Symposium on Security and Privacy, pp. 48–62 (2012)
4. Ma, K.-K., Yit Phang, K., Foster, J.S., Hicks, M.: Directed symbolic execution. In: Yahav, E. (ed.) Static Analysis. LNCS, vol. 6887, pp. 95–111. Springer, Heidelberg (2011)
5. Godefroid, P., Klarlund, N., Sen, K.: Dart: directed automated random testing. In: ACM Sigplan Conf. on Programming Language Design and Implementation (2005)
6. Wheeler, D.: Flawfinder (2011), http://www.dwheeler.com/flawfinder
7. Evans, D.: Splint, http://www.splint.org
8. Kim, M., Kim, Y., Jang, Y.: Industrial application of concolic testing on embedded software: Case studies. In: IEEE Int'l Conf. on Software Testing, Verification and Validation, pp. 390–399 (2012)
9. Gabel, M., Yang, J., Yu, Y., Goldszmidt, M., Su, Z.: Scalable and systematic detection of buggy inconsistencies in source code. In: ACM Int'l Conf. on Object Oriented Programming Systems Languages and Applications (2010)
10. Jiang, L., Misherghi, G., Su, Z., Glondu, S.: Deckard: Scalable and accurate tree-based detection of code clones. In: Int'l Conf. on Software Engineering, pp. 96–105 (2007)
11. Cadar, C., Dunbar, D., Engler, D.: Klee: Unassisted and automatic generation of high-coverage tests for complex systems programs. In: USENIX Symp. on Operating Systems Design and Implementation, vol. 8, pp. 209–224 (2008)
12. Zhang, D., Liu, D., Lei, Y., Kung, D., Csallner, C., Wang, W.: Detecting vulnerabilities in c programs using trace-based testing. In: IEEE/IFIP Int'l Conf. on Dependable Systems and Networks, pp. 241–250 (2010)

13. Broder, A., Mitzenmacher, M.: Network applications of bloom filters: A survey. Internet Mathematics 1(4), 485–509 (2004)
14. Sinks, http://code.google.com/p/domxsswiki/wiki/Sinks
15. Li, H., Kim, T., Bat-Erdene, M., Lee, H.: Software vulnerability detection using backward trace analysis and symbolic execution. In: Int'l Conf. on Availability, Reliability and Security, pp. 446–454 (2013)
16. Vulnerabilities, C.: Exposures cve., http://cve.mitre.org
17. Yamaguchi, F., Wressnegger, C., Gascon, H., Rieck, K.: Chucky: exposing missing checks in source code for vulnerability discovery. In: ACM SIGSAC Conference on Computer & Communications Security, pp. 499–510 (2013)
18. Burnim, J., Sen, K.: Heuristics for scalable dynamic test generation. In: IEEE/ACM Int'l Conf. on Automated Software Engineering, pp. 443–446 (2008)

Modeling the Effect of Infection Time
on Active Worm Propagations

Hui Liu[1,2,*], Xiaolong Ma[1], Tianzuo Wang[1], Bo Ding[1], and Qiang Lu[1]

[1] College of Computer
[2] PDL Laboratory
National University of Defense Technology, Changsha, China
`kay_liu@aliyun.com`, `mars11235813@sina.com`,
`{phoenixwtz,luqiangjfj}@163.com`, `dingbo.nudt@hotmail.com`

Abstract. Addressing the problem overlooked by those continuous time worm propagation models, namely it must take each worm instance a certain period of time delay to completely infect a targeted vulnerable host after it has scanned the host, the paper analyzes in depth the reasons which cause the well-known discrete time AAWP model also overestimating the spread speed of active worm propagations. Then the paper puts forward a more proper states transition of vulnerable hosts during active worm propagations. Last but the most important, a new model named Optimized-AAWP is proposed with more reasonable understanding of this time delay, i.e. infection time of a worm, in each round of worm infection. The simulation results show that the Optimized-AAWP model can reflect the important effect of infection time on active worm propagations more accurately.

Keywords: Optimized-AAWP, worm propagation model, infection time.

1 Introduction

Along with the continuous developments of internet, numerous vulnerabilities have been exposed. Although the number of vulnerabilities doesn't increase obviously in every recent year, network attacks which exploited these vulnerabilities reveal an obvious trend of growth [1]. Due to the existence of these vulnerabilities, lots of malicious codes, especially internet worms which are capable of self-replicating and active-propagating, have increasingly become one of the most serious threats to network security.

So far, those worms have successfully employed random scanning, sequential scanning, localized scanning, hit-list scanning and so on [2-6]. As one of the important fields of the study on worms, a worm propagation model is devoted to properly study the propagation of worms which may use different scanning strategies by means of mathematical modeling. Based on a logical worm propagation model, some potential factors which may have important effect on worm propagations would be analyzed thoroughly, which could facilitate the research or deployment of the defenses and mitigations toward worms.

---

* Corresponding author.

L. Batten et al. (Eds.): ATIS 2014, CCIS 490, pp. 123–134, 2014.
© Springer-Verlag Berlin Heidelberg 2014

The remainder of the paper is organized as follows. Section 2 provides some information on related worm modeling efforts. Section 3 analyzes our simulations of the imperfection of the well-known AAWP model in depth. Section 4 describes in detail our theoretic analysis of the effect of worms' infection time on their spread, and then presents some results from the simulation based experiments of our Optimized-AAWP model. Section 5 gives some concluding remarks of the paper.

2   Related Works

Internet worms are similar to biological viruses regarding their propagation behaviors, therefore some researching methods and mathematical models used for epidemics would be adapted to the study on worm propagations, forming some classic worm propagation models such as SEM model [7], SIS model [8], SIR model [9], two-factor model [10] and so on.

Simple epidemic model (SEM) assumes that every vulnerable host in the network may be in the state of susceptible or infectious during worm propagation. Every infectious host will try to infect other susceptible hosts in the network with the same probability. And once an individual is infected, it will stay in the infectious state forever [7]. If N means the number of vulnerable hosts in the susceptible state before a worm starting its propagation, $I(t)$ stands for the number of hosts which have been infected by the worm at a moment t, then the SEM model could be explained by the differential equation (1), in which β means the infection rate, it represents the infectious intensity of the infectious hosts on remaining susceptible hosts at this moment t.

$$dI(t)/_{dt} = \beta I(t)[N - I(t)] \tag{1}$$

Based on the similar assumptions of SEM model and its analysis methods of continuous time approximation, considering the hosts which were infected may change their states back to susceptible owing to the elimination of worm instances on them, some other well-known worm propagation models have been proposed, such as SIS model [8] and Kermack-Mckendrik model [9] (i.e., KM model, also known as SIR model). While two-factor model which was based on the KM model analyzes deeply that the susceptible hosts may change their states because of patching the corresponding vulnerabilities, as well as network congestions caused by the large amount of worm scanning traffics and other factors, which have effects on worm propagations too [10].

When Z. Chen et al. analyzed the spread of the worm Code-Red, they came up with that every worm instance must need some time delay to infect a next vulnerable host which was in the susceptible state. Before the susceptible individual is completely infected, it will not transform into the infectious state, that is, it will not have been infected 'entirely'. But those classic epidemic worm models which use continuous time approximation as the foundation to study on worms are difficult to reflect the effect of this time delay on active worm propagations properly. Based on this, Z. Chen et al. put forward the well-known AAWP model using discrete time and deterministic approximation [11]. In the AAWP model, the time delay needed for each worm instance to scan and infect a next potential target was called a time tick.

If η indicates the rate of average worm scanning and t stands for the length of each time tick, m_i means the total number of vulnerable hosts and n_i stands for the number of hosts which were in the infectious state at the end of a time tick i ($i \geq 0$), then the expected number of infected hosts n_{i+1} can be calculated by the equation (2) at the end of time tick $i+1$.

$$n_{i+1} = n_i + (m_i - n_i)[1 - (1 - \frac{1}{2^{32}})^{\eta n_i}]$$ (2)

On the basis of the AAWP model, many important factors, including some classic or novel scanning strategies [12-15], and the heterogeneity of network environments [17-20], have been further analyzed of their potential effects on active worm propagations. While these studies have promoted our understandings on worms greatly, their accuracy, reasonability and effectiveness are strongly connected to the analysis of the AAWP model.

3   Analysis of the Imperfection of AAWP

Apparently speaking, if a worm could complete a next scanning and infection in a shorter time, namely, the worm will have a smaller time tick in the analysis of the AAWP model, then the worm will spread more quickly in the network, vice-versa. Therefore, compare with those worm propagation models using continuous time approximation, the AAWP model should reflect the potential effect of different scanning and infection time delay of worms, i.e., different length of their time tick on active worm propagations, especially the speed of worm spread, more accurately.

However, as shown in figure 1, our simulations of the AAWP model expressed by equation (2) got a completely unexpected result. During the simulations, according to the analysis of the Code-Red worm by CC. Zou [16], we assumed that in the initial state,

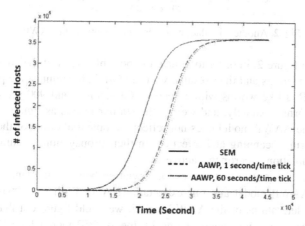

Fig. 1. Worm propagations with different length of time tick in AAWP

the number of *infectious* host $n_0=1$, the number of vulnerable hosts $m_0=\ldots=$ $m_i=359{,}000$, and the average scanning rate $\eta=6$. With Matlab simulink, we simulated the propagations of some Code-Red like worms, namely the dynamic growth of the number of infected hosts when these worms spread, using 1 second and 60 seconds as these 2 worms' time tick separately according to the AAWP model. At the same time, we also simulated the propagation of the Code-Red worm according to the SEM model with the same parameters as a comparison.

From the simulation results in figure 1, on the one hand, we can see that the propagations of worms in the AAWP model is lagging behind the SEM model relatively considering the time delay for scanning and infection, which matches the intuition. But on the other hand, according to the simulation results of the AAWP model above, there is no significant difference between the worm which only needs 1 second and the other which needs 60 seconds to complete a round of scanning and infection (we think that 60 seconds is a long enough time tick, and it is relatively rare in real worm propagations), which seems to be somewhat illogical.

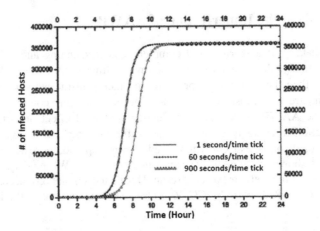

Fig. 2. Another simulation of worm propagations in AAWP

As shown in figure 2, in order to reduce the possible effect of the choice of simulator on our simulations and their results, we used Origin to simulate the propagations of these Code-Red like worms with 1 second, 60 seconds and 900 seconds as time tick for each worm separately, and we got the similar results as figure 1. Therefore, we think that the AAWP model does not reflect the potential effect of the time delay of different worms' scanning and infection on their propagations accurately enough through our simulation experiments above.

Then what is the reason that causes the deviation between the simulation results based on the AAWP model and our expectation? After further analysis on the assumptions and derivations of the AAWP model, we could figure out that the key of the problem lies on the misunderstanding by the AAWP model for its analysis on worm infection in a time tick. The AAWP model assumes that a worm instance on an infected host will complete its scanning and infection to a next potential target within a time tick. Then, when a time tick is over, all of those susceptible hosts which are scanned by this worm instance within this time tick will be infected completely, i.e., the states of these susceptible hosts will be changed into infectious, so they can scan and infect other susceptible hosts at the beginning of the next time tick.

But obviously, due to the limitation of its scanning rate, a worm instance on an infected host could not send out all of its scans to potential targets at the beginning of a time tick. In fact, it will send out its scans in batches in a time tick, and then continue the subsequent infections to them in batches too. That is, in a time tick, a worm instance on an infected host will begin its scanning and infection to different susceptible hosts at different moments in the time tick. Further, the worm instance needs certain time delay to complete the infection to a susceptible host which has been scanned. So at the end of each time tick, there may be some vulnerable hosts are still under the transition from the susceptible state to infectious state, i.e., they aren't infectious immediately at the beginning of the next time tick. But in the AAWP model, these susceptible hosts which haven't to be infected completely will be regarded as in the infectious state, and begin to scan and infect other potential targets at the beginning of the next time tick, which leads to overestimate the number of infected hosts in the network. And as shown in figure 2, the longer the time tick is, the more serious the overestimation of infected hosts in the AAWP model is.

Take the worm propagations described in [11] as an example. When the scanning rate is η and the time tick is 1 second, a worm instance on an infected host will send out η scans in each time tick and completely infect those susceptible hosts which are targeted in these η scans. At this time, if the time tick of another worm is 30 seconds, then an instance of the second worm on an infected host will send out 30η scans in each time tick. That is, along with the increase of the length of time tick, the scans that a worm instance sends out in a time tick will increase accordingly. So the probability of susceptible hosts to be scanned by the worm instance in a time tick will also increase accordingly. But the assumption that once a susceptible host is scanned in a time tick, it will be infected completely at the end of the same time tick in the AAWP model, actually means that compared with the first worm with a time tick of 1 second, the capabilities of scanning and infection of the second worm using 30 seconds as its time tick are amplified in probability accordingly. Thus, it leads to the fundamental reason why there is no obvious difference among the above simulations of worm propagations, in which these Code-Red like worms use different length of time tick according to the AAWP model.

Therefore, the AAWP model notices an important factor neglected before in some classic epidemic based worm propagation models, that is, the time delay for a worm instance needs to completely infect a susceptible host which has been scanned will play an important role on the spread of the worm. However, the accuracy of the AAWP model on analyzing the effect of this factor is holdbacked by the misunderstanding that the scanned susceptible hosts in a time tick will be infected completely at the end of the same time tick.

4   Analysis on the Effect of Worm's Infection Time

4.1   States Transition of Vulnerable Hosts in Worm Propagations

In fact, the process in which a susceptible host is infected by a worm instance can be subdivided into two phases. In the first phase, a worm instance uses some scanning strategies to select and then determine some susceptible hosts as its potential targets, which means these susceptible hosts have been scanned. In the second phase, the worm instance usually establishes TCP connections to each of these scanned hosts after three-handshakes, and then exploits potential vulnerabilities to gain access of them. After a successful access to a targeted host, the worm instance will also copy itself to the targeted host through different distribution mechanism. Only after these two phases are completed, the targeted host will become infectious to other vulnerable hosts. Then the above process of worm infection would be repeated.

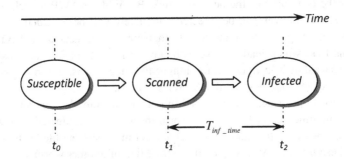

Fig. 3. States transition of a targeted vulnerable host in the two phases of worm infection

During the course of the two phases in which a worm instance scans and infects a vulnerable host, the vulnerable host will be in one of the following three states as *susceptible*, *scanned*, and *infected*. The possible transition of its states in the worm propagation will be *susceptible->scanned->infected*, as shown in figure 3.

4.2   Infection Time of a Worm

According to the process of these two phases in a round of worm infection and the states transition of vulnerable hosts during this process, we give the following understanding about infection time of a worm.

Infection time: During the worm propagation, the time interval between a vulnerable host been *scanned* and been *infected* is called the infection time of the worm, denoted by T_{inf_time}.

For example, as shown in figure 3, if a worm instance starts a round of infection at the moment t_0, a *susceptible* host is scanned at the moment t_1, and the two phases of worm infection is completed at the moment t_2, then the infection time T_{inf_time} of the worm is $t_2 - t_1$.

Compared with the time tick used in the AAWP model which covers the whole period of two phases in a round of worm infection (i.e., $T_{time\_tick} = t_2 - t_0$), the infection time of a worm defined in the paper pays more attention to the second phase of worm infection, that is the time interval between which the state of a vulnerable host may be changed from *scanned* to *infected*. Our following analysis will further demonstrate that the factor of this time interval has more important effect on active worm propagations.

4.3   The Worst Case of Worm Infection in AAWP Model

After the introduction of the infection time of a worm, it can be seen clearly that the assumption of the AAWP model that a scanned vulnerable host will be infected completely at the end of the same time tick is actually an ideal case during worm propagations. Meantime, all of the hosts infected in each time tick $t_2 - t_0$ must be scanned before the moment t_1 in the time tick, and then could be infected completely at latest in the moment t_2 in the same time tick. This is also the situation simulated above in figure 1 and figure 2.

Considering the worst case during active worm propagations that all the *susceptible* hosts would be scanned after the moment t_1 in each time tick, so all scanned vulnerable hosts are still in the *scanned* state at the end of each time tick. If we adopt the discrete time and deterministic approximation as the AAWP model, the vulnerable hosts still in the *scanned* state at the end of time tick i will be delayed to *infected* state, they wouldn't be infectious until the end of the next time tick $i+1$. Then these *infected* hosts will scan and infect other potential targets since the beginning of the time tick $i+2$.

If we continue to use the symbols as the AAWP model and the assumption that a vulnerable host doesn't to be infected repeatedly, and denote the number of vulnerable hosts which would have been scanned in the time tick i by s_i, then s_i could be expressed by equation (3).

$$s_i = (m_{i-1} - n_{i-1} - s_{i-1})\left[1 - (1 - \frac{1}{2^{32}})^{\eta t n_{i-1}}\right] \tag{3}$$

So at the end of time tick $i+1$, the expected number of infected hosts n_{i+1} will be

$$n_{i+1} = n_i + s_i \tag{4}$$

Therefore, the expected number of infected hosts at the end of time tick $i+1$ could be expressed by equation (5) according to the equations (3) and (4).

$$n_{i+1} = n_i + (m_{i-1} - n_{i-1} - s_{i-1})\left[1 - \left(1 - \frac{1}{2^{32}}\right)^{\eta t n_{i-1}}\right]$$

$$= n_i + (m_{i-1} - n_i)\left[1 - \left(1 - \frac{1}{2^{32}}\right)^{\eta t n_{i-1}}\right] \tag{5}$$

Similarly, with the parameters that $n_0=1$, $m_0=...=m_i= 359,000$ and $\eta=6$, we have simulated the worst case in the propagations of Code-Red like worms which use 1 second, 60 seconds, and 900 seconds as their time tick separately according to the

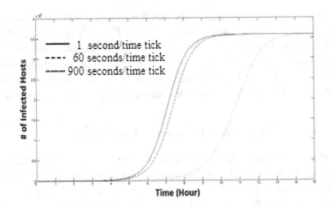

Fig. 4. Worm propagations with different length of time tick in the worst case of AAWP

equation (5), and the simulation results are shown in figure 4. As we can see in the worst cases, all of these worm propagations lag those in the ideal case of the AAWP model, and the longer the time tick is, the more obvious the lag is.

If we ignore other potential factors, the results of normal worm propagations should be between these two cases simulated and analyzed above. The following of the paper will apply this analysis process of the worst case above not only to the normal worm propagations but also the conjunction of the optimization for AAWP model. We hope it can reflect the important effect of different infection time on active worm propagations more accurately with a logical worm propagation model named Optimized-AAWP.

4.4   The Optimization for AAWP

It can be seen from the above analysis that the key point concerned by our Optimized-AAWP model should be T_{inf_time}, i.e., the infection time of a worm, not the time tick mentioned in the AAWP model. Therefore, in the Optimized-AAWP model, the time tick will only be regarded as a time unit, and no longer has any meanings of time related to the actions of worm's scanning, infection and so on. At the same time, in order to simplify the complexity of analysis and without loss of generality, in the following section we will take 1 second as the length of a time tick in our Optimized-AAWP model.

If we continue to use the symbols and the assumption that a vulnerable host doesn't to be infected repeatedly as the AAWP model and the equation (5) (Note: now t is not the length of the time tick as it in the AAWP model, but the length of the infection time of a worm, i.e., T_{inf_time}) , as well as each worm instance will send out its η scans at the beginning of each second, i.e. each time tick, then the number of vulnerable hosts scanned in the time tick $i +1$ could be expressed as equation (6).

$$s_{i+1} = \begin{cases} \left(m_i - n_i - \sum_{k=0}^{i} s_k\right)\left[1-(1-\dfrac{1}{2^{32}})^{\eta n_i}\right], & 0 \le i \le t-1 \text{ and } s_0 = 0 \\[4mm] \left(m_i - n_i - \sum_{k=1}^{t} s_{i+1-k}\right)\left[1-(1-\dfrac{1}{2^{32}})^{\eta n_i}\right], & i \ge t \end{cases} \tag{6}$$

Similarly, at the end of the time tick $i+1$, the expected number of infected hosts is

$$n_{i+1} = \begin{cases} n_0, & 0 \le i \le t-1 \\ n_i + s_{i+1-t}, & i \ge t \end{cases} \tag{7}$$

Therefore, according to the equations (6) and (7), the expected number of infected hosts at the end of the time tick $i+1$ could be calculated as

$$n_{i+1} = \begin{cases} n_0, & 0 \le i \le t-1 \\[2mm] n_i + \begin{cases} \left(m_{j-1} - n_{j-1} - \sum_{k=1}^{t} s_{j-k}\right)\left[1-(1-\dfrac{1}{2^{32}})^{\eta n_{j-1}}\right], & j \ge t \\[4mm] \left(m_{j-1} - n_{j-1} - \sum_{k=0}^{j-1} s_k\right)\left[1-(1-\dfrac{1}{2^{32}})^{\eta n_{j-1}}\right], & 1 \le j \le t-1 \end{cases} \\[8mm] \qquad\qquad i \ge t \text{ and } j = i+1-t \end{cases} \tag{8}$$

With the same parameters that $n_0=1$, $m_0=...=m_i=359{,}000$ and $\eta=6$, the simulation results of the propagations of Code-Red like worms with 5 seconds ($t=5$), 60 seconds ($t=60$) and 180 seconds ($t=180$) as their infection time separately according to the equation (8) are shown in figure 5. It can been seen clearly from the simulation results that the longer the infection time of a worm is, the slower the speed of the worm spread is.

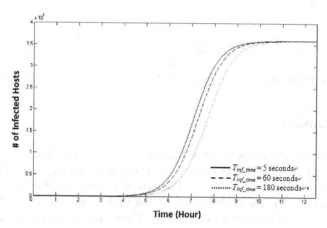

Fig. 5. Worm propagations with different length of infection time in Optimized-AAWP

Meanwhile, we compare the simulation results of the AAWP model and the Optimized-AAWP model in figure 6 and figure 7 respectively. It is clear too that in the both scenarios, all of the worm propagations simulated by Optimized-AAWP model rest between the ideal case and the worst case of the AAWP model using the same simulation parameters. Therefore, we think the Optimized-AAWP model can help us understand the important effect of different infection time on active worm propagations more accurately.

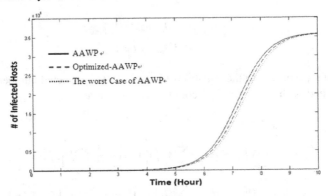

Fig. 6. Comparing Optimized-AAWP with AAWP, 60 seconds per time tick or infection time

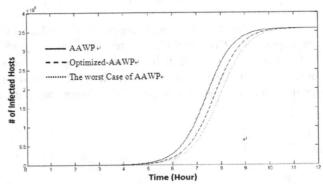

Fig. 7. Comparing Optimized-AAWP with AAWP, 180 seconds per time tick or infection time

5   Conclusion

The AAWP model notices the important factor of the time delay that a worm instance needs to infect a targeted host completely in active worm propagations. But because of the misunderstanding of time tick and actions of a worm instance on scanning and infection in a time tick, the AAWP model doesn't reflect the effect of different time delay on active worm propagations accurately. Therefore, the conception of infection time of a worm is presented more reasonably through the analysis of the states transition of vulnerable hosts in the two phases of worm infection. And then, with a systematic study on worm infection time, the Optimized-AAWP model is proposed by using discrete time and deterministic approximation. The simulation results show the Optimized-AAWP model can reflect the important effect of different infection time on active worm propagations more accurately.

References

1. DVLabs, TippingPoint IPS and Application Security Center. SECURE Your Network: 2010 Full Year Top Cyber Security Risk Report, Tech. Rep., HP Corporation (2011)
2. Weaver, N., Paxson, V., Staniford, S., Cunningham, R.: A Taxonomy of Computer Worms. In: Proceedings of the 1st ACM Workshop on Rapid Malcode (WORM 2003), Washington DC, USA, pp. 11–18 (2003)
3. Staniford, S., Paxson, V., Weaver, N.: How to Own the Internet in Your Spare Time. In: Proceedings of the 11th USENIX Security Symposium (Security 2002), San Francisco, CA, USA, pp. 149–167 (2002)
4. Weaver, N.: Potential Strategies for High Speed Active Worms: A Worst Case Analysis, White Paper, BRASS Group, UC Berkeley (2002)
5. Wu, J., Vangala, S., Gao, L., et al.: An Effective Architecture and Algorithm for Detecting Worms with Various Scan Techniques. In: Proceedings of the 11th Annual Network and Distributed System Security Symposium (NDSS 2004), San Diego, CA, USA, pp. 143–156 (2004)
6. Scandariato, R., Knight, J.C.: The Design and Evaluation of a Defense System of Internet Worms. In: Proceedings of the 23rd IEEE International Symposium on Reliable Distributed Systems (SRDS 2004), Florianpolis, Brazil, pp. 164–173 (2004)
7. Daley, D.J., Gani, J.: Epidemic Modeling: An Introduction, pp. 120–126. Canbridge University Press, Cambridge (1999)
8. Kephart, J.O., White, S.R.: Measuring and Modeling Computer Virus Prevalence. In: Proceedings of IEEE Computer Society Symposium on Research in Security and Privacy, Oakland, CA, USA, pp. 2–3 (1993)
9. Frauenthal, J.C.: Mathematical Modeling in Epidemiology, pp. 78–93. Springer, New York (1980)
10. Zou, C., Gong, W., Towsley, D.: Code Red Worm Propagation Modeling and Analysis. In: Proceedings of the 9th ACM Conference on Computer and Communication Security, Washington DC, USA, pp. 143–148 (2002)
11. Chen, Z., Gao, L., Kwiat, K.: Modeling the Spread of Active Worms. In: Proceedings of IEEE INFOCOM 2003, San Franciso, CA, USA, pp. 1890–1900 (2003)
12. Chen, Z., Chen, C., Ji, C.: Understanding localized-scanning worms. In: Proceedings of 26th IEEE International Performance Computing and Communications Conference (IPCCC 07), New Orleans, LA, pp. 186–193 (2007)
13. Chen, C., Chen, Z., Li, Y.: Characterizing and Defending against Divide-conquer-scanning Worms. Computer Networks 54(18), 3210–3222 (2010)
14. Chen, Z., Ji, C.: Optimal worm-scanning method using vulnerable-host distributions. International Journal of Security and Networks 2(1), 71–80 (2007)
15. Choi, Y.H., Liu, P., Seo, S.W.: Creation of the importance scanning worm using information collected by Botnets. Computer Communications 33(6), 676–688 (2010)
16. Zou, C.C., Towsley, D., Gong, W.: On the Performance of Internet Worm Scanning Strategies. Journal of Performance Evaluation 63(7), 700–723 (2006)

17. Rajab, M., Monrose, F., Terzis, A.: On the Effectiveness of Distributed Worm Monitoring. In: Proceedings of the 14 th USENIX Security Symposium, Baltimore, MD, USA, pp. 225–237 (2005)
18. Rajab, M., Monrose, F., Terzis, A.: On the Impact of Dynamic Addressing on Malware Propagation. In: Proceedings of the 2006 ACM Workshop on Recurring Malcode (WORM), Alexandria, VA, USA, pp. 145–153 (2006)
19. Chen, Z., Chen, C.: Heterogeneity in vulnerable hosts slows down worm propagation. In: Global Communications Conference (GLOBECOM 2012), pp. 923–928 (2012)
20. Liu, B., Wang, H., Xiao, F., Chen, X.: Enhanced-AAWP, a heterogeneous networkoriented worm propagation model. Journal on Communications 32(12), 103–113 (2011) (in Chinese with English abstract)

Location Privacy Preserving
for Semantic-Aware Applications

Lefeng Zhang[1], Ping Xiong[1], and Tianqing Zhu[2]

[1] School of Information and Security Engineering,
Zhongnan University of Economics and Law, China
[2] School of Information Technology, Deakin University, Australia
{loveyifine,tianqing.e.zhu}@gmail.com, pingxiong@znufe.edu.cn

Abstract. With the increase use of location-based services, location privacy has recently raised serious concerns. To protect a user from being identified, a cloaked spatial region that contains other k-1 nearest neighbors of the user is used to replace the accurate position. In this paper, we consider location-aware applications that services are different among regions. To search nearest neighbors, we define a novel distance measurement that combines the semantic distance and the Euclidean distance to address the privacy preserving issue in the above-mentioned applications. We also propose an algorithm kNNH to implement our proposed method. The experimental results further suggest that the proposed distance metric and the algorithm can successfully retain the utility of the location services while preserving users' privacy.

Keywords: Location Privacy, k-anonymity, Logarithm Spiral.

1 Introduction

In recent decades, the popularity of mobile devices such as smart phones and tablets has lead to a growing use of location based services (LBSs). By submitting the location information to the LBS providers, a user can access location-aware applications such as Points of Interest (POI) retrieval, GPS navigation, location social networks, and etc. [1].

However, while enjoying the convenience of LBSs, users actually trade the services with his/her privacy [8]. It is widely believed that LBSs also pose a serious threat to users' privacy since the location can reveal sensitive information about the user to an adversary (which may be the LBS itself). A series of case studies have demonstrated even the identifying features of the users have been removed, location data still can reveal sensitive information. For example, Hoh et al. [6] used a database of week-long GPS traces from 239 drivers to find plausible home locations; Matsuo et al. [7] presented an algorithm to infer users' long-term properties such as gender, age, profession, and interests from their respective location histories. Accordingly, how to protect users' privacy against potentially compromised LBS providers is of vital importance.

L. Batten et al. (Eds.): ATIS 2014, CCIS 490, pp. 135–146, 2014.

In the past several years, various privacy preserving methods have been proposed for location-based systems [4,13]. Among them, k-anonymity based methods are the most popular solutions to the location privacy preserving. K-anonymity requires the user's location is indistinguishable among a set of other k-1 points and amounts of methods were proposed to achieve this goal by creating a cloaking region [2,14]. Specifically, when a user queries the service provider, a cloaked spatial region that covers k-1 nearest neighbors of the user is submitted instead of his/her accurate position. Pan et al. [10] proposed an incremental clique-based cloaking algorithm *ICliqueCloak* to generate *cloaked regions* containing k nodes. Nergiz et al. [9] created a generalization-based method to achieve k-anonymity for anonymization of trajectories.

However, in real world scenario, the user will encounter sematic problem, especially on the boundary of two regions. The user normally prefers services in the same region of him/her, rather than in other regions. For example, the prices of car gas may be different among regions. When querying for the locations of gas stations, the car drivers could prefer more choices located in the cheaper region within the recommender list, besides of considering the physical distance. Intuitively, to achieve a better tradeoff between privacy and utility in such applications, three requirements should considered. Firstly, for privacy preserving, a cloaked region covers k users should be generated instead of the accurate location. Secondly, from the utility perspective, the size of the cloaked region should be as small as possible to get an accurate response from the service provider. Finally, the service difference among regions should be considered.

Thus, we present a novel distance measurement that combines the semantic and the Euclidean distance. The semantic distance and the Euclidean distance are mapped into a 2-dimension space and the relationship between them is defined by introducing the *logarithm spiral*. Exploiting the new distance metric, we present an algorithm to implement our method. The experimental results suggest that the proposed distance metric as well as the algorithm can efficiently meet the requirements mentioned above.

The rest of this paper is organized as follows. Preliminaries are presented in Section 2. In Section 3, we propose the distance measurement as well as the algorithm of privacy preserving for semantic-aware applications. Section 4 presents the experimental results, followed by the conclusion in Section 5.

2   Preliminaries

2.1   Notation

Let a and b be two location points where users submit queries for location-based services. Generally, a point is definitely located in some region. For example, Empire State Building is located in Midtown Manhattan. Suppose a and b belong to region A and B respectively, the Euclidean distance between them is denoted by d_{ab}^E. For those location-based services that differ across regions, the distance between regions should be considered. We denote the distance between A and B by d_{AB}^E, which may be represented by the Euclidean distance between the centre points of the two regions. By combining the two kind of distances, we define the Hybrid-distance, denoted by d_{ab}^H, to abstract a comprehensive measurement on the distance between a and b. Intuitively, given fixed d_{ab}^E, when a and b belong to the same region, d_{ab}^H will be smaller than that when a and b belong to different regions. Moreover, we define the semantic distance, denoted by d_{ab}^S, to describe the relationship between the Euclidean distance and region distance.

2.2 Location Privacy Preserving Mechanisms

To protect location privacy from disclosure, various Location Privacy Persevering Mechanisms (LPPMs) are proposed, such as *k-anonymity*. *k-anonymity* requires that each individual is indistinguishable from at least other *k*-1 ones. Thus, in most of LPPMs, a clocking region covering the user as well as other *k*-1 users is sent to the LBS provider instead of the user's accurate location.

On the other hand, to guarantee the *utility* of the LBS, the region submitted to the service provider should be relatively small to get accurate response. Thus, the nearest *k*-1 neighbors are generally selected according to the Euclidean distance. However, considering the semantic requirements, it brings a problem to the *k-anonymity* mechanism that *Is the Euclidean distance adequate for choosing the nearest k-1 users?*

In this paper, we use *k-anonymity* as the location privacy preserving mechanism and attempt to find a new distance measurement to meet the reqirements of semantic-aware applications.

2.3 Related Work

Existing privacy protection schemes can be classified into two categories: *location perturbation and obfuscation*, and *PIR-based approaches*.

location perturbation and obfuscation aims to separate users' sensitive information and actual identities, usual practices are to obfuscate a user as a small piece of region when querying to a LBS, or add perturbation noises in data publishment. Gedik et al. [3] model the anonymization constraints as a constraint graph and propose a personalized *k-anonymity* model, in which users can adjust their minimum level of anonymity, the maximum temporal and the spatial resolutions they can tolerate. Pingley et al. [11] use a quad tree to maintain road-density information and conducted the Various-grid-length Hilbert Curve mapping to employ *k-anonymity* in mobile based protection mechanisms.

Some other approaches have made use of Private Information Retrieval (PIR). PIR protocol allows a user to retrieve an item from a server in possession of a database without revealing which item is retrieved. Ghinita et al. [5] demonstrated the practicality of applying computational PIR to the protection of LBS users' privacy by solving the nearest neighbor (NN) search in a theoretical setting. Pingley et al. [12] designed DUMMY-Q to hide the real query with a number of dummy queries of different attributes from the same location.

Our work is similar with the perturbation and obfuscation scheme. Combining the region feature and traditional Euclidean distance, we propose a hybrid distance measurement and efficient algorithm for solving semantic problems.

3 kNNH Algorithm

3.1   Overview of kNNH

To deal with the problem, we consider *tree* structure to represent locations in different hierarchies. With the help of *tree* structure, we define a *semantic distance* d^S, the sum of Euclidean distance between points and Euclidean distance between regions. Our aim is to combine semantic distance and Euclidean distance to create a new distance measurement that satisfies semantic requirements. Therefore, we need to figure out the potential relationship between semantic distance and Euclidean distance, and further apply the relationship to new distance creation. However, the distances are 1-Dimension numbers, which means the data has only one feature. It is struggle to find useful information in such low dimension data. Higher dimension data will provide more features and make the relationship more precious. But mapping 1-Dimension data to higher dimension will surely import more parameters, which may complicate the problem. Therefore, to increase data dimension and avoid too many parameters, we use *Logarithm Spiral*, to equally map a 1-Dimension point to a 2-Dimension vector.

We consider every radius of a logarithm spiral as a vector. Vectors with different lengthes represent corresponding distances. Every distance has its unique vector after mapping. As for two mapped vectors, they usually have different lengthes and directions. However, the angle of a radius can represent both direction and length, because once the angle is decided, the length can be uniquely solved from the logarithm function. Therefore, the most representative relationship for vectors in logarithm spiral is angle, *i.e*, the angle between two vectors.

We need to find a proper angle metric ψ to represent the relationship between random two vectors, and define a hybrid distance d^H to help select k-1 users in a novel way. The framework is presented as below.

- Apply tree structure to incorporate hierarchy factor in data distribution.
- Equally expand 1-Dimension distance points to 2-Dimension vectors by *Logarithm Spiral*.
- Find the relationship ψ between two expanded vectors.
- Create a hybrid distance measurement d^H.

The pseudocode k Nearest Neighbor based on Hybrid-distance (kNNH) algorithm is shown in Algorithm. 1.

The first two lines of kNNH creates a region set that contains region U and its neighbors. The following *While* loop will guarantee selected regions contain at least k users. The *for* loop calculates semantic distance in line 8, finds relationship ψ and restrains its range in line 10. The hybrid distance is born in line 11. *For* loop will update different hybrid distances into set H after each

---

Algorithm 1. kNNH

Input: Privacy level k; User u's location (x_u, y_u); Spiral parameter β; Region distance matrix M_D; Current location of all other users.
Output: k nearest neighbors of user u based on hybrid distance.
1. Compute u's location region U according to (x_u, y_u)
2. $N_U = U \cup \{$all the neighbor regions of $U\}$
3. **while** the number of points in N_U is less than k **do**
4. $N_U = N_U \cup \{$all the neighbor regions of $N_U\}$
5. **end while**
6. $H = \varnothing$
7. **for** each point x in N_U **do**
8. $d_{ux}^S = d_{ux}^E + d_{UX}^E$
9. $\psi = \frac{1}{|\beta|} \cdot \ln(\frac{d_{ux}^S}{d_{ux}^E})$
10. $\psi_r = \frac{1}{1+e^{-\psi}}$
11. $d_{ux}^H = e^{\psi_r} \cdot d_{ux}^E$
12. $H = H \cup d_{ux}^H$
13. **end for**
14. Return k nearest neighbors according to H

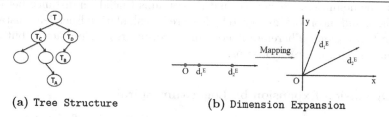

(a) Tree Structure   (b) Dimension Expansion

Fig. 1. Data Structure and Dimension Expansion

iteration. Finally, k nearest neighbors of user u can be selected in the order of hybrid distance.

The following sections will explain how these methods are implemented and demonstrate why they are feasible.

3.2 Data Structure and Semantic Distance Definition

To satisfy with semantic requirements we adopt a *tree* structure, as being shown in Fig. 1a, to represent the hierarchy feature of the location dataset.

We consider every node in the tree as a *region*. Nodes T_A, T_B, T_C, T_D represent region A, B, C, D and they have a same parent node T. T_C, T_D are the first two parents nodes of node T_A and T_B along their branches, we call them *top nodes* of T_A and T_B. Consider two location points, a and b, who are located in region A and B respectively. The traditional privacy preserving obfuscation will use the Euclidean distance between region C and D to replace the real Euclidean distance between point A and B.

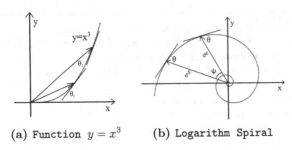

(a) Function $y = x^3$ (b) Logarithm Spiral

Fig. 2. Neutral Logarithm Spiral

However, as we mentioned above, the Euclidean distance does not consider the semantic requirement and the hierarchy feature. Therefore, we define the semantic distance d_{ab}^S between two location points a and b as following,

$$d_{ab}^S = d_{ab}^E + d_{CD}^E. \tag{1}$$

From the definition, we can see that d^S contains Euclidean distance between two points, and incorporates hierarchy feature by calculating Euclidean distance between two regions. Therefore it not only incorporates region factor, but also represents geographic relationships.

3.3 Dimension Expansion by Logarithm Spiral

From the definition, we can see that the semantic distance d_{ab}^S consists of two Euclidean distances, d_{ab}^E and d_{CD}^E. To have a better implementation of semantic distance, we need to figure out the relationship between d^E and d^S. However, distances are real numbers located in 1-Dimension number axis, the relationships between them are simply '>', '<', and '=', which cannot well represent inner relationships. As a result, we need to *expand* the data to a relatively higher dimension, and find potential relationships in high dimension space. Therefore, we import a map function Ψ, to map 1-Dimension distance points to 2-Dimension *vectors*, and then find the relationship in 2-Dimension space, as is shown in Fig.1b.

However, simply mapping from 1-Dimension to 2-Dimension will not solve the problem properly. There is another problem to settle: *equality*. Taking 1-Dimension axis as an example, it is a common sense that the unit length should be identical. *i.e*, numbers should have a uniform distribution along the number axis. Otherwise, it will cause problems on calculation or comparison.

Therefore, We use an equal mapping function, *logarithm spiral*, to achieve this equality requirement. In polar coordinates system (ρ, θ), logarithm spiral can be described as

$$\rho = \alpha \cdot e^{\beta\theta}, \tag{2}$$

where $e = 2.718...$, $\alpha, \beta \neq 0$. Its equiangular property is as follows:

Theorem 1. *If a line* $\mathbb{L}$ *goes through the origin, and intersects a logarithm spiral at point* P*, then the angle between* $\mathbb{L}$ *and* P*'s tangent line* $\mathbb{L}_\partial$ *will be always the same.*

Theorem. 1 tells us that every angle θ in Fig. 2b is equal. It means that logarithmic spiral is *self-similar*, so that the result of applying any similarity transformation to the spiral is congruent to the original untransformed one. However, other functions do not have this property. Take polynomial function $y = x^3$ for example, as is shown in Fig. 2a, the angle θ_1 and θ_2 is unequal. It means that the vectors from origin to any points in $y = x^3$ are unequally distributed in the 2-Dimension space. Therefore, logarithm spiral is a kind of neutral curve that it measures its radius under the same standard.

We tend to map 1-Dimension distance points to 2-Dimension vectors, and Theorem.1 will guarantee the map equality. The map function is

$$\Psi : \{Distance\ points \longrightarrow logarithm\ spiral\ radius\}.$$

3.4 Relationship in New Space

We will identify the relationship between d^S and d^E in new expanded space. We consider N_Ψ as all the potential relationships in Ψ space, ψ is a possible one from N_Ψ's value set, *i.e*, $\psi \in N_\Psi(d^E, d^S)$.

From the logarithm spiral equation 2, we can figure out that once parameters are fixed, the spiral radius ρ can be uniquely represented by θ. Remember that we use spiral radius to represent 2-Dimension vectors.

Therefore, ψ is defined to be the angle between vector d^E and vector d^S. As is shown in Fig. 2b. In 2-Dimension space, the angle between two vectors evaluates their difference. Larger ψ means bigger difference. Note that ψ is always more than zero and it will be larger than 2π if the difference is huge enough.

3.5 Hybrid Distance Definition

After finding relationship ψ between d^S and d^E, we can finally define our hybrid distance d^H. Although we have found the relationship between d^E and d^S, considering the range of the earth, in the worst case, the angle ψ between two vectors may become drastically big, so it is necessary to restrain them in a controllable range. We use the most common Sigmod function to further process data ψ in order to restrain their range. This restraint is called *Sigmod Procession*:

$$\psi_r = Sigmod(\psi) = \frac{1}{1 + e^{-\psi}}. \tag{3}$$

Please note that in *Research Issues*, d^H has to represent both sematic and geographic relationships. We will define a combination function f to combine ψ and d^E together to produce d^H:

$$d^H = f(\psi_r, d^E). \tag{4}$$

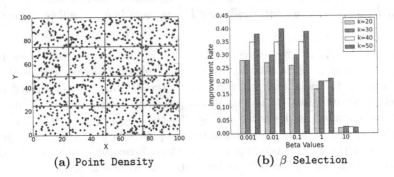

(a) Point Density   (b) β Selection

Fig. 3. Point Density and β selection

After Sigmod procession, $\psi_r \in [0.5, 1]$, which is a narrow interval. To shrinkage this interval slightly, we finally define d^H,

$$d^H = f(\psi_r, d^E) = e^{\psi_r} \cdot d^E. \tag{5}$$

In summary, with the application of tree structure, after dimension expansion and the d^H definition, we can experiment with real data to evaluate the feasibility of our new method.

4   Experiment and Evaluation

4.1   Experiment Data and Configuration

We use a 1000×1000 2-Dimension square to represent the whole geographic location map. We also set separate lines at $x, y = 25, 50, 75, ..., 1000$ to divide the square area into 1600 small regions, to represent the top nodes in a region tree. The location points (x_i, y_i) are randomly picked up from the interval $[0, 1000]$. We generate 100000 location points in total and the point distribution density is approximate 60 per region, which is shown in Fig. 3a. The most important parameter is the value k in k-anonymity algorithm, which represents the privacy level in the protection procession. We will set different k values to evaluate the measurement performance.

Our aim is to find more querier-located points in a query, thus we define

$$r_A^k(\chi) = \frac{the\ number\ of\ points\ in\ region\ A}{k-1}(\chi \in \{d^E, d^H\}) \tag{6}$$

as an effectiveness metric to compare different distance measurements. $r_A^k(.)$ is the ratio that the number of points in region A divided by k-1. It describes the proportion of querier-located users in an obfuscation group, which contains k-1 users in total. Larger $r_A^k(.)$ means we find more obfuscation users in querier-located area, also means the distance measurement satisfies with semantic requirements.l

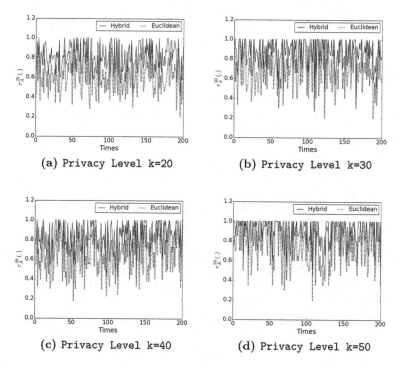

(a) Privacy Level k=20   (b) Privacy Level k=30

(c) Privacy Level k=40   (d) Privacy Level k=50

Fig. 4. Randomly Selected Points

4.2   Choose Logarithm Spiral Parameters

The first step of the experiment is choosing proper parameters for logarithm spiral. As described before, angle ψ between two vectors is used to represent their relationship.

According to the *self-similar* property of logarithm spiral, the parameter α is irrelative with final results because it only controls the spiral shrinkage. Therefore the logarithm spiral has only one parameter β influential in this experiment.

Note that the logarithm spiral function is in exponential form. To avoid exponent explosion in computation, parameter β should not be too large. Thus we choose 10^{-3}, 10^{-2}, 10^{-1}, 1 and 10 as different β values. Considering generous cases, we set privacy level k equals $20, 30, 40, 50$ respectively for comparison.

We define *Improvement Rate* (IR) as a metric to evaluate the experiment results. IR represents the improvement of querier-located points found by hybrid distance. The IR is calculated as following,

$$IR = \frac{r_A^k(d^H)}{r_A^k(d^E)} - 1. \tag{7}$$

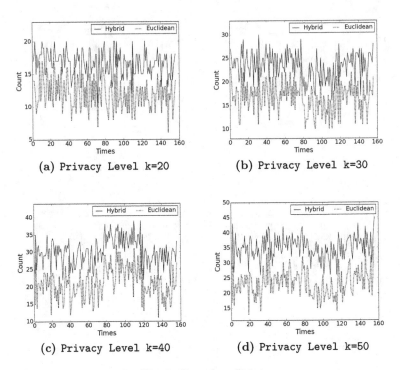

Fig. 5. Boundary Points

We run 600 times in different k values for $\beta = 10^{-3}, 10^{-2}, 10^{-1}, 1$ and 10. The averaged IR results is shown in Fig. 3b. From the figure we can see that, given a specific β, changes of privacy level does not influence much about IR, but if privacy value k is fixed, different β may cause IR drastically changes. What's more, large β may degenerate the improvement rate. If $\beta = 10$, the IR is merely about 0.0022 in different k value conditions. However, if β is less than 1, i.e, $\beta = 10^{-3}, 10^{-2}, 10^{-1}$, different β values may lead to similar results. In the following sections, we use $\beta = 10^{-2}$ to conduct further experiment.

4.3 Overall Effectiveness Evaluation

To discuss the effectiveness of our algorithm, firstly we consider the most generous case. We randomly choose 200 points, regard them as queriers in region A, and compute $r_A^k(.)$ in different distance measurement. The results is shown in Fig. 4. From the result we can see that in different privacy levels, $r_A^k(d^H)$ is always larger than $r_A^k(d^E)$. That means hybrid distance always incorporates more querier-located points than traditional Euclidean distance.

4.4 Boundary Points Evaluation

Considering different qualities of service in different regions, we select about 160 points near boundary as potential users, to see wether hybrid distance can incorporate more querier-located users in obfuscation process. We set privacy level k to be $20, 30, 40, 50$ respectively. For a better illustration, we assume y axis represent the number $r_A^k(.) \times (k-1)$, it counts querier-located users in the whole obfuscation group. The results are shown as Fig. 5.

Fig. 5a shows the condition when privacy level k equals 20. From the figure we can see that every time the program runs, our hybrid distance measurement incorporate more querier-located points of users than traditional Euclidean distance measurement, which is represented by dashed line.

Fig. 5b and Fig. 5c show the conditions where privacy level k increases. We can see again that among 156 running times, the solid line is always higher that the dashed line. Although both lines become lower simultaneously some time, the distance of vertical height is keeping the same. Therefore our hybrid distance performs better than Euclidean distance in different privacy level k.

The final Fig. 5d is the case of privacy level k equals 50. As is explained before, we generate 100000 points in a 1000×1000 square area, so that the average number of points is about 62. This time we assign a high privacy level to a boundary neighbouring querier, the result shows that even the cloaking area approaches to the whole region, our hybrid distance measurement also performs better in this extreme condition.

5 Conclusions

In this paper, we consider a semantic situation where different regions have different qualities of service. In this situation, a querier may want a LBS server return more querier-interested location points in his/her region. Therefore, the LPPM algorithms should draw in more querier-located points in an obfuscation group. To guarantee privacy level, traditional algorithms usually choose the nearest k-1 users in the order of Euclidean distance. However, Euclidean distance is helpless when considering special semantic requirement. We define semantic distance on the basis of Euclidean distance, and map every distance number to a 2-Dimension vector by logarithm spiral. The angle between two vectors is used to represent their relationship. With the definition of semantic distance and relationship, we present kNNH algorithm and create a hybrid distance that incorporate semantic requirement to help select k-1 users. The experiment results show the effective of our hybrid distance measurement.

References

1. Andrés, M.E., Bordenabe, N.E., Chatzikokolakis, K., Palamidessi, C.: Geo-indistinguishability: Differential privacy for location-based systems. In: Proceedings of the 2013 ACM SIGSAC Conference on Computer & Communications Security, CCS 2013, pp. 901–914. ACM, New York (2013)

2. Bamba, B., Liu, L., Pesti, P., Wang, T.: Supporting anonymous location queries in mobile environments with privacygrid. In: Proceedings of the 17th International Conference on World Wide Web, WWW 2008, pp. 237–246. ACM, New York (2008)

3. Gedik, B., Liu, L.: Protecting location privacy with personalized k-anonymity: Architecture and algorithms. IEEE Transactions on Mobile Computing 7(1), 1–18 (2008)

4. Gedik, B., Liu, L.: Location privacy in mobile systems: A personalized anonymization model. In: Proceedings of the 25th IEEE International Conference on Distributed Computing Systems, ICDCS 2005, pp. 620–629. IEEE Computer Society Press, Washington, DC (2005)

5. Ghinita, G., Kalnis, P., Khoshgozaran, A., Shahabi, C., Tan, K.-L.: Private queries in location based services: Anonymizers are not necessary. In: Proceedings of the 2008 ACM SIGMOD International Conference on Management of Data, SIGMOD 2008, pp. 121–132. ACM, New York (2008)

6. Hoh, B., Gruteser, M., Xiong, H., Alrabady, A.: Enhancing security and privacy in traffic-monitoring systems. IEEE Pervasive Computing 5(4), 38–46 (2006)

7. Matsuo, Y., Okazaki, N., Izumi, K., Nakamura, Y., Nishimura, T., Hasida, K., Nakashima, H.: Inferring long-term user properties based on users' location history. In: Proceedings of the 20th International Joint Conference on Artifical Intelligence, IJCAI 2007, pp. 2159–2165. Morgan Kaufmann Publishers Inc, San Francisco (2007)

8. Mokbel, M.F., Chow, C.-Y., Aref, W.G.: The new casper: Query processing for location services without compromising privacy. In: Proceedings of the 32nd International Conference on Very Large Data Bases, VLDB 2006, pp. 763–774. VLDB Endowment (2006)

9. Nergiz, M.E., Atzori, M., Saygin, Y.: Towards trajectory anonymization: A generalization-based approach. In: Proceedings of the SIGSPATIAL ACM GIS 2008 International Workshop on Security and Privacy in GIS and LBS, SPRINGL 2008, pp. 52–61. ACM, New York (2008)

10. Pan, X., Xu, J., Meng, X.: Protecting location privacy against location-dependent attacks in mobile services. IEEE Transactions on Knowledge and Data Engineering 24(8), 1506–1519 (2012)

11. Pingley, A., Yu, W., Zhang, N., Fu, X., Zhao, W.: Cap: A context-aware privacy protection system for location-based services. In: 29th IEEE International Conference on Distributed Computing Systems, ICDCS 2009, pp. 49–57 (June 2009)

12. Pingley, A., Zhang, N., Fu, X., Choi, H.-A., Subramaniam, S.S., Zhao, W.: Protection of query privacy for continuous location based services. In: 2011 Proceedings IEEE INFOCOM, pp. 1710–1718 (April 2011)

13. Shokri, R., Theodorakopoulos, G., Boudec, J.-Y.L., Hubaux, J.-P.: Quantifying location privacy. In: Proceedings of the 2011 IEEE Symposium on Security and Privacy, SP 2011, pp. 247–262. IEEE Computer Society Press, Los Alamitos (2011), http://dx.doi.org/10.1109/SP.2011.18, doi:10.1109/SP.2011.18

14. Xue, M., Kalnis, P., Pung, H.K.: Location diversity: Enhanced privacy protection in location based services. In: Choudhury, T., Quigley, A., Strang, T., Suginuma, K. (eds.) LoCA 2009. LNCS, vol. 5561, pp. 70–87. Springer, Heidelberg (2009)

Analysis on the Reliability of Non-repairable and Repairable Network Storage Systems

MingYong Yin[1], Chun Wu[2], and Yizheng Tao[1]

[1]Institute of Computer Application, Mianyang, China
{yinmy,taoyz}@caep.cn
[2]Southwest University of Science and Technology, Mianyang, China
wuchun_swust@126.com

Abstract. The reliability analysis is of great significance for assessing the performance of network storage systems. This paper aims to analyze reliability of network storage system, either with or without maintenance requirement, using quantitative calculation and simulation evaluation. When the devices were non-repairable, a FC-SAN network storage system was tested in three typical redundancy modes (i.e. simplicity, dual-FC switches, dual-server & dual-FC switches).Reliability calculation was performed with help of reliability block diagram and mathematical analytical method. For the repairable devices, Markov analysis and Monte Carlo stochastic simulation were introduced to assess the reliability of the network storage systems. In addition, simulations were carried out to measure a number of reliability indices of the network storage systems. These indices, including availability, mean time to first failure, and the mean up time, are used for analysis and comparison of simulation data. This analysis can provide useful guidance for designing future network storage systems.

Keywords: reliability, network storage systems, reliability block diagram, Monte Carlo.

1 Introduction

In today's digital and Internet era, more and more human production and daily information are being transformed into digital forms. The volume of data is growing exponentially and viewed as the most valuable asset of all. Corporate networks and Internet data traffic have shown an increasing dependence and demand for storage systems. Among different storage systems, the network storage systems feature outstanding flexibility making them the main solution to massive data storage. Data storage reliability is one of the core features in these systems to ensure network traffic works properly and continuously. Therefore, it is essential to carry out the reliability analysis for network storage systems in terms of its system evaluation and design improvement.

Paris et al. studiedshared parity disks mechanism to improve the reliability of RAID arrays[1]. Xin et al. investigated the reliability mechanisms for detecting and recovering form drive failures and nonrecoverable read errors in a network attached storage system (BBSDs, object-based storage devices)[2]. Chaarawi et al. proposed a

L. Batten et al. (Eds.): ATIS 2014, CCIS 490, pp. 147–158, 2014.

method of adding a shared storage class memory device to improve the reliability of RAID arrays [3]. Lu et al. presented a new RAID data layout to improve disk recovery reliability and analyzed its performance with Markov model[4]. Elerath et al. presented a flexible model for estimating reliability of RAID storage system [5]. Qiu et al. made reliability assessment for storage area network by calculating the long-term average downtimes, service failure rates, and service availability[6].

All of these existing works focus on exploring how the storage technology can be improved, and how reliability assessment can be performed on single storage subsystem. When it comes to the reliability analysis for complete network storage systems, especially the network equipment in the repairable and non-repairable cases, limited studies are reported on the relevant quantitative reliability analysis and evaluation.

2   Model

Reliability is generally defined as a probability to complete the specified tasks in a specified time and under specified conditions (ISO8402 and British Standard BS4778). Typical data network system have the storage reliability index that can be expressed using the probability of a read-and-write task done correctly, i.e., the Reliability $R(t)$. Reliability analysis of a storage system isusually performed under static conditions (non-repairable) and under dynamic conditions (repairable). Subject to the failure model and service strategy, dynamic reliability analysis is generally more complex than the static one. Non-repairable network storage system may be indicated with reliability, failure rate, annual failure rate.Repairable network storage systems may cover more reliable indicators, including reliability, mean time to first failure, the mean up time, the mean down time , fault frequency, etc.

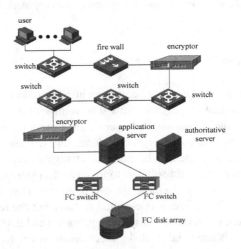

Fig. 1. A typical model of network storage system

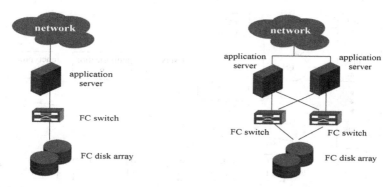

Fig. 2. A simple FC-SAN storage subsystem   **Fig. 3.** FC-SAN storage subsystem with dual-server and dual-FC Switch

A typical network storage system is shown in Figure 1. This is a safe storage system that works with FC-SAN, including network transmission components (switches), network security components (encryption machines, firewalls, authorization servers) and network storage components (application servers, FC switches, FC disk arrays). In order to improve the reliability of the data storage, the network system requires more than the selected storage and network devices of high reliability.Asuitable redundancy mechanism is generally located to further improve the data storage reliability of the network system, including the server redundancy, FC switch redundancy, and disk redundancy. This paper focuses on the reliability of network storage system under three typical redundancies, including simple mode of FC-SAN(Figure 2), dual-FC switches (Figure 1), and dual-server & dual-FC switches(Figure 3).Each mode of FC disk group usesRAID0, RAID1, RAID5, RAID6 as their disk redundancy mechanism.

3   Calculation of the Static Network Storage Reliability Based on the Block Diagram and Analytical Method

Starting with the reliability, the block diagram is a logic diagram of the system and the components, as a graphic expression of the connection between meaning and re-liability of the system unit [7]. Each block represents a subsystem, a component or a device in a status (normal or fault) respectively. Figure 4 representsthe reliability block diagram of a typical network storage system shown in Figure 1. It is assumed that the disk array in RAID5 mode subjects to the logical relationship $k-out-n$ .Of all these five disks, at least four or more disks in normal service may be considered as in a normal array state. In this network, two of the redundant FC switches were placed in parallel. If one works properly, the entire FC system is normal. The other server blocks,including switch blocks, firewall blocks, and encryptor blocks, are connected in a linear manner, which means a system failure will occur when any of these blocks fails.

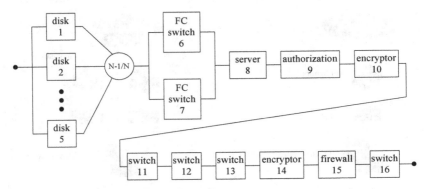

Fig. 4. Reliability block diagram of network storage system

In the reliability block diagram of a network system, there is a logic relationship between the blocks, each of which represents the probability of failure on the basic equipment. Here, the quantitative analytical method may be employed to complete the reliability analysis of the static network storage system. Analytical method is one of the rigorous mathematical methods. A typical network storage systems involves the actual use of network systems to simplify and simulate their typical structure and characteristics, where the network structure is generally not too complex, fitting well with the analytical method. With a simple structure, the system gives full play to the more obvious features on clear concept and accurate model.

The first stepfor calculating the reliability of data storage in a network system is to determine the reliability of the frame unit (subsystems or devices or components) in the block diagram.According to Microsoftand DELL's research reports [8,9], $1 \times 10^{-6} \sim 1 \times 10^{-5}$ hourly failure rate is deemed as an appropriate parameter on single networks and storage devices. The second step for computing the reliability is to determine the basic logic relations between frame units in reliability diagram and the approach for reliability calculation after units being emerged.

4   Reliability Analysis of Dynamic Network

4.1   Reliability Analysis Based on Markov Process

Highly reliable network systems typically have a redundant design. In casepart of the equipment in the system fails, redundant equipment and hot standby equipment are combined to keep the whole network storage system working properly. The fault device (even not to cause the entire system failure) requires timely repair or replacement to maintain high system reliability. Under the consideration of the network system equipment as a repairable unit, a single device can either be in normal operating condition or in a failure status. The whole network works as a system in a plurality of states that can be switched between each other. In this paper, the Markov process is introduced to describe the faulty equipment as to their service state transferred and the time spent. Since, Markov process is used to describe the system, it is possible to use its analytical methodology to obtain the system availability indicators. Figure 2 shows a simple FC-SAN network (disk array using a single disk mode of RAID0), which is composed of three separate units in series - Unit 1:The application server; Unit 2:FC switch; Unit 3:Disk.

Assuming unit i in the system has a constant failure rate λ_i and a constant service rate μ_i ($i=1,2,3$), each unit designated with a separate maintenance personnel. The unitsare responsible for repair and maintenance of the unit to be restored to its original state, i.e. "repaired as new". In the system modeling, the possibilities of multiple units being invalidated or repaired simultaneously are ignored.

The System has its corresponding state transition as shown in Figure 5, whose transformation matrix is

$$A = \begin{pmatrix} -(\mu_1+\mu_2+\mu_3) & \mu_1 & \mu_2 & 0 & \mu_3 & 0 & 0 & 0 \\ \lambda_1 & -(\lambda_1+\mu_2+\mu_3) & 0 & \mu_2 & 0 & \mu_3 & 0 & 0 \\ \lambda_2 & 0 & -(\mu_1+\lambda_2+\mu_3) & \mu_1 & 0 & 0 & \mu_3 & 0 \\ 0 & \lambda_2 & \lambda_1 & -(\lambda_1+\lambda_2+\mu_3) & 0 & 0 & 0 & \mu_3 \\ \lambda_3 & 0 & 0 & 0 & -(\mu_1+\mu_2+\lambda_3) & \mu_1 & \mu_2 & 0 \\ 0 & \lambda_3 & 0 & 0 & \lambda_1 & -(\lambda_1+\mu_2+\lambda_3) & 0 & \mu_2 \\ 0 & 0 & \lambda_3 & 0 & \lambda_2 & 0 & -(\mu_1+\lambda_2+\lambda_3) & \mu_1 \\ 0 & 0 & 0 & \lambda_3 & 0 & \lambda_2 & \lambda_1 & -(\lambda_1+\lambda_2+\lambda_3) \end{pmatrix} \quad (1)$$

By calculating the probability of each system in steady state, we get the average time for which the system may be staying in each state, thereby further computing the system availability (average proportion of time for the system to work properly) and other indicators.

The steady-state of the system $P=[P_0,P_1,\cdots,P_7]$ must meet $P\times A=0$, where $\sum_{j=0}^{7} P_j = 1$. The average availability is steady state probability of status 7, and it can be obtained as follows

$$A_s = P_7 = \frac{\mu_1\mu_2\mu_3}{(\lambda_1+\mu_1)(\lambda_2+\mu_2)(\lambda_3+\mu_3)} \quad (2)$$

4.2   Monte-Carlo

For simple repairable systems, the Markov method can be used for analysis as described in previoussection.The Markov analysis were conducted on the three components of the storage system connected in series, with the availability of the system being calculated. The actual network storage system consists of more components. The system may have the number of states that increases rapidly with the number of components. The failure and maintenance of each component may be in various distributions. At this point, the mere Markov approach can be quite difficult for system analysis. The present work takes the Monte Carlo simulation for the usability evaluation on the repairable network storage system. Before conducting the random Monte Carlo simulation, there is a need to determine the probability distribution model of failure time and repair time of each unit. Exponential distribution and Weibull distribution are widely used distributions in reliability analysis.

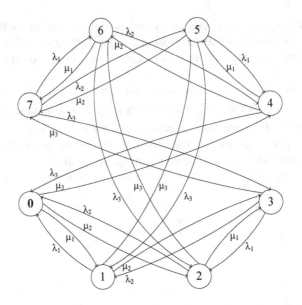

Fig. 5. Diagram of the system state transition of three independent units in series

Failure time of product unit T is called a Weibull distribution with parameters $\alpha(>0), \lambda(>0)$, recorded as $T \sim \text{Weibull}(\alpha, \lambda)$, if the distribution function satisfies

$$F(t) = \Pr(T \le t) = \begin{cases} 1 - e^{-(\lambda t)^{\alpha}}, & t > 0 \\ 0, & \text{ot her s} \end{cases} \tag{3}$$

Corresponding probability density function is

$$f(t) = \frac{d}{dt} F(t) = \begin{cases} \alpha \lambda^{\alpha} t^{\alpha-1} e^{-(\lambda t)^{\alpha}}, & t > 0, \lambda > 0 \\ 0, & \text{ot her s} \end{cases} \tag{4}$$

where, λ is the scale parameter, and α is the shape parameter. Weibull distribution is a key distribution form in reliability engineering, which isadaptive to simulate a variety of failure rate variations. When $\alpha = 1$, the distribution form changes to exponential distribution.When $\alpha = 2$, the distribution form changes to the Rayleigh distribution.When α takes the value between $3 \sim 4$, the distributing form is close to a normal distribution.

When using the Monte Carlo simulation of each unit in the cases of the system failure and maintenance, the first thing is to complete the sampling of the failure time for Weibull distribution and repair time for the exponential distribution.

Theorem: If a random variable X has a continuous distribution function $F(x)$, then $r = F(x)$ can be uniformly distributed on the interval. $(0,1)$.

Solving with Eq.(3), Weibull distribution for random variables follows the sampling formula

$$x = \frac{1}{\lambda}(-\ln r)^{\frac{1}{\alpha}} \tag{5}$$

5   Simulation and Results

5.1   Reliability Simulation on Non-repairable Network Storage System

Figure 1 above showsa network storage system, which consists of the storage subsystems, including simple FC-SAN, dual-FC switches FC-SAN, dual server & dual-FC Switches FC-SAN. In this section, a reliability block diagram is established for the parsing, computing and simulating, on the reliability and the failure rate of the network storage system. In view of the market models that vary in price and reliability, this simulation was set up with two kinds of reliability indices for each network and storage devices. For instance, the hourly failure rate is set to $P_H = 1 \times 10^{-6}$ for high reliability equipment, and $P_L = 1 \times 10^{-5}$, for low reliability equipment.

Figure 6 shows the annual failure rates of the network storage system in the cases of simple FC-SAN, dual-FC switches FC-SAN, dual-server &dual-FC switches FC-SAN. It is worth noting that the combination of the high-reliability network equipment and the low-reliability storage devices is selected($p_n = P_H, p_s = P_L$).The system may have a failure ratethat is lower than the case where the low-reliability network equipment is combined with the high-reliability storage devices ($p_n = P_L, p_s = P_H$). The reason is that the part of the network transmission needs to go through a longer path (containing more devices). In view of the reliability diagram in series, the reliability of the network equipment may have a greater impact on the overall system. The system normally works in models RAID0, 1, 5, 6, where RAID0 comes with non-redundant mechanism, its reliability was significantly lower than the other three. The annual failure rate of the three ways RAID1,5,6 are very close, through careful comparison, we can find RAID1 is slightly lower than the reliability of RAID5, and RAID6 is of the highest reliability.

5.2   Reliability Simulation of the Repairable Network Storage System

Figure 2 above shows a storage subsystem with three units in series., Results for Markov steady-state analysis and the Monte Carlo simulation method, for solving system availability, are   shown in Table 1. The table shows 20 times of Monte Carlo simulation (each lasting 8760 hours). The obtained result has a very small error with the numerical solution from Markov analysis (less than 0.2%). The error of the simulation was reduced further by 80 ~ 90%, with 2000 times of Monte Carlo simulation, in comparison with 20 times simulation.

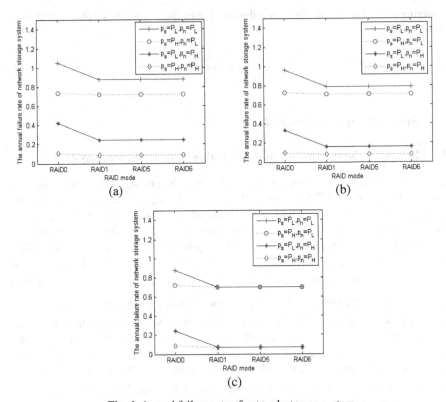

Fig. 6. Annual failure rate of network storage system

Table 1. Availability of storage subsystems with three units in series

Parameters	Numerical solution	Simulation times	Monte Carlo Simulation solution	Relative error
$\lambda = 1 \times 10^{-6}$ $\mu = 0.1$	0.999970006	20	0.99992580	0.0044%
		2000	0.99996113	0.00089%
$\lambda = 1 \times 10^{-5}$ $\mu = 0.1$	0.99970006	20	0.99936644	0.033%
		2000	0.99967369	0.0026%
$\lambda = 1 \times 10^{-6}$ $\mu = 0.01$	0.99970006	20	0.99981735	0.012%
		2000	0.99966473	0.0035%
$\lambda = 1 \times 10^{-5}$ $\mu = 0.01$	0.99700599	20	0.99896119	0.20%
		2000	0.99718265	0.018%

Besides, 4 cases were considered for the typical network storage system, as shown in Figure 1.These includes RAID0, RAID1, RAID0 (no encryption machine), RAID1 (no encryption machine). Monte Carlo simulation was performed to reflect the impact of both the disk redundancy mechanism and the encryptor that may have on system reliability.

Figure 7 shows the availability of the Monte Carlo simulated network system. Under the conditions of four set of parameters ($PG1: \lambda = 1 \times 10^{-5}, \mu = 0.01$, $PG2: \lambda = 1 \times 10^{-5}, \mu = 0.1$, $PG3: \lambda = 1 \times 10^{-6}, \mu = 0.01$, $PG4: \lambda = 1 \times 10^{-6}, \mu = 0.1$, each including $\alpha = 1$), system availability is mainly determined by the ratio u/λ . The smaller the ratio u/λ (PG1) is, the longer the service time for each unit of the system is, which result the shorter time for failure and lower the availability of the system. On the other hand, the greater the ratio u/λ (PG4) is, the shorter the service time for each unit of the system is, which result the longer time for failure, and higher the availability of the system.RAID1 has system availability higher than RAID0. WithPG1 parameters, the former is 0.2% higher than the latter. As the ratio u/λ increases, there was only 0.002% higher between the two.When the system is highly available, adding some redundancy mechanism is not much helpful as expected. Networks with high level of security are usually deployed with an encryption machine to ensure that the only encrypted data are transmitted over the network. Nevertheless, introducing encryption machine also naturally increases the probability of failure of the whole system, thereby reducing the availability of the system. The comparison between non-encryption systems with the original system can be also seen from Figure 7. In the case of parameter set PG1, where the system is available at a lower degree, the introduction of the encryption machine brings a slight decrease tosystem availability. The degree of reduction is closely relatedto the reliability of the encryption machine itself. Namely,encryption machine reduced by app. 0.2%with PG1 parameter set,by app. 0.02%withPG2 and PG3 parameter set, and by app. 0.002% with PG3 parameter set only.

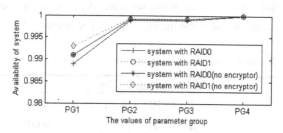

Fig. 7. Availability of network storage system

Figure 8 shows the average number of failures (in 50 years) for simulated network storage systems and disk components. Plainly, the average number of failures is dramatically affected by the failure model parameters λ of unit. For a large failure rate ($\lambda = 1 \times 10^{-5}$), the average failure of RAID0 system is app. 48 times; when the failure rate is reduced to one tenth ($\lambda = 1 \times 10^{-6}$), the average number of system failure is also reduced to the degree slightly larger than one tenth.The reliability of disk arrays are also particularly concerned,even more than the overall reliability of network storage systems.

Because, the failure of a disk array may result in serious consequences of data loss, for which, simulated assessment is needed for the probability of occurrence of such situations. As shown in the figure 8, RAID0 and the average numbers of failures in the case of $\lambda = 1 \times 10^{-5}$ and $\lambda = 1 \times 10^{-6}$ were8.7 and 0.9 times; RAID1 and the average number of failuresin the case $\lambda = 1 \times 10^{-5}$, is app. 0.005. At $\lambda = 1 \times 10^{-6}$, the entire 2000 times of simulation were found with none of RAID1 disk array failure event (i.e., the event that two disks are simultaneously in maintenance state). Apparently, the redundant disk mode (e.g. RAID1) is quite essential to the system data protection.

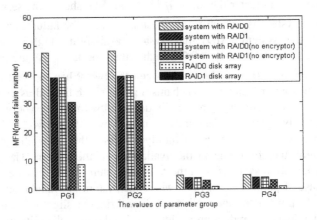

Fig. 8. Mean failure number in network storage system and disk array

Table 2 shows the mean up time in network storage systems. This tablemainly depends on the parameters of the failure time distribution λ, while the value of service rate μ has a slight effect on the mean up time. As they are the same λ, an increased repair rate μ may result in the mean up time to be decreased slightly.

Table 2. Mean up time of network storage systems

System type	MUT (mean up time)			
	$\lambda = 1 \times 10^{-5}$ $\mu = 0.01$	$\lambda = 1 \times 10^{-5}$ $\mu = 0.1$	$\lambda = 1 \times 10^{-6}$ $\mu = 0.01$	$\lambda = 1 \times 10^{-6}$ $\mu = 0.1$
System with RAID0	9121.7	9095.0	87840	86552
System with RAID1	11135.8	11119.6	104083	100280
System with RAID0 (no encryptor)	11172.8	11108.9	103108	101229
System with RAID1 (no encryptor)	14341.6	14295.7	120928	118960
System with RAID1 (no encryptor)	101.40	10.509	99.30	10.559

For the model in unit failure,the shape parameter α of the Weibull distribution can be set to different values. The unit failure time exhibits different distribution curves, $\alpha = 1$ for exponential distribution, $\alpha = 2$ for Rayleigh distribution, and $\alpha = 4$ for approximate normal distribution. Figure 9 shows the average network storage system with the mean time to first failure and its standard deviation in the three kinds of values α ; Figure 10 shows the mean up time and its standard deviation. Clearly, MTTFF significant increases in the systemas the value α increases,. This attributes to the failure probability of the exponential distribution at the beginning of the unit life. It iswhen there was a high density of the failure probability, andthen continued to decrease. In the Rayleigh distribution, the initial failure probability had a relatively lower density than exponential distributionin comparison to the Gaussian distribution.In the initial period with a failure probability density, that was even lower. In Figure 10, an increased value α causes little effect on the mean up time of the system, but significant influence on the standard deviation. With the added value α , standard deviation of the mean up time is gradually reduced, due to the normal distribution and the Rayleigh distribution.,Because, they provided a failure probability density concentrating more in the vicinity of some point of time. As the failure time is also getting close, standard deviation is getting lower.

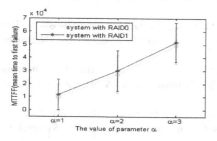 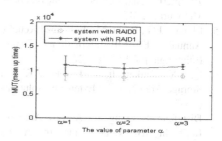

Fig. 9. Mean time to first failure in network storage system

Fig. 10. Mean up time in network storage system

6   Conclusions

This paperfirst employed the reliability block diagram to establish logical relationships between network devicesunder static conditions when network equipment maintenance is not taken into consideration. Analytical methods are then employed to performreliability calculation of network storage. Comparative analysis of the data showed that a single network device reliability comes with some basic indicators, whichmay have impact on the overall reliability of the network storage systems. In addition, a variety of server redundancy, FC switch redundancy and disk redundancy may pose impact on system reliability. In view of the dynamic condition on network equipment being repairable, the Markov process was completed modeling for the state conversion of network equipment. Afterwards, Markov steady-state analysis took over, and reliability analysis was performed with the simple network storage subsystem. For the complete network storage system containing more components, the Monte Carlo stochastic simulation was performed to simulate the failure and maintenance events for each network component. Finally, the data were statistically analyzed to obtain reliability indicators includingavailability of the system, the average number of failures, mean time available, and the average time unavailable.

References

1. Paris, J.-F., Amer, A.: Using Shared Parity Disks to Improve the Reliability of RAID Arrays. In: 28th IEEE International Performance Computing and Communications Conference, pp. 129–136. IEEE Press, Scottsdale (2009)
2. Xin, Q., Miller, E.L., Schwarz, T., Long, D.D.E., Brandt, S.A., Litwin, W.: Reliability Mechanisms for Very Large Storage Systems. In: 20th IEEE/11th NASA Goddard Conference on Mass Storage Systems and Technologies, pp. 146–156. IEEE Press (2003)
3. Chaarawi, S., Paris, J.-F., Amer, A., Schwarz, T.J.E., Long, D.D.E.: A Using a shared storage class memory device to improve the reliability of RAID arrays. In: 5th Petascale Data Storage Workshop, pp. 1–5. IEEE Press, New Orleans (2010)
4. Lu, J., Zhang, X., Zhou, X.: Based on Markov Model Analyze a NewRAID Reliability. In: 7th International Conference onComputer Science & Education, pp. 211–213. IEEE Press, Melbourne (2012)
5. Elerath, J.G., Pecht, M.: Enhanced Reliability Modeling of RAID Storage Systems. In: 37th Annual IEEE/IFIP International Conference on Dependable Systems and Networks, Edinburgh, pp. 175–184 (2007)
6. Qiu, X., Telikepalli, R., Drwiega, T., Yan, J.: Reliability and Availability Assessment of Storage Area NetworkExtension Solutions. IEEE Communications Magazine 43(3), 80–85 (2005)
7. Distefano, S., Xing, L.: A New Approach to Modeling the System Reliability: Dynamic Reliability Block Diagrams. In: Annual Reliability and Maintainability Symposium, Newport Beach, pp. 189–195 (2010)
8. Jim, G., Catharine, V.I.: Empirical Measurements of Disk Failure Rates and Error Rates. Microsoft Research Technical Report, MSR-TR-2005-166 (2005)

Homomorphic Cryptography-Based Privacy-Preserving Network Communications

Antoine Guellier, Christophe Bidan, and Nicolas Prigent

CIDre Team, SUPELEC/Inria/CNRS/Université de Rennes 1/IRISA
Supélec Rennes, Cesson-Sévigné, France
{first.lastname}@supelec.fr

Abstract. This work presents a novel protocol for privacy preserving network communications, using homomorphic cryptography. The malleability properties of homomorphic encryption allows routing without ever disclosing the sender or receiver of a message, while resisting against basic end-to-end attacks. We first present our protocol in an abstract network model, and instantiate it for ad-hoc networks as a use-case example.

Keywords: Privacy, Anonymous, Network, Communications, Routing, Protocol, Homomorphic Cryptography.

1 Introduction

Ubiquitous computing and worldwide communications are now part of the daily life of many individuals. We expect from these systems availability and security in order to provide reliable, confidential, and authenticated communications. Since the Snowden revelations [9], we also expect these systems to provide strong privacy. This is especially important in very constrained context. For instance, in a censored or totalitarian regime, a nonconformist reporter *needs* privacy to exercise her freedom of speech and communicate with the outside. Indeed, the simple fact of connecting to a blacklisted website or participating in a network exposes her to serious consequences [3]. We focus on private communications within contexts where privacy is a necessity.

Anonymity and privacy for network communications begin with Chaum's MIX-nets [1]. They inspired a large portion of works in this field [5], although some may differ by modifying the number of MIX nodes or points in their functioning. Solutions introducing *high latency* between the sending of a packet and its reception are in general more resistant to end-to-end attacks and traffic analysis than their *low latency* counterparts. On the other hand, they are not suited for time-critical or interactive applications such as web surfing or SSH. Tor [6] and more generally onion routing is a low-latency protocol, while Mixmaster or Babel [5] aim at resisting against end-to-end attacks and induce high latency.

Our main contribution is to propose a routing protocol that allows strongly private bidirectional interactive communication using homomorphic cryptography. To the best of our knowledge, it is the first routing protocol relying on

L. Batten et al. (Eds.): ATIS 2014, CCIS 490, pp. 159–170, 2014.

this technology. By distributing the trust and using a *proactive topology dissemination*, our protocol resists both internal and external passive adversaries. In addition, our protocol not only hides the relation between senders and receivers, but also decorrelates every message from its sender and receivers everywhere in the network. We further provide an analysis of our protocol in terms of privacy, and study its integration in a real-world example.

Using homomorphic cryptography is motivated by the limitation of traditional cryptography. Indeed, homomorphic encryption (HE) [8] schemes allow to publicly compute the encrypted value $\mathsf{HEnc}(f(m_1, m_2, \ldots, m_k))$ for some function f using the encryptions $\mathsf{HEnc}(m_i)$ for $i \in [0..k]$. Because they are sufficient for our purposes, we only consider *partial* HE schemes as Paillier or ElGamal [8].

The rest of the paper is organized as follows. In Sect. 2 we present the required tools, our models, and privacy goals. The protocol itself is presented in Sect. 3, while Sect. 4 discusses its properties and further improvements. Before concluding, Sect. 5 investigates its integration in ad-hoc networks [2].

2   Preliminaries

2.1   Cryptographic Tools

This work makes extensive use the ElGamal cryptosystem [7], for its good efficiency compared to other partial schemes and its scalar exponentiation capacity. To make this cryptosystem secure, it must work within a group $\mathbb{G}$ where the Decisional Diffie-Hellman (DDH) assumption holds, *i.e.* in a group of prime order q. Typically, $\mathbb{G} \subset \mathbb{Z}_p^*$ is a subgroup of the multiplicative group of prime order $p = k.q + 1$ for some integer k. Keys are of the form $(pk, sk) = (h = g^x, x) \in \mathbb{G} \times \mathbb{Z}_q$ where $\mathbb{G} = \langle g \rangle$. The encryption of a message $m \in \mathbb{G}$ is $c = \mathsf{HEnc}(pk, m) = (g^r, m.h^r) \in \mathbb{G}^2$ for some random value $r \in \mathbb{Z}_q$. ElGamal supports multiplication of ciphertexts $\mathsf{HEnc}(pk, m_1) \times \mathsf{HEnc}(pk, m_2) = (g^{r_1+r_2}, m_1.m_2.h^{r_1+r_2}) = \mathsf{HEnc}(pk, m_1.m_2 \mod p)$, scalar multiplication $\mathsf{ScMult}(m_1, \mathsf{HEnc}(pk, m_2)) = (g^r, m_1.m_2.h^r) = \mathsf{HEnc}(pk, m_1.m_2 \mod p)$, and scalar exponentiation $\mathsf{ScExp}(\mathsf{HEnc}(pk, m_1), m_2) = (g^{r.m_2}, m_1^{m_2}.h^{r.m_2}) = \mathsf{HEnc}(pk, m_1^{m_2} \mod p)$. ElGamal also supports *re-randomisation*: a ciphertext $c = (c[0], c[1])$ for some message can be turned into a different looking, randomly distributed ciphertext for the same message: $\mathsf{ReRand}(pk, c) = (c[0].g^{r'}, c[1].h^{r'})$.

We also use a *threshold homomorphic encryption* (THE) scheme [4]. This type of homomorphic scheme can have its secret keys split into parts and distributed among several entities. As a result, for some threshold t, t entities or more can collaboratively decrypt ciphertexts, but less than t entities do not learn anything on the underlying plaintexts. In practice, key generation is performed by an authority who publicizes the public key and distributes shares of the secret key. Encryption is performed as usual, but decryption requires at least t share holders: each one locally decrypts the ciphertext using its share, and the outputs are then combined to recover the plaintext. Although any THE scheme may be suitable, this work uses the threshold variant of Paillier from Damgård *et al.* [4].

We denote the encryption, decryption using a share, and combining primitives of a THE scheme by $\mathsf{THEnc}(pk, m)$, $\mathsf{THDec}(share, c)$, and $\mathsf{THComb}(\hat{c}_1, \ldots, \hat{c}_t)$.

Note that standard public-key encryption (PKE) is denoted by Enc, and symmetric-key encryption using key K is denoted $\{\cdot\}_K$.

2.2 Models and Goals

In the rest of the paper, we denote the node initiating a connection *source*, and its intended receiver *destination*. We should however mention that once the connection is established, information may flow in both directions. Nodes between a source and a destination *relay* the messages on a multi-hop path. We call a *message* any data transiting through the network, whether it is application-level data or routing information.

Distributed trust. We rely on a *distributed trust* model, where any node may initiate, relay or be the receiver of a connection. By distributing the routing and removing all hierarchy among the nodes, we limit the consequences of node corruption. As there is no central network entity nor dedicated relays, corrupting a node brings very little power on the network as a whole. Actually, in our model, a node is unable to make use of the routing information on its own to run the protocol: it must collaborate with other network members. This suggests a corrupted node alone can not break the privacy of our protocol.

Privacy Goals. We refer to Pfitzmann and Köhntopp [15] to define the concept of *unlinkability* in our setting: two *items of interest* are unlinkable if the adversary is unable to distinguish whether they are related or not. Using this terminology, we aim at ensuring the following properties.

Source/message unlinkability (SMU) Given a message m and a node S, it is impossible to distinguish whether S is the source of m or not;

Destination/message unlinkability (DMU) Given a message m and a node D, it is impossible to distinguish whether D is the destination of m or not;

Source/destination unlinkability (SDU) Given two nodes, it is impossible to distinguish whether they communicated or not;

Message/message unlinkability (MMU) Given two messages, it is impossible to distinguish whether they belong to the same source-destination pair communication or not;

Adversary Model. We consider two adversary models: a *passive, non-collusive* adversary *internal* to the network (also called *honest-but-curious*) (AdvI), and a global eavesdropper (AdvII). The first type of adversary participates in the network and is compliant with the protocol, but tries to get as much knowledge as possible on the network and other nodes. The second is still passive but more powerful, although it does not participate in the network. We do not give the adversary the ability to tamper with the network by dropping, replaying, or performing DoS or Sybil attacks for instance. Note that when considering information theoretic adversaries, notably against cryptographic primitives, we use the probabilistic polynomial-time (PPT) model. In any case, the goal of the adversary is to break the properties stated above.

Non-goals. We do *not* intend to provide an implementation-ready, nor an efficient protocol. Also, protecting messages at the application level, although necessary, is outside the scope of this work.

3   The Protocol

Bearing in mind the desired privacy properties, we aim at designing a protocol that constructs and uses routes so that any node can contact any others at any time. This section describes our solution in two steps: it first shows how to disseminate topology without using nodes' identities, and then how the routing information is used to allow message sending.

Initially, we consider an abstract network model where nodes are randomly placed and connected to their neighbors through a bare physical medium. Prior to describing our protocol, we introduce several values associated to a node X.

- ID_X: X's network identity. It is a random value chosen by X prior to network setup, typically extracted from a large public set so that collisions between two nodes' identifiers occur with negligible probability. Generally speaking, nodes are willing to keep their identity concealed to other network members.
- $(pk_X^{perm}, sk_X^{perm})$: the permanent key pair of X, possibly certified or publicly linked to X's identity.
- (pk_X, sk_X): one of X's *temporary* key pairs, decorrelated from X's identity. A node may own many temporary keys and dynamically generate them.
- src_X: a value generated by X and used in its routing activity as a source (or relay) node. This value is unconditionally kept secret by X.
- dst_X: a value generated by X and used in its routing activity as a destination node. This value is unconditionally kept secret by X.

We assume that prior to network setup, nodes willing to communicate exchanged their respective network identifiers, long term public keys, and possibly some auxiliary information, in the same manner as PGP keys are exchanged. In a very constrained context such as a censorship, a highly private and secure protocol allowing the transport of small data, such as MIAB [11], can be used.

3.1   Routing while Concealing Identities

As we aim at concealing every node's identity, the main challenge we have to face is to route messages *without network members knowing other nodes' network-wide identities*. For this, we introduce the notion of *local identifiers*: instead of using a destination D's identity ID_D to designate it, a node X uses a value derived from values belonging to D and itself. This value is collaboratively computed by X and D upon creation of the route. It should allow X to route messages towards D, but must prevent X from making the link with ID_D. We denote this value $LocalID_D^X$ and define it as:

$$LocalID_D^X = ID_D.g^{srcx.dst_D}, \text{ where } \langle g \rangle = \mathbb{G}$$

Because most of our operations are performed *within* the ElGamal group $\mathbb{G} \subset \mathbb{Z}_p^*$, the local identifiers and more generally all values in our protocol are modulo p.

The local identifiers resolve the question of destination addressing. However, we also need a way for node to forward messages towards some local identifier on a multi-hop path. Indeed, a message must travel from node to node in order to reach its destination. This implies that nodes must be able to address specific neighbors, still without knowing their identities. To enable private neighborhood discovery, we borrow a technique from Zhang *et al.* [16]. It consists, for every pair of neighboring node, in engaging in a Diffie-Hellman (DH) handshake so as to obtain a common secret, and to derive symmetric keys and *link identifiers* from this secret using cryptographic key derivation functions. A link identifier between two nodes X and Y, denoted $L_{X,Y}$ or $L_{Y,X}$ indifferently, acts as a MAC address in a traditional LAN. The key $K_{X,Y}$ associated to $L_{X,Y}$ is used to encrypt the messages on the link. The particularity of this construction is that link identifiers and keys are only used one time. New ones are generated for each message (without the need for a new handshake), in such a way that it is impossible to relate two links (or keys) stemming from the same handshake.

We now describe how to disseminate the topology without revealing any node identity. The general idea works as follows: when a node knows a route, it *proposes* this route to its neighbors. Said otherwise, it offers its neighbors to forward messages towards some destination for them. We make use of the elements defined above, and store routing information into two different tables: a *Destination Route Table* (DRT) and a *Forwarding Route Table* (FRT). To explain how these tables are filled, we use the example from Fig. 1 depicting a toy network of 4 nodes in a row.

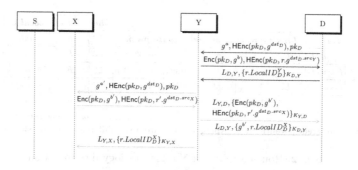

Fig. 1. Topology dissemination in a toy network

In a first phase (in blue), D broadcasts to all its neighbors a *route proposal*: it proposes itself as destination. The goal of this route proposition is to make neighboring nodes aware of D and compute their local identifiers towards D. For this, the neighboring node Y generates a random number r, and computes

$\mathsf{ScMult}\left(r, \mathsf{ScExp}(\mathsf{HEnc}(pk_D, g^{dst_D}), src_Y)\right)$ using the homomorphic properties of ElGamal. It sends a re-randomization of the result so as to ensure the ciphertext looks random, and a second half of a DH handshake (encrypted, to avoid *man-in-the-middle* attacks). D decrypts the ciphertext, computes $ID_D.r.g^{dst_D.src_Y} = r.LocalID_D^Y$ and sends the result back using the newly generated link identifier and key. Y recovers $r.LocalID_D^Y$ and simply multiplies by $(r^{-1} \mod p)$. After these exchanges, D inserts a new entry in its FRT: $\langle L_{D,Y}, K_{D,Y}, null\rangle$. The *null* value indicates the end of a route, and allows D to know that it is the intended receiver of messages incoming from the link $L_{D,Y}$. As for Y, it inserts an entry in its DRT: $\langle LocalID_D^Y, L_{Y,D}, K_{Y,D}, pk_D, \mathsf{ReRand}(pk_D, \mathsf{HEnc}(pk_D, g^{dst_D}))\rangle$, where the last value is simply a re-randomized copy from D's first message.

In the second phase (in green), Y proxies the route proposal from D to its own neighbors. D silently discards the proposal upon noticing it is the destination. The protocol is then very similar, except that Y must act as proxy between X and D because D is the only node able to decrypt X's answer. After the exchanges, Y inserts in its FRT $\langle L_{X,Y}, K_{X,Y}, LocalID_D^Y\rangle$, and X insert in its DRT $\langle LocalID_D^X, L_{X,Y}, K_{X,Y}, pk_D, \mathsf{ReRand}(pk_D, \mathsf{HEnc}(pk_D, g^{dst_D}))\rangle$. D does not insert any new entry.

This procedure is repeated, X proposing the route to S, and X and Y proxying S's answer. In the general case, the procedure is repeated until the whole network is aware of D's presence. Furthermore, all nodes self-propose in the same manner as D to advertise their presence. As a result, each node's presence in the network will eventually be known by all, while its identity remains undisclosed. In our example, Y's tables are eventually filled as described in Fig. 2.

Using regular timeouts for table entries and periodical keep-alive messages, tables can be updated in case a node leaves the network. Although the complexity of this topology dissemination method is considerable (at least quadratic in the number of nodes), it is only necessary to run it once at network setup.

Local id	Link id	Key	Dest. pk	Route prop.
$LocalID_D^Y$	$L_{Y,D}^{(1)}$	$K_{Y,D}^{(1)}$	pk_D	$\mathsf{HEnc}(pk_D, g^{dst_D})$
$LocalID_X^Y$	$L_{Y,X}^{(1)}$	$K_{Y,X}^{(1)}$	pk_X	$\mathsf{HEnc}(pk_X, g^{dst_X})$
$LocalID_S^Y$	$L_{Y,X}^{(2)}$	$K_{Y,X}^{(2)}$	pk_S	$\mathsf{HEnc}(pk_S, g^{dst_S})$

Destination Table

Link id	Key	Local id
$L_{Y,D}^{(2)}$	$K_{Y,D}^{(2)}$	null
$L_{Y,X}^{(3)}$	$K_{Y,X}^{(3)}$	null
$L_{Y,D}^{(3)}$	$K_{Y,D}^{(3)}$	$LocalID_X^Y$
$L_{Y,D}^{(4)}$	$K_{Y,D}^{(4)}$	$LocalID_S^Y$
$L_{Y,X}^{(4)}$	$K_{Y,X}^{(4)}$	$LocalID_D^Y$

Forwarding Table

Link ids with different parenthesized exponents stem from two different DH handshakes.

Fig. 2. Routing tables of Y after topology dissemination

3.2 Sending a Message

At this point, each node has at least one route towards every other node. Note that completely anonymous communications are possible: the two tables allow any two nodes in the network to connect to each other using local identifiers. However, nodes can not know who they are connecting with, and the tables do not directly allow a source to reach a specific destination of its choice.

In order to allow connection of S to D without breaching privacy, S and D not being 1 hop neighbors, our solution makes S ask for help to another node. Also, we use a THE scheme with threshold $t = 2$ and make the assumption that there exist a pair of keys (pk_*, sk_*) for this scheme such that pk_* is publicly known, but sk_* is unknown to all network members. However, every node X owns a share of the decryption key sk_*, noted sh_X. The key pair and shares can be generated by a third party for instance. Finally, we suppose that, in addition to its identity and public key, D gave S the auxiliary value $\mathsf{THEnc}(pk_*, dst_D)$.

Figure 3 describes the message sequence for S to be able to send a message to D. The first phase (in blue) is called *route initialization*: this is the part where S and X cooperate using THE to find a route from X to D[1]. Before running this protocol, S generates a random number r and computes $C = \mathsf{ReRand}(pk_*, \mathsf{ScMult}(r, \mathsf{THEnc}(pk_*, dst_D)))$. S and X then use their respective decryption shares sh_S and sh_X to cooperatively decrypt C. X obtains a blinded value of dst_D, $v = r.dst_D$, by using the THComb primitive. X then computes in the clear $(g^{src_X})^v$, encrypts it under one of its keys using ElGamal, and sends back the result C'. If r and $p - 1$ are co-prime, applying $\mathsf{ReRand}(pk_X, \mathsf{ScMult}(ID_D, \mathsf{ScExp}(C', r^{-1} \bmod (p - 1))))$ on the ciphertext C' received by S yields a random-looking encryption of $LocalID_D^X$, which X is able to decrypt. X looks up in its DRT for a route towards this local identifier, and forwards the payload encrypted under D's permanent key. The second phase (in green) simply consists in table look ups. Upon receiving the message, Y looks up in its FRT to find the entry corresponding to $L_{X,Y}$. Y recovers the relevant local identifier from this entry, looks up in its DRT for a route toward it, and forwards accordingly. If at any moment, a table look up fails, a notification is sent back. D knows it is the destination thanks to the *null* value in its FRT entry corresponding to $L_{Y,D}$.

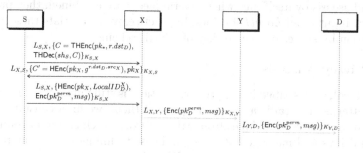

Fig. 3. S initializes a route and sends a message to D

4 Discussion

4.1 Interaction and THE in Route Initialization

In our model, the interaction in the route initialization is necessary in order to ensure DMU. Indeed, because of the way routes are built, the same local identifiers

---

[1] In the general case, S can choose any node in the network to play the role of X.

may be used both to emit or to forward a message to a given destination. Suppose a source S could, on its own, find a route towards a specific destination D, *i.e.* S can find the value $LocalID_D^S$ in its DRT and knows it actually designates D. Later on, if S is asked to forward a message towards the same destination D, S will use the value $LocalID_D^S$ (as explained in Sect. 3.2). Thus, S will infer the message is for D and break DMU. Therefore, for DMU to hold, a source S *must not* be able to initiate a communication alone.

The most straightforward solution is for S to hand all its messages to some other node X, and for X to forward messages towards the actual destination D. This means that X must find the relevant $LocalID$ to send the messages to, but for DMU to hold, it must not uncover the actual intended destination. In other words, through an oblivious interaction with S, X must learn $LocalID_D^X$.

To achieve secure computation of $LocalID_D^X$, a strong assumption need to be done: every node must possess a *universal auxiliary information* on the network. That is to say, a value that does not relate to a particular node, but on the contrary relates to *all* nodes. We actually show in the full version of this paper[2], that without such auxiliary information, an efficient and secure route initialization is impossible in our model[3]. In a nutshell, if we do not use universal auxiliary information, we show that, because X can not use any knowledge it has on D (else X would know the intended destination beforehand, which is absurd), X does not bring any input to the computation of $LocalID_D^X$ except src_X. This means that S must know the rest of the inputs necessary to compute it, *i.e.* S knows ID_D and dst_D. Therefore, S can compute $LocalID_D^S$ by itself, and break DMU as explained above. The proposed solution is to give the power to S and X to compute *together* something they could not compute by themselves. We achieve this *via* a piece of information that each node keeps secret, different for each node and useless by itself, but when several pieces are combined, they produce a necessary input to all $LocalID$ values. In practice, we instantiate these auxiliary information by shares of a secret key of a THE scheme.

4.2 Privacy Analysis

Our protocol, as described in the previous section, is still vulnerable to many end-to-end attacks and traffic analysis. To prevent them, we fix a constant message size[4] and we borrow techniques from MIX networks such as the introduction of random delays and message batching [5]. These techniques unfortunately incur additional latency in communications. We reject the use of dummy messages, for their prohibitive cost compared to the additional privacy they provide [14].

Preliminary properties Intuitively, our design ensures the following properties:
(1) By construction, *routes are partially disjoint*: for a given source-destination pair there may exist several routes, and for two different source-destination

---

[2] Available at http://hal.inria.fr
[3] There is a way to achieve route initialization by performing an *exhaustive search* in both S and X's DRTs, but this yields a quadratic complexity in the number of nodes.
[4] Large messages are split into several parts, and padding is used if necessary.

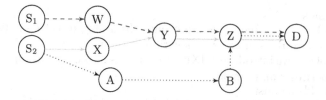

Fig. 4. An example of partially disjoint routes

pairs, routes may overlap. Thus, in Fig. 4, Z can not know whether messages come from S_1 or S_2, as the link identifier is the same for both routes.

(2) If the Decisional DH assumption holds and secure cryptographic key derivation functions exist, link identifiers are *secure*: for a given pair of neighboring nodes (X, Y), link messages are unlinkable for AdvI and AdvII. That is to say, the pairs $(L_{X,Y}^{(1)}, K_{X,Y}^{(1)})$ and $(L_{X,Y}^{(2)}, K_{X,Y}^{(2)})$ stemming from two different DH handshakes are unlinkable.

(3) The local identifiers are *secure*: for all X and D, $LocalID_D^X$ is known only to X; if the Computational DH assumption holds, given $LocalID_D^X$ it is not possible to recover the inputs that formed it; and if the DDH assumption holds, for any X, D_1, D_2, $LocalID_{D_1}^X$ and $LocalID_{D_2}^X$, X is unable to know which local identifier points to which destination.

(4) Route propositions are *indistinguishable* for AdvI. Because, locally, the messages exchanged are the same in both cases, whether a route proposition emanated from the destination itself or a proxy is indistinguishable for AdvI.

(5) If properties 2 and 4 hold, if the encryption schemes are semantically secure, and if we use MIXing techniques in the route proposal, then up to a certain point, AdvII can not distinguish whether a proposition emanated from the destination itself or a proxy[5].

(6) If local identifiers are secure, route initialization is *oblivious* for AdvI: S never makes the link between D and its value $LocalID_D^S$, and V never learns that the destination is D. In addition, the blinding factor r hides dst_D and if the discrete logarithm problem is hard, src_X is concealed.

(7) If we use MIXing techniques, and if link identifiers are secure, route initialization is indistinguishable from standard communication for AdvII.

Proof sketches of these properties are available in the long version of this paper. We merely note here that property 3 seem to hold for the same reason that ElGamal is semantically secure. Indeed, $LocalID_D^X$ can be seen as an ElGamal encryption of ID_D under key dst_D using randomness src_X. However, the proof can not be the same, as in our case, the random coins src_X are known to X.

Privacy properties Assuming the properties stated above hold, our protocol fulfills our privacy goals. We provide proof sketches in the full version of this paper.

---

[5] Up to a certain point, because when the proxy is far from the destination, a basic timing analysis is sufficient to distinguish the two cases.

- **SMU** holds against
    - **AdvI**, because messages are exempt from any direct or indirect information on the source or its location in the network.
    - **AdvII**, if we introduce MIXing techniques in the forwarding process and properties 2 and 7 hold.
- **DMU** holds against
    - **AdvI**, if properties 3, 4 and 6 hold, and if the encryption schemes are receiver-anonymous [12].
    - **AdvII**, if properties 2 and 5 hold, and if the destination, upon receiving a message, simulates a relay.
- **SDU** holds against **AdvI** and **AdvII** if SMU *or* DMU hold.
- **MMU** holds against
    - **AdvI**, if property 1 holds. Except in the special case of node X in Fig. 3.
    - **AdvII**, if property 2 holds.

4.3   Shortcomings and Future Improvements

Because we focused on privacy, our solution is neither efficient nor optimized. In particular, it does not give any guarantee on the connectivity of the network, does not handle routing loops and does not limit the size of the routes. For a practical routing algorithm, mechanisms handling those points are necessary. The difficulty is to design such mechanisms while preserving privacy.

Our protocol is vulnerable to a collusion of merely 2 nodes: if S and X collude in the route initialization protocol, they uncover the secret value dst_D of D and S eventually break DMU. To resist against a collusion of more than 2 nodes, we can ask the relay nodes between S and X (assuming X is not neighbor to S) to participate in the threshold decryption protocol.

It would also be interesting to remove the strong assumption of universal auxiliary information. Indeed, although it is acceptable for particular contexts, assuming that each node owns a share of a common secret is unrealistic in general. A solution is to distribute the secret and secret shares generation, but in this case, the dynamic insertion of nodes is very complex. Other choices, models or assumptions might allow circumventing the impossibility result while enabling efficient route initialization. For instance, decorrelating the activities of sources and relays, so as to avoid issues raised in Sect. 4.1, would remove the need for interaction and universal auxiliary information.

Future work should focus on testing the protocol against typical network attacks, and on assessing the practical usability of our design by measuring efficiency, available bandwidth and scalability through simulations. Also, formal proofs of privacy properties are desirable. To this end, we envision using the framework of Hevia *et al.* [10] that provides a formal definition of unlinkability against adversary models that are very close to ours.

5   Adaptation to a Real-Wold Example: Ad-Hoc Networks

We defined our protocol in a general, abstract network. As in our model, only a simple physical medium is necessary, our protocol can work on top of any bare network graph. Now, this section investigates how our protocol can be instantiated to a real world example. Because of the similarities with our model, we envision an adaptation to ad-hoc networks [2].

Indeed, these networks are infrastructure-less: there is no central node(s), and the routing is completely distributed. Ad-hoc routing protocols are either *reactive* or *proactive*. In the formers, routes are created only when necessary in an on-demand fashion while the others behave more as IP routing, where topology is flooded in the network. Although anonymous reactive routing designs are overwhelming, proactive ones are quite rare [13]. Our solution stands out by its proactive nature, by the strong privacy it provides, and by the use of homomorphic cryptography, which has never been used before in ad-hoc networks.

These networks allow a smooth integration of our protocol. Indeed, we can directly work above the MAC layer, assuming that nodes are able to function in *promiscuous* mode and to set their address to the broadcast address. Thus, nodes always use MAC broadcasting to communicate, and link identifiers to address neighbors, as described originally by Zhang *et al.* [16]. Thanks to the broadcast nature of ad-hoc networks, privacy is actually improved. Indeed, when a node emits using link identifiers, AdvII can not know which neighbor is addressed. This is not the case with wired networks, where links are point-to-point.

If we envision an adaptation to ad-hoc networks, the main shortcoming of our protocol is its inefficiency. The cost of cryptographic primitives is prohibitive for ad-hoc network nodes, which are typically small devices with limited battery.

6   Conclusion

This preliminary work lays the foundations for strongly private network communications using homomorphic encryption. We presented a privacy preserving routing protocol suitable for distributed environments, exhibited its main features, and provided elements of proof for its privacy properties. As a practical use-case, we showed that an adaptation to ad-hoc networks is at hand.

Many points need to be addressed, and several others can be improved. In particular, future work will include advanced experimentations to attest the gain in privacy provided by our protocol, and its efficiency. Even though we do not expect our protocol to perform as good as the state-of-the-art, we assume our users are willing to trade some efficiency against strong privacy (a feature often lacking in presently deployed solutions[6]). If possible, privacy properties should be proved formally, but how to do so is still an open question. Even technologies already widely deployed, which benefit from years of experience, regularly suffer attacks. Of course, we do not intend to replace these solutions, but merely to complete them. We see our work as a proof of concept for new strongly private interactive communications, offering free communications in any circumstances.

Acknowledgment. This work is partially funded by the *Collège International Doctoral de l'Université Européenne de Bretagne* and the Regional Council of Brittany

---

[6] A list of works is available at `http://www.cs.kau.se/philwint/censorbib/` (thanks to Phillip Winter).

(France). The authors would like to thank Simon Boche and Cristina Onete for their insightful suggestions and discussions during the writing of this paper.

References

1. Chaum, D.L.: Untraceable electronic mail, return addresses, and digital pseudonyms. Commun. ACM 24(2), 84–90 (1981)
2. Chlamtac, I., Conti, M., Liu, J.J.N.: Mobile ad hoc networking: imperatives and challenges. Ad Hoc Networks 1(1), 13–64 (2003)
3. Cohn, W.A.: Yahoo's china defense. The New Presence 9(3), 30–33 (2007)
4. Damgård, I., Jurik, M.: A generalisation, a simplification and some applications of paillier's probabilistic public-key system. In: Kim, K.-c. (ed.) PKC 2001. LNCS, vol. 1992, pp. 119–136. Springer, Heidelberg (2001)
5. Diaz, C., Preneel, B.: Taxonomy of mixes and dummy traffic. In: Deswarte, Y., Cuppens, F., Jajodia, S., Wang, L. (eds.) Information Security Management, Education and Privacy. IFIP, vol. 148, pp. 217–232. Springer, Heidelberg (2004)
6. Dingledine, R., Mathewson, N., Syverson, P.: Tor: The second-generation onion router. In: Proceedings of the 13th Conference on USENIX Security Symposium, SSYM 2004, vol. 13, p. 21. USENIX Association, Berkeley (2004)
7. El Gamal, T.: A public key cryptosystem and a signature scheme based on discrete logarithms. In: Blakely, G.R., Chaum, D. (eds.) CRYPTO 1984. LNCS, vol. 196, pp. 10–18. Springer, Heidelberg (1985)
8. Fontaine, C., Galand, F.: A survey of homomorphic encryption for nonspecialists. EURASIP J. Inf. Secur., 15:1–15:15 (January 2007)
9. Greenwald, G.: No Place to Hide. Metropolitan Books (May 2014)
10. Hevia, A., Micciancio, D.: An indistinguishability-based characterization of anonymous channels. In: Borisov, N., Goldberg, I. (eds.) PETS 2008. LNCS, vol. 5134, pp. 24–43. Springer, Heidelberg (2008)
11. Invernizzi, L., Kruegel, C., Vigna, G.: Message in a bottle: Sailing past censorship. In: Proceedings of the 29th Annual Computer Security Applications Conference, ACSAC 2013, pp. 39–48. ACM, New York (2013)
12. Kohlweiss, M., Maurer, U., Onete, C., Tackmann, B., Venturi, D.: Anonymity-preserving public-key encryption: A constructive approach. In: De Cristofaro, E., Wright, M. (eds.) PETS 2013. LNCS, vol. 7981, pp. 19–39. Springer, Heidelberg (2013)
13. Liu, M.J., Kong, J., Hong, X., Gerla: Performance evaluation of anonymous routing protocols in manets. In: Wireless Communications and Networking Conference, WCNC 2006, vol. 2, pp. 646–651. IEEE (April 2006)
14. Oya, S., Troncoso, C., Pérez-González, F.: Do dummies pay off? Limits of dummy traffic protection in anonymous communications. In: De Cristofaro, E., Murdoch, S.J. (eds.) PETS 2014. LNCS, vol. 8555, pp. 204–223. Springer, Heidelberg (2014)
15. Pfitzmann, A., Köhntopp, M.: Anonymity, unobservability, and pseudonymity - A proposal for terminology. In: Federrath, H. (ed.) Designing Privacy Enhancing Technologies. LNCS, vol. 2009, pp. 1–9. Springer, Heidelberg (2001)
16. Zhang, Y., Liu, W., Lou, W., Fang, Y.: Mask: anonymous on-demand routing in mobile ad hoc networks. IEEE Transactions on Wireless Communications 5(9), 2376–2385 (2006)

The 0-1 Knapsack Polytope – A Starting Point for Cryptanalysis of Knapsack Ciphers?

Vicky H. Mak-Hau and Lynn M. Batten

School of Information Technology, Deakin University, Australia
{vicky.mak,lynn.batten}@deakin.edu.au

Abstract. The Knapsack Cryptosystem of Merkle and Hellman, 1978, is one of the earliest public-key cryptography schemes. The security of the method relies on the difficulty in solving Subset Sum Problems (also known as Knapsack Problems). In this paper, we first provide a brief history of knapsack-based cryptosystems and their cryptanalysis attacks. Following that, we review the advances in integer programming approaches to $0 - 1$ Knapsack Problems, with a focus on the polyhedral studies of the convex hull of the integer set. Last of all, we discuss potential future research directions in applying integer programming in the cryptanalysis of knapsack ciphers.

1 Introduction: The 0-1 Knapsack Problem and Knapsack Ciphers

The security of cryptographic systems is often based on the intractability of underlying mathematical problems. One such problem, known as the 'subset sum' problem, considers a set A of positive integers and asks, given a fixed number, say W, whether it is possible to write W as a sum of a subset of the numbers in A (possibly in only one way). This can be stated mathematically as follows: Let $A = \{a_1, a_2, \ldots a_n\}$ where each a_i as well as n and W are fixed integers. Letting $\boldsymbol{a}$ represent the vector $(a_1, a_2, \ldots, a_n)$, the problem asks to find a vector $\boldsymbol{x} = (x_1, x_2, \ldots x_n)$ of $0's$ and $1's$ such that $\boldsymbol{a} \cdot \boldsymbol{x} = W$ where $\cdot$ denotes the vector product. There are obvious variations possible, including the idea of allowing the vector $\boldsymbol{x}$ to contain values other than 0 and 1. In fact, the x_is can be thought of as *weights*. In the form described, the corresponding subset sum problem is a special case of the *0-1 knapsack problem*.

The Knapsack Cryptosystem of Merkle and Hellman is one of the first public-key cryptography schemes and its security relies on the difficulty of solving subset sum problems. Many variations and extensions of the idea have been introduced in the subsequent literature in response to attacks by researchers. The one-iteration version was broken by [28] in 1982 while attacks on multi-iteration versions have been proposed in, for instance, [3,22,13]. All these attacks are successful for low-density knapsack ciphers. Because of these attacks, a number of stronger variations on knapsack ciphers were proposed in, for example, [7] and

L. Batten et al. (Eds.): ATIS 2014, CCIS 490, pp. 171–182, 2014.
© Springer-Verlag Berlin Heidelberg 2014

[23]; these were almost immediately followed by cryptanalysis attacks in, e.g., [27] and [20]. These attacks are not successful in all circumstances.

Cryptanalysis efforts for knapsack ciphers have since been shifted from recovering the private keys to directly solving the 0-1 knapsack problem which is known to be NP-hard as indicated by [17]. While Dynamic Programming can solve such problems in pseudo-polynomial time (e.g., [36]), the time is a function of the order of the knapsack capacity. A $0-1$ knapsack problem can be solved in polynomial time only when the knapsack capacity is polynomial w.r.t. the size of the knapsack problem; such is not the case for most knapsack cryptosystems.

An alternative interpretation of the knapsack concept is that of combining a set of fixed weights in order to achieve a target weight; such a combinatorial problem has many applications. Thus, the combinatorial optimization research community has found opportunities for developing algorithms which can solve various versions of the subset sum problem. In fact, in recent years, well-known meta-heuristic methods developed for combinatorial optimization problems have been used in the cryptanalysis of knapsack ciphers (see, for example, [31,1,4,11]). These heuristic algorithms, however, do not guarantee finding an optimal solution to any given combinatorial optimization problem, and consequently do not guarantee to break any knapsack cipher. In any case, these proposed meta-heuristic based cryptanalysis methods provided few experimental results.

Integer programming, on the other hand, if given enough time and memory space, can guarantee optimality of a combinatorial optimization problem. If the complete polyhedral description of the convex (integer) hull of the integer set can be found, then the optimal linear programming relaxation solution will be naturally integer, and consequently any knapsack cipher can be broken in polynomial time. Hence, identifying facets of the $0-1$ knapsack polytope and deriving polynomial time separation algorithms of these facets should contribute significantly to the cryptanalysis of knapsack-based cryptosystems.

In this paper, we review the literature on integer programming for $0-1$ knapsack problems and suggest possible further research for the use of integer programming techniques to attack the $0-1$ knapsack cryptosystems.

In Section 2, we describe the original Merkle-Hellman knapsack-based public key cryptosystem. In Section 3, we consider known 0-1 knapsack solution methods based on Dynamic Programming or meta-heuristics. Section 4 considers recent advances in this regard by using integer programming methods; in particular, this section also examines facets of the $0-1$ knapsack polytope which may lead to efficient algorithms. We draw these results together in Section 5, making recommendations for further work in this direction.

2   A Brief History of the Knapsack Public Key Cryptosystem (PKC)

Merkle and Hellman [18] presented the first knapsack-based PKC, (seven months after the RSA cryptosystem developed by [26]). The one-iteration additive knapsack cipher is explained as follows.

Key generation – Alice first chooses a sequence of *superincreasing* numbers a'_j, for $j \in N = \{1, \ldots, n\}$, i.e.,

$$a'_j > \sum_{\ell=1}^{j-1} a'_\ell, \quad \forall j = 2, \ldots, n. \tag{1}$$

She then chooses numbers α and ω such that $\omega > \sum_{j=1}^{n} a'_j$ and $\gcd(\alpha, \omega) = 1$, and calculates:

$$a_j \equiv \alpha a'_j \pmod{\omega}, \quad \forall j = 1, \ldots, n. \tag{2}$$

Now, $(\boldsymbol{a'}, \alpha, \omega)$ are kept as the private key where $\boldsymbol{a'} = (a'_1, a'_2, \ldots a'_n)$, whilst $\boldsymbol{a}$ is published as a public (encryption) key.

Encryption – Bob encrypts a plaintext $\boldsymbol{x} = (x_1, \ldots, x_n)$ into a ciphertext by calculating $W = \boldsymbol{a} \cdot \boldsymbol{x}$, and sends W to Alice. With α, ω co-prime and $\boldsymbol{a}$ generated by (2), we are guaranteed that the encryption is unique–no two distinct subsets will result in the same W. As a generalisation of [18], a'_j can be chosen randomly from the interval $[(2^{j-1} - 1)2^n + 1, 2^{j-1}2^n]$ for all $j \in N$ and ω can be chosen randomly from $[2^{2n+1} + 1, 2^{2n+2} - 1]$, hence W is clearly exponential in n.

Decryption – When Alice receives the ciphertext, W, she calculates $W' = \beta W \pmod{\omega}$, for $\beta = \alpha^{-1} \pmod{\omega}$, and solves $\sum_{j=1}^{n} a'_j x_j = W'$ to decrypt the message. Notice that this equation does have a unique solution and can be solved in linear time as explained next. If $W' \geq a'_n$, then $x_n = 1$ and the problem is reduced to $\sum_{j=1}^{n-1} a'_j x_j = W' - a_n$, otherwise $x_n = 0$, and we solve $\sum_{j=1}^{n-1} a'_j x_j = W'$. This process is repeated until we obtain the value of each x_i.

Cryptanalysis studies on the Merkle-Hellman cryptosystem soon followed, see, e.g., [30]. The one-iteration implementation of the cipher has been broken by [28] wherein a toy-sized integer programming problem was solved to find an integer k_1 such that the fraction k_1/a_1 provides an approximation to β/ω. See [15] for an excellent description of Shamir's attack.

An iterative additive cipher was also described in [18]. If T iterations are to be implemented, we select (α_t, ω_t), with $\gcd(\alpha_t, \omega_t) = 1$, $\omega_t > \sum_{\ell=1}^{j-1} a'_\ell$, for all $t = 1, \ldots, T$, and iteratively calculate:

$$a_j^t \equiv \alpha_t a_j^{t-1} \pmod{\omega_t}, \quad \forall j = 1, \ldots, n, \tag{3}$$

for all $t = 1, \ldots, T$, resulting in T vectors $\boldsymbol{a}^t = (a_1^t, a_2^t, \ldots a_n^t)$; we set $\boldsymbol{a}^0 = \boldsymbol{a'}$. Encryption and decryption in their paper are implemented in a similar way as in the one-iteration system. On the other hand, [29] proposed that all $\boldsymbol{a}^t$ be used simultaneously to produce a T-dimensional ciphertext $\boldsymbol{b}$. In this case, let B be the binary matrix formed by taking all T vectors $\{\boldsymbol{a}^t\}$ over GF(2), and $\tilde{\boldsymbol{b}}$ be the least significant digit of $\boldsymbol{b}$, the plaintext can be retrieved by solving $\boldsymbol{x} = B^{-1}\tilde{\boldsymbol{b}}$.

A few other knapsack ciphers were proposed and were soon followed by cryptanalysis attacks. For a thorough exposition of the numerous knapsack-based ciphers and cryptanalysis attacks, see, for example, [8]. A number of these attacks treated the cryptanalysis problem as a lattice problem, and the L^3 lattice basis reduction algorithm in [14] was implemented in some of them. See also [3], and [13]. The attack reported in [13], worked only for low-density problems, typically for $\frac{n}{\log_2 \tilde{a}} < 0.645$, where $\tilde{a} = \max_{1 \leq j \leq n}\{a_j\}$, which translates to $n < 182$ for superincreasing $\boldsymbol{a}'$ as described in the Merkle and Hellman scheme.

In addition to the additive knapsack ciphers, a few multiplicative knapsack ciphers have been proposed (e.g., [18]). These ciphers exploit the difficulty not only in solving the knapsack problem, but also in solving the discrete logarithm problem. Merkle and Hellman choose n pairwise relatively prime numbers $p_1, \ldots, p_n$, a prime $q > \Pi_{i=1}^n p_i$, and a primitive root $b \pmod{q}$, then find a_i by solving $p_i \equiv b^{a_i} \pmod{q}$, for all $i = 1, \ldots, n$. Again, $\boldsymbol{a}$ is published as the public key, and b, q are kept as the private key. Encryption of a plaintext $\boldsymbol{x}$ is obtained by calculating $W = \boldsymbol{a} \cdot \boldsymbol{x}$, and decryption consists of computing $b^W \pmod{q}$. [22] proposed an attack that can discover b and q in polynomial time with a high probability, but only under the assumptions that at least a large subset of $\{p_i\}$ is known and that $q \in 2^{\mathcal{O}(n \log n)}$.

A knapsack cryptosystem that generates encryption and decryption keys by taking a discrete logarithm in finite fields has been proposed in [7]. To generate the key, first a prime p and a positive integer $h \leq p$ are chosen such that discrete logarithms in $GF(p^h)$ (polynomials of degree $\leq h-1$ with coefficients in $GF(p)$) can be computed efficiently. Then they compute a p-dimensional vector $\boldsymbol{a} = (a_1, a_2, \ldots, a_p)$ with $a_i = \log_g(t + \alpha_i)$ for all $\alpha_i \in GF(p)$, where $t \in GF(p^h)$ is algebraic of degree h over $GF(p)$ chosen at random, and $g \in GF(p^h)$ is a multiplicative generator of $GF(p^h)$ also chosen at random. Afterwards, $\boldsymbol{a}$ is scrambled by a random permutation π to form $\pi(\boldsymbol{a})$, and a random noise $0 \leq d \leq p^h - 2$ is then added to form $c_i = \pi(\boldsymbol{a})_i + d$. Now, $\boldsymbol{c} = \{c_1, \ldots, c_p\}, p, h$ are published as the public key; and t, g, π, d are kept as private keys. To encrypt a message $\boldsymbol{x}$ of length p with exactly h 1's, we calculate $W = \sum_{i=1}^p c_i x_i \pmod{p^h - 1}$. Clearly, W is exponential in p. To decrypt the message, we first calculate $W' = W - hd$ $\pmod{p^h - 1}$, then $p(t) = g^{W'} \pmod{f(t)}$, for $f(t)$ a random irreducible monic polynomial of degree h in $GF(p)[t]$. Let $r(t) = t^h \pmod{f(t)}$ be a polynomial of degree $\leq h-1$, we obtain $d(t) = t^h + q(t) - r(t) = (t + \alpha_{i_1}) \cdot (t + \alpha_{i_2}) \cdot \ldots \cdot (t + \alpha_{i_h})$. The h roots α_{i_j}, for $j = 1, \ldots, h$, can be obtained by successive substitution. Applying the inverse of the permutation, the original message is recovered.

An attack on the [7] scheme was attempted by [27] wherein improvements to the L^3 lattice basis reduction algorithm were proposed. (See [21] for a history of the L^3 algorithm and the recent advances.) It appeared that the work of [27] was still ineffective against high-density knapsacks as the algorithm was reasonably successful for the $n = 103$ Chor-Rivest ciphers, but not for the $n = 151$ ones.

Over the years, more knapsack ciphers were developed (examples include [23], [19], [10], [33], and [25]). These also, were soon followed by cryptanalysis attacks (e.g., [20], and [24]). Even though the background mathematics used for the different knapsack ciphers may vary, from the point of view of an attacker, the single target is to determine the private key, and to do so efficiently and

effectively. Therefore, recent cryptanalysis attempts turned to solving the subset
sum problems directly using well-known meta-heuristic methods established for
combinatorial optimization (see, e.g., [31,1,4,11]).

3   0-1 Knapsack Solution Methods

Most heuristic methods for knapsack cipher attacks fall within the meta-heuristics
framework. A Genetic Algorithm (GA)-based attack was proposed in [31]; the authors tested the GA method on five letters of the alphabet represented by a byte
derived from the corresponding ASCII code. The average run time was 83 seconds (on a 1993 or earlier computer) with number of chromosomes ranging from
40 to 1860. The vectors were of length 15. Sixteen years later, [4] applied some
variations to the GA method of [31], using vectors of length 8 and reported faster
convergence. It would be beneficial, however, to experiment with GA problems on
a much larger scale. Binary Partical Swarm Optimization methods have been proposed in [11] and [1] (who tested their method on the same five letters as in [31] and
[4]). There is, however, some work in the literature on other meta-heuristic algorithms, not specifically for the cryptanalysis of knapsack ciphers, but for 0-1 knapsack problems in general, (see, e.g., [16] for a Simulated Annealing algorithm). One
important issue with any meta-heuristic approach (or heuristic methods in general), is that optimal solutions are _not_ guaranteed.

   A 0-1 knapsack problem can be solved by Dynamic Programming, (an exact
algorithm), in $\mathcal{O}(nW)$ time where n and W are as described at the beginning
of Section 2. The method is described in many textbooks, (see, e.g., [36]). Let
λ be the "states" with values from 1 to n. The dynamic programming recursion
formula is given by:

$$f_r(\lambda) = \max\{f_{r-1}(\lambda), \quad c_r + f_{r-1}(\lambda - a_r)\},$$

with $f_0(\lambda) = 0$, for all $\lambda \geq 0$. Since we calculate the value of $f_r(\lambda)$ for each $r =
1, \ldots, n$ and each $\lambda = 1, \ldots, W$, it follows that the complexity of the algorithm is
of order $\mathcal{O}(nW)$. If W is exponential in n (as in most cases discussed in Section
2), then the computation time will be exponential in n. This might have been the
reason researchers have turned to inexact modern heuristics methods; however,
in the context of cryptanalysis of knapsack ciphers, we _do_ need exact solutions.
We thus turn our attention to exact solution methods: Integer Programming.

4   Integer Programming Advances in Solving 0-1 Knapsacks

In this section, we present some Binary Integer Programming (BIP) basics and
review polyhedral studies on the 0-1 knapsack.

4.1 Integer Linear Programming Basics

An Integer Linear Programming (ILP) problem typically takes the following form: $z_{IP} = \max\left\{ cx \ : \ Ax \leq b, \ x \geq 0, \ x \in \mathbb{Z}^n \right\}$, for $A \in \mathbb{Q}^{m \times n}$, $c \in \mathbb{Q}^n$, and $b \in \mathbb{Q}^m$. If $x \in \{0,1\}^n$, then this is a Binary Integer Programming (BIP) problem.

A Linear Programming Relaxation (LPR) of an ILP is given by $z_{LPR} = \max\left\{ cx \ : \ Ax \leq b, \ x \geq 0 \right\}$, (in the case of a BIP, $0 \leq x_j \leq 1$ for all $j \in N$). Let $\mathcal{P}$ be the polytope defined by $\mathcal{P} = \{x \ : \ Ax \leq b, \ x \geq 0\}$, and $\mathcal{Q}$ be the polytope defined by the *convex hull* of the integer points in $\{x \in \mathcal{P} \ : \ x \in \mathbb{Z}^n\}$. As $\mathcal{P} \supseteq \mathcal{Q}$, $z_{LPR} \geq z_{IP}$. We call the value $z_{LPR} - z_{IP}$ the *IP-LP gap*.

A face $\mathcal{F}$ of $\mathcal{Q}$ is defined as $\mathcal{F} = \{x \in \mathcal{Q} : \boldsymbol{\pi} \cdot \boldsymbol{x} = \pi_0\}$, for some given π_0 and $\boldsymbol{\pi} = \{\pi_1, \ldots, \pi_n\}$. If $\dim(\mathcal{F}) = \dim(\mathcal{Q}) - 1 = n - 1$, then $\mathcal{F}$ is called a *facet*. A 'valid' inequality (one that contains all feasible solutions) is the half space defined by $\boldsymbol{\pi} \cdot \boldsymbol{x} \leq \pi_0$ such that $\mathcal{Q} \subseteq \{x \ : \ \boldsymbol{\pi} \cdot \boldsymbol{x} \leq \pi_0\}$. If we know all the facets of $\mathcal{Q}$, then by solving the LPR of these facets we will get the optimal solution to the ILP. Linear Programming problems can be solved in polynomial time. Most ILPs, on the other hand, require an exhaustive search and therefore in general cannot be solved in polynomial time.

To date, a complete description of all facets of the convex hull of the 0-1 knapsack is not known. Several faces and facets have been found in the literature, most of them based on "strong covers" (which we will explain in the next section). There may well be an exponential number of such strong covers in any given 0-1 knapsack. Even if we are able to exhaustively enumerate these strong covers, it would not be practical to include all associated constraints into an LP/IP solver. The standard technique that deals with IP/LP problems with a very large number of constraints is the cutting plane algorithm, where only a small number of constraints which are not satisfied (are 'violated') by those solutions are added iteratively as they are found. Such a problem is commonly referred to as the *separation problem* in ILP (see, e.g. [36]).

A commonly used exact method for solving an ILP or a BIP problem is the branch-and-bound (BNB) method. The BNB is an exhaustive tree search algorithm that begins with an LPR of the ILP at root node of the tree. If the optimal solution to the LPR is naturally integer, then it is the optimal solution to the ILP. Otherwise, one of the variables x_j^* with a fractional value will be used as a "branch" to create two nodes (sub-problems), one with the extra constraint $x \leq \lfloor x_j^* \rfloor$ and the other with $x \geq \lceil x_j^* \rceil$. This procedure is repeated until all nodes on the BNB tree are explored. A node on the BNB tree can be "pruned" if a feasible solution is found (i.e., one in which all variables are integer), or if the subproblem is infeasible, or if the LPR bound is no better than the best feasible solution found so far. The branch-and-cut (BNC) algorithm is a variation of the BNB, in which at each node of the BNB tree, only a small collection of the constraints is included in the LPR, and the cutting plane algorithm is implemented to generate constraints as they are violated. For finding exact solutions to 0-1 knapsack ciphers, BNC is likely to be the method of choice.

4.2   The 0-1 Knapsack Polytope: Valid and Facet-Defining Inequalities

Using the notation of Section 2 with $N = \{1, 2, \ldots, n\}$ and $\boldsymbol{x} = \{x_1, x_2, \ldots, x_n\}$, we now formally define the 0-1 knapsack polytope to be:

$$\mathcal{K} = \text{conv}\Big\{ \boldsymbol{x} \in \mathbb{R}^n \ : \ \sum_{j \in N} a_j x_j \leq W, \quad x_j \in \{0, 1\}, \ \forall j \in N \Big\}.$$

We assume that $a_j \leq W$, for all $j \in N$, and hence $\dim(\mathcal{K}) = n$.

Now we define a *minimal cover* as in, for example, [5] or [35]. W.l.o.g., we assume that the set $A = \{a_1, a_2, \ldots, a_n\}$ is sequenced in descending order, $a_j \geq a_{j+1}$, for $j = 1, \ldots, n-1$. A subset $S \subset N$ is called a *minimal cover* of W if

$$\sum_{j \in S} a_j > W; \quad \text{and} \quad \sum_{j \in S \setminus \{i\}} a_j \leq W, \ \forall i \in S. \tag{4}$$

As demonstrated in [35], (with procedures described therein), every strong cover S can produce at least one valid constraint. Let Ω be the set of all minimal covers of W. The set of all minimal cover constraints is given by:

$$\sum_{j \in S} x_j \leq |S| - 1, \quad \forall S \in \Omega. \tag{5}$$

Every minimal cover can be used to produce at least one facet-defining constraint in the form of:

$$\sum_{j \in S} x_j + \sum_{j \in N \setminus S} \beta_j x_j \leq |S| - 1, \quad \forall S \in \Omega. \tag{6}$$

These constraints are referred to as the *'simple' Lifted Cover Inequalities* (LCI) in [12]. In some cases the lifting is done sequentially, (i.e. one β_j at a time), however in other cases, it is done simultaneously. A more general form of LCI is given by [32] as follows:

$$\sum_{j \in S \setminus \Psi} x_j + \sum_{j \in N \setminus S} \alpha_j x_j + \sum_{j \in \Psi} \beta_j x_j \leq |S \setminus \Psi| + \sum_{j \in \Psi} \beta_j - 1, \quad \forall S \in \Omega, \tag{7}$$

for S a cover, and $\Psi \subset S$. Here, the α_j are known as "up-lifting" coefficients, and β_j as "down-lifting" coefficients. See, e.g., [6,37,9] for more work on constraint lifting for cover inequalities.

On the other hand, [5] described an extended version of the minimal cover inequality (5) which, in a way, can also be viewed as "lifting". Let $j_1 = \arg \max_{j \in S} \{a_j\}$, $S' = \{j \in N \setminus S \ : \ a_j \geq a_{j_1}\}$, and $E(S) = S \cup S'$. We further define $\bar{\Omega}$ to be the set of *strongly minimal covers*, where:

$$\bar{\Omega} = \{S \in \Omega \ : \ E(S) \not\subset E(T), \quad \forall T \in \Omega \setminus S, \ s.t., |T| = |S|\}.$$

In this case, let $i_1 = \arg max_j\{a_j \ : \ j \in N \setminus E(S)\}$. Then a set S is a *strongly minimal cover* if $E(S) = N$ or if

$$\sum_{j \in (S \setminus \{j_1\}) \cup \{i_1\}} a_j \leq W, \quad \text{for } E(S) \neq N.$$

In the rest of the paper, for simplicity, we will call these strongly minimal covers the *strong covers*. The class of strong cover inequalities is given by:

$$\sum_{j \in E(S)} x_j \leq |S| - 1, \quad \forall S \in \bar{\Omega}. \tag{8}$$

From the strong covers in (8), [35] has demonstrated that every strong cover inequality can generate another valid inequality, although, there is no guarantee that all valid inequalities can be generated in this manner. Further, if $\mathcal{K}$ comprises only inequalities with 0-1 coefficients, then

$$\mathcal{K} = \left\{ \boldsymbol{x} : \sum_{j \in E(S)} x_j \leq |S| - 1, \quad \forall S \in \bar{\Omega}, \ 0 \leq x_i \leq 1 \right\}.$$

As mentioned earlier, we do not have complete knowledge of $\mathcal{K}$, but some of the facet-defining inequalities for the 0-1 knapsack polytope have been found in the literature (which we will review below). In Binary Integer Programming, we call the bound constraints of the binary decision variables (i.e., $x_i \geq 0$ and $x_i \leq 1$, for all $i \in N$), *trivial inequalities*.

Proposition 1. *([5] – Proposition 2, Page 149) Let $\boldsymbol{a} = \{a_1, a_2, \ldots, a_n\}$, $\boldsymbol{x} = \{x_1, x_2, \ldots, x_n\}$, and $j^* = \arg max_i\{a_i \ : \ i \in N \setminus \{j\}\}$. The trivial inequalities $x_j \leq 1$ are facet-defining for $\mathcal{P}$ iff $a_{j^*} + a_j \leq W = \boldsymbol{a} \cdot \boldsymbol{x}$.*

For non-trivial constraints, we have the following results. Let S be a strong cover, j_1 be as previously defined, and $j_2 = \arg max_j\{a_j \ : \ j \in S \setminus \{j_1\}\}$.

Theorem 41. *([5] – Theorem 1, Page 151) Letting $\boldsymbol{a}$ and $\boldsymbol{x}$ be defined as in Proposition 1, then the strong cover constraint*

$$\sum_{j \in E(S)} x_j \leq |S| - 1 \tag{9}$$

defines a facet iff $E(S) \geq 2$ and

$$\sum_{j \in S \setminus \{j_1, j_2\} \cup \{1\}} a_j \leq W.$$

Though the necessary and sufficient conditions listed above are easy to check, identifying strong covers $S \in \bar{\Omega}$ is nontrivial. If, however, we have an efficient method to generate $\bar{\Omega}$, each strong cover can be used to generate a valid constraint that is facet-defining under certain sufficient conditions.

Theorem 42. (*[5] – Theorem 2, Page 156) Let* $Q = \{0, \ldots, q\}$, *for* $1 \leq q \leq \pi_0$, *the constraint*

$$\sum_{j \in N} \pi_j x_j \leq \pi_0 \tag{10}$$

is valid for $\mathcal{K}$ *if:*
1. *there exists a partition of* N *into* $q + 1$ *mutually pairwise disjoint sets* N_h, *for* $h \in Q$, *such that* $\pi_j = h$, *for all* $j \in N_h$ *and all* $h \in Q$; *and*
2. *for the sets* N_h *of the partition in (1),* $M = \bigcup_{h=1}^{q} N_h = E(S)$, *for some minimal cover* $S = \{j_1, \ldots, j_r\} \subseteq N_1$, *with* $\pi_0 = |S| - 1$; *and*
3. $N_0 = N \setminus M$, $N_1 = M \setminus N_0$, *and* $N_h = \left\{ i \in N \ : \ \sum_{j \in S_h} a_j \leq a_i < \sum_{j \in S_{h+1}} a_j \right\}$, *for all* $h = 2, \ldots, q$, *where* $S_h = \{j_1, \ldots, j_h\}$, *for* $h = 2, \ldots, q + 1$.
Further, (10) is facet-defining if $\sum_{j \in S \setminus S_h} a_j + a_i \leq W$, *for all* $i \in N_h$, *and all* $h \in Q$, *and if conditions (1), (2), and (3) also hold.*

More facet-defining results on minimal covers can be found in, e.g., [6]. In non-cover based inequalities, [34] proposed a class of "weight inequalities" and some extensions of this idea with polyhedral results in some special cases. Let $T \subseteq N$ with $\sum_{j \in T} < W$ (T defined this way is referred to as a "pack" in the literature). An obvious constraint is given by:

$$\sum_{j \in T} a_j x_j \leq \sum_{j \in T} a_j. \tag{11}$$

These are also known as the *Pack Inequalities* (PI). A stronger version of the constraint, called *weight inequalities* is proposed in [34]. Let $r = W - \sum_{j \in T} a_j + 1$; N_j the subset of N with $a_i = j$, for all $i \in N_j$; and that $\bigcup_{i \geq r+1} N_i \setminus T \neq \emptyset$. The weight inequalities are given as follows:

$$\sum_{j \in T} a_j x_j + \sum_{i \geq r} \sum_{j \in N_i \setminus T} (i - r) x_j \leq \sum_{j \in T} a_j. \tag{12}$$

Some extensions of the weight inequality were also proposed in the paper. For example, the *weight-reduction inequality* is valid for $\mathcal{K}$ while others are valid or facet-defining for some special cases of $\mathcal{K}$.

Most of the strong valid inequalities or facet-defining inequalities are based on strong covers, but there may well be exponentially many of them, and therefore it is impractical to include them all in an IP/LP solver. For this reason, separation algorithms for some 0-1 knapsack constraints have been studied in the literature. See, e.g., [12] for an excellent exposition of separation algorithm, including some of their own algorithms along with thorough implementations.

In [12], we can find an extensive set of experiments on the LP relaxation of the 0-1 knapsacks, using various separation algorithms for simple cover inequalities, strong cover inequalities, (referred to as the *Extended Cover Inequalities* therein), lifted cover inequalities, weight inequalities, sequentially-lifted pack inequalities, as well as the general knapsack facets. They first solve the LP relaxation of the

0-1 KP and obtain the IP-LP gap. Then, for each knapsack constraint, one or more separation algorithms will be called. If any violated inequalities are found, they will be added to the LP and the new LP is re-optimised. This procedure is iterated until no more violated constraint is found. The dual simplex algorithm is used in the re-optimization, however the initial LP relaxation is solved using the primal simplex algorithm. An improvement to the original IP-LP gap is reported. For the separation of extended cover inequalities and lifted cover inequalities, [12] proposed an $\mathcal{O}(n^2 W)$ exact algorithm and an $\mathcal{O}(nW)$ exact algorithm. Surprisingly, they reported that the latter was in fact slower than the former in practice. In any case, since Dynamic Programming can solve a 0-1 knapsack in $\mathcal{O}(nW)$ time, a much faster separation algorithm is desired. [12] also presented an $\mathcal{O}(n^2)$ time heuristics separation algorithm that in most test instances, closed approximately the same amount of IP-LP gap as the exact separation algorithms. Regarding the weight inequalities, [12] improved the $\mathcal{O}(nW\tilde{a})$ separation algorithm of [34], (for $\tilde{a} = \max_{j \in N}\{a_j\}$) and proposed an $\mathcal{O}((n + \tilde{a})W)$ algorithm as well as a heuristic algorithm. For the lifted pack inequalities, an $\mathcal{O}(nW)$ time dynamic programming method is proposed for computing lifting coefficients for packs discovered from the weight inequality heuristic separation algorithms. As for the separation of general knapsack facets, several improvements to an existing separation algorithm has been proposed and tested.

5   Future Research Directions

The test problems used in [12] are from MIPLIB 2003 (see [2]). These test instances are 0-1 BIPs with not one, but many knapsack constraints (ranging from 6 to 756). The number of variables (n) in these test problems ranges from 27 to 2756. In a way, these are "harder" problems, as they are highly constrained. On the other hand, the feasible set is much smaller when a problem has more than one knapsack constraint. To summarise, the major differences between the MIPLIB 2003 problem instances and the 0-1 knapsack ciphers problem instances are: (1) the latter have one single knapsack constraint whereas the former have multiple knapsack constraints; (2) the latter have a unique optimal solution whilst the former may contain multiple optimal solutions; (3) the latter typically have a lower density than the former; and (4) the optimal value for the latter is already known but we are interested instead in finding the actual optimal solution in order to break the cipher whereas for the former, most of the time the optimal value is not known in advance. Further, past experiments are focused on the improvement to IP-LP bounds induced by the strong constraints. We aim to solve the 0-1 knapsack problem for optimality.

As future research directions, one may wish to conduct further study on the 0-1 knapsack polytope to exploit the special features of the 0-1 knapsack ciphers, including the fact that they have a unique optimal solution, and that they have a lower than usual density. As the optimal value is known for 0-1 knapsack ciphers, we now finally have the means to evaluate the strong constraints found so far for 0-1 knapsack problems in order to see how much of the

IP-LP gap has been closed. As soon as more strong valid (or even facet-defining) constraints are identified, one can implement a full-on BNC algorithm for solving the 0-1 knapsack for optimality (hence recovering the optimal solution). Given the sparse structure of these 0-1 knapsack ciphers, it would be interesting to see whether any improvement to the $\mathcal{O}(nW)$ computational complexity of the Dynamic Programming method can be achieved.

References

1. AbdulHalim, M.F., Attea, B.A., Hameed, S.M.: A binary particle swarm optimization for attacking knapsacks cipher algorithm. In: International Conference on ICCCE 2008, pp. 77–81 (May 2008)
2. Achterberg, T., Koch, T., Martin, A.: MIPLIB 2003. Oper. Res. Lett. 34(4), 361–372 (2006)
3. Adleman, L.M.: On breaking generalized knapsack public key cryptosystems. In: Proceedings of the Fifteenth Annual ACM Symposium on Theory of Computing, STOC 1983, pp. 402–412. ACM, NY (1983)
4. Al-Dabbagh, R.D.H.: Compact genetic algorithm for cryptanalysis trapdoor 0-1 knapsack cipher. Journal of Al-Nahrain University 12(2), 137–145 (2009)
5. Balas, E.: Facets of the knapsack polytope. Math. Prog. 8(1), 146–164 (1975)
6. Balas, E., Zemel, E.: Facets of the knapsack polytope from minimal covers. SIAM Journal on Applied Mathematics 34(1), 119–148 (1978)
7. Chor, B., Rivest, R.L.: A knapsack type public key cryptosystem based on arithmetic in finite fields. In: Blakely, G.R., Chaum, D. (eds.) CRYPTO 1984. LNCS, vol. 196, pp. 54–65. Springer, Heidelberg (1985)
8. Desmedt, Y.G.: What happened with knapsack cryptographic schemes? In: Skwirzynski, J.K. (ed.) Performance Limits in Communication Theory and Practice. NATO ASI Series, vol. 142, pp. 113–134. Springer, Netherlands (1988)
9. Gu, Z., Nemhauser, G.L., Savelsbergh, M.W.P.: Sequence independent lifting in mixed integer programming. J. Comb. Optim. 4(1), 109–129 (2000)
10. Huang, M., Lee, C., Tzeng, S.: A new knapsack public-key cryptosystem based on permutation combination algorithm (2008),
    http://isrc.ccs.asia.edu.tw/www/myjournal/P123.pdf
11. Jain, A., Chaudhari, N.S.: Cryptanalytic results on knapsack cryptosystem using binary particle swarm optimization. In: de la Puerta, J.G., et al. (eds.) International Joint Conference SOCO'14-CISIS'14-ICEUTE'14. AISC, vol. 299, pp. 375–384. Springer, Heidelberg (2014)
12. Kaparis, K., Letchford, A.N.: Separation algorithms for 0-1 knapsack polytopes. Math. Prog. 124(1-2), 69–91 (2010)
13. Lagarias, J.C., Odlyzko, A.M.: Solving low-density subset sum problems. J. ACM 32(1), 229–246 (1985)
14. Lenstra Jr., A.K., Lenstra, H.W., Lováz, L.: Factoring polynomials with rational coefficients. Mathematische Annalen 261(4), 515–534 (1982)
15. Lenstra Jr, H.W.: Integer programming and cryptography. The Mathematical Intelligencer 6(3), 14–21 (1984)
16. Liu, A., Wang, J., Han, G., Wang, S., Wen, J.: Improved simulated annealing algorithm solving for 0/1 knapsack problem. In: Proceedings of the 6th ISDA, ISDA 2006, vol. 2, pp. 1159–1164. IEEE Computer Society, DC (2006)

17. Menezes, A.J., Van Oorschot, P.C., Vanstone, S.A.: Handbook of applied cryptography. CRC Press (2010)
18. Merkle, R.C., Hellman, M.E.: Hiding information and signatures in trapdoor knapsacks. IEEE Transactions on Information Theory 24(5), 525–530 (1978)
19. Naccache, D., Stern, J.: A new public-key cryptosystem (1997)
20. Nguyên, P.Q., Stern, J.: Merkle-hellman revisited: A cryptanalysis of the qu-vanstone cryptosystem based on group factorizations. In: Kaliski Jr., B.S. (ed.) CRYPTO 1997. LNCS, vol. 1294, pp. 198–212. Springer, Heidelberg (1997)
21. Nguyen, P.Q., Vallée, B.: The LLL Algorithm: Survey and Applications, 1st edn. Springer Publishing Company, Incorporated, Heidelberg (2009)
22. Odlyzko, A.: Cryptanalytic attacks on the multiplicative knapsack cryptosystem and on Shamir's fast signature scheme. IEEE Trans. Inf. Theor. 30, 594–601 (1984)
23. Qu, M., Vanstone, S.A.: The knapsack problem in cryptography. In: Finite Fields. Contemp Math., vol. 168, pp. 291–308. A.M.S (1994)
24. Rastaghi, R.: Cryptanalysis of a new knapsack type public-key cryptosystem. CoRR, abs/1210.8375:1–5 (2012)
25. Ray, A., Bhat, A.: Enhancement of merkle-hellman knapsack cryptosystem by use of discrete logarithmics (2013)
26. Rivest, R.L., Shamir, A., Adleman, L.: A method for obtaining digital signatures and public-key cryptosystems. Communications of the ACM 21, 120–126 (1978)
27. Schnorr, C.-P., Hörner, H.H.: Attacking the chor-rivest cryptosystem by improved lattice reduction. In: Guillou, L.C., Quisquater, J.-J. (eds.) EUROCRYPT 1995. LNCS, vol. 921, pp. 1–12. Springer, Heidelberg (1995)
28. Shamir, A.: A polynomial time algorithm for breaking the basic merkle-hellman cryptosystem. In: Advances in Cryptology: Proceedings of CRYPTO 1982, pp. 279–288. Plenum (1982)
29. Shamir, A.: Embedding cryptographic trapdoors in arbitrary knapsack systems. Information Processing Letters 17(2), 77–79 (1983)
30. Shamir, A., Zippel, R.: On the security of the Merkle–Hellman cryptographic scheme (corresp.). IEEE Trans. Inf. Theor. 26(3), 339–340 (1980)
31. Spillman, R.: Cryptanalysis of knapsack ciphers using genetic algorithms. Cryptologia 17(4), 367–377 (1993)
32. Van Roy, T.J., Wolsey, L.A.: Solving mixed integer programming problems using automatic reformulation. Operations Research 35(1), 45–57 (1987)
33. Wang, B., Hu, Y.: Quadratic compact knapsack public-key cryptosystem. Computers & Mathematics with Applications 59(1), 194–206 (2010)
34. Weismantel, R.: On the 0/1 knapsack polytope. Math. Prog. 77(3), 49–68 (1997)
35. Wolsey, L.A.: Faces for a linear inequality in 0-1 variables. Math. Prog. 8, 165–178 (1975)
36. Wolsey, L.A.: Integer programming. Wiley-Interscience, NY (1998)
37. Zemel, E.: Easily computable facets of the knapsack polytope. Mathematics of Operations Research 14(4), 760–764 (1989)

Forensic Identification of Students Outsourcing Assignment Projects from Freelancer.com

Michael Monnik and Lei Pan

School of IT, Deakin University, Melbourne, Australia
{mdmonnik,l.pan}@deakin.edu.au

Abstract. This paper reports the increasing popularity of outsourcing academic works by university students motivated by the lure of lucrative dividends and visa opportunities. Due to a lack of formal methods in detecting such transactions, freelance websites are thriving in facilitating the trade of outsourced assignments. This is compounded by the fact that many university staff have neither the time nor training to perform complex media analysis and forensic investigations. This paper proposes a method to aid in the identification of those who outsource assignment works on the most popular site `freelancer.com`. We include a recent real-world case study to demonstrate the relevancy and applicability of our methodology. In this case study, a suspect attempts to evade detection via use of anti-forensics which demonstrates the capability and awareness of evasion techniques used by students.

1 Introduction

Plagiarism is mistakenly believed to be a short path to academic success by some students. From their perspective, paying someone else to do their assignments is a shortcut for accelerating the time needed to complete their enrolled degree and hence gaining better opportunities for employment, work permits, and visa applications which may yield bigger financial returns and permanent residency in the near future. These lucrative dividends lure many innocent minds to participate in the outsourcing of assignments.

Despite of the increased use of commercial plagiarism detection software, students seek alternative means to bypass the automated checkers such as *TurnItIn*. One typically used attempt includes outsourcing assignment works via online freelance websites. As of mid 2014, about 65,000 university assignment projects are listed on `freelancer.com` out of the total 6,300,000 projects.

Had attention not been brought to the public on this issue, the consequences could have been severe. Nevertheless, this issue deserves the utmost attention in the coming future. Outsourced assignments bring distrust to the quality of graduates, disbelief in the education system, and even discredit the institution's long-standing reputation. In particular, university staff cannot always perform complex media analysis in the hopes of revealing an online identity. Such lack of technical training needed to tackle this challenge alone, requires the involvement of the digital forensics community in addressing this issue. Realistically, forensic

L. Batten et al. (Eds.): ATIS 2014, CCIS 490, pp. 183–190, 2014.

experts are rare in number and short in time. Any solution should consider this constraint in its process.

In this paper, we propose a method to aid in the identification of those who outsource assignment works on freelance websites. Our first step is to locate the URL of the completed and relevant projects, as many advertised projects are fraudulent or phantom in nature; our second step is to identify the project hirer and provide evidence of association with a student. In order to alleviate the effort and intensity of training an assistant, we propose a step-wise keyword search method based on necessity level, using commercial search engines to return a manageable amount of retrieved information. Hence, our contributions are three-fold — 1) An assistant is allocated the task of performing web searches which lowers the workload of the forensic expert; 2) the case study visualizes and interprets bidder information; 3) our case study involves the use of anti-forensic measures taken by the student, in an attempt to evade detection via the use of photographic imagery and the disabling of GPS functionality on the device.

This paper is organized as follows: Section 2 surveys the existing literature to identify the current plagiarism detection methods and justify the research opportunity. Section 3 presents our four-component method which is conducted by both an university assistant and a forensic expert. Section 4 presents a case study demonstrating the application of our method, and significant conclusions are elaborated in Section 5.

2 Literature Review

Traditional plagiarism detection attempts to find out whether a fragment of text has been copied from known sources. Its successful operation relies upon the availability of these texts in the database; without the presence of these texts, the successful detection of outsourced solutions is not plausible. For example, *TurnItIn* is a commercial plagiarism-detection tool which compares submitted texts to that of a predefined database. Having compared with the cached phrases, a result report indicates the percentages of similarity between the suspected text and retrieved source documents. However, hiring a freelancer to write the assignment will completely bypass *TurnItIn* and the products alike.

Failing to address the genuine identification of the author, in outsourced assignments, exaggerates the effectiveness of traditional plagiarism detection. As such, detection techniques exclude web-based documents and important information pertaining to a transaction of work. Specifically, this includes bidder information, project description, user feedback scores, bidding price, and deadlines. This omitted information is essential in detecting outsourced assignments and revealing the genuine identity of the submitter.

Time is a critical factor. Garfinkel et al. [1] introduce a differential algorithm for digital forensic investigation. That is, the investigators should focus on the characteristics of the storage media that have been changed between two snapshots in time. Ideally, there exists an operation which describes changes to metadata of the two byte strings collected at different times. To derive the operations causing changes, the authors [1] present a list of abstract rules for common operations such as deleting, creating, moving, copying, or renaming files on a storage image. Accordingly, we observe that the assignment due date is directly related to the project deadline advertised on freelance websites, which gives us a reliable reference point to create a meaningful timeline.

Additionally, the quality of query terms significantly affects the search results. In order to improve the chance of relevant documents, Zhao and Callan [2] define "term necessity" as the probability that a query term appears in relevant documents. That is, the term necessity value indicates the percentage of relevant documents retrieved by the query term — the higher a term's necessity value, the more relevant the retrieved documents. Specifically, there are four important features — necessary term, necessity level of synonyms, necessity level of unlike terms, and abstract but rare terms. Using these four principles, Zhao and Callan [2] achieve a significant increase (over 40% in average) of retrieval accuracy by applying term necessity estimates as coefficients of query terms.

3 Locating an Outsourced Assignment Project

In order to locate outsourced assignments, our method consists of four components — creating search terms, constructing queries, filtering out projects of little interest, and identifying the wrongdoer. We suggest the first three components are carried out by an assistant who possesses little forensic knowledge; the last component is more appropriately handled by a forensic expert. The assistant recommends the selected URLs of the outsourced projects to the forensic expert, and thereafter the expert attempts to identify the hirer.

3.1 Query Term Selection

According to our observation, the selection of query terms, irrespective of grammar or spelling, determines the success rate of retrieving related projects. We propose an algorithm to select query terms according to their level of necessity which is based upon the idea proposed by Zhao and Callan [2].

1. An assistant proposes the necessity terms covering the information of the subject, discipline, institution and nature of the assignment.
2. The assistant sorts the terms according to their perceived centeredness of the advertised projects. Terms will be ranked higher if more likely to appear in the project description or title.
3. The assistant discards the terms that are more likely to be replaced by its more prevalent synonyms.
4. The assistant also discards the terms that are unlikely to coexist with their synonyms on the project page.
5. The assistant discards the terms with a highly abstract meaning.

The involvement of a human assistant is crucial to the quality of query terms, as automated programs are incapable of effectively abstracting academic contents in just a few words. Moreover, the efficiency of selecting query terms is significantly improved with personnels' familiarity of the assignments.

3.2   Keyword Search via Google Search Engine

The assistant may freely choose any search engine, however in this paper
google.com is used. One of the main advantages is that it requires minimal
training as most internet users are familiar with Google. That is, amateur users
would be quite familiar with the concept of bag of words, which applies basic
logical operations — AND, OR, and NOT. To search for a bag of words, *Google
Search* defines the logical operators OR as "|" and NOT as "-". The AND op-
erator is assumed by default. These symbols should be prefixed in front of the
particular query term. Furthermore, sites, their titles and text can be targeted
by using parameters "site:", "intitle:" and "intext:". Additionally, we consider
the time window information which the assignment project is most likely to be
posted on a freelance site. We use the parameter "daterange:" implemented by
Google search engine. In this context, the dates should be in Julian calendar
format. We can also apply further constraints to the query if more detailed information is available to us. If we expect a PDF file to be attached to the project
page, then we use the parameter "filetype:pdf" in the query.

   At the end of this stage, the assistant constructs a search query by supplying
the parameters with appropriate values. The top 20 project pages returned by
Google search are then collected for visualization analysis described in the next
subsection. If there are an insufficient number of results, the assistant will use
different search engines making appropriate adjustments of the query.

3.3   Visualization and Analysis of Bidding Information

In order to filter out incomplete, phantom, and possibly fraudulent projects
posted on freelancer.com, we propose an analytical visualization method for
non-technical personnel. This method requires only the bidder information from
a project page which is in the public domain, and automatically updated by the
freelance websites. This information enables us to pinpoint the specific projects
that fit the requirements of being completed by outsourced workers.

   According to our observation of successfully completed projects, we identified
the following three critical characteristics of such projects and their corresponding bidders — 1) Feedback is the amount of reviews that the worker received
from the past projects hirers which indicates the popularity of the worker. 2) The
reputation is a ranking the average satisfactory score each hirer provides regarding the deliverables, which is often derived as a combination of multiple factors
including communication, quality, expertise, professionalism, and rehireability.
There is a positive correlation between the reputation score and the likelihood
of project completion. 3) The completion rate is a percentage of projects that
are completed on time and satisfactory to the hirer. In summary, the three indicators represent a history of bidders' profile. Specifically, the feedback indicates
the number of past projects; whereas, the product of reputation and completion
rate indicates the quality of past projects. We observe that the bidders with the
highest score of these three factors combined are to be the most likely winners
of the bid.

Before conducting visualization, we collect the raw data of the three indicators of all bidders from a project page into a spreadsheet; we normalize the value of feedback by setting a constant as a denominator; we then sort bidders on feedback value by the incremental order; lastly, we set x-axis to be the sorted bidders and y-axis to be the three values.

To use the visualization results, we check the position of the winning bidder in our plot. If the winner of the bid resides on the right hand side of the plot, then the project is likely to be completed; and if the winner of the bid resides on the left hand side of the plot, then the project is likely to be canceled. Such judgements can be made by people with little technical background knowledge. Hence, the assistant may recommend the projects with the high likelihood of completion for further analysis.

3.4   Forensic Analysis of Digital Media

After we receive the recommendation from the assistant, we conduct a traditional forensic analysis according to the following steps: 1) We download any attachment from the URL of the project page. 2) We use a forensic tool such as Forensic Toolkit or EnCase to investigate the contents and the meta-data of the downloaded file. The extracted contents will be used to establish connection between the hirer and any wrongdoing activity. Additionally, the extracted meta-data may provide extra information such as personal identity, device information and positional data. Combining all available information, a short list of suspects might be deduced. 3) We then inspect HTML page elements of the project page to search for timestamps necessary for a timeline. Usually freelance websites preserve these timestamps after the bidding window is closed and often hide them in JavaScript variables which can be revealed by inspecting the source code of the page. 4) Lastly, we inspect the user profile page of the hirer. We search for the badges which often contain personal information and timestamps of some completed projects. Sometimes, the user may post a personal photo in the user profile if the hirer is careless. After these four steps, we would be able to file a case against the person in question.

4   Case Study

On the 21st of January 2014 we received an auditory request for possible cases of EBMA students outsourcing their academic work. In anticipation of our expected outcome, we hope to identify such students and subject in question. Our first step was to collect information on `freelancer.com`; subsequently, our second step was to obtain the specific time and date the unit assignments were released and due from the EBMA body. Additionally, we set our date window to cover the past three months before the start of the investigation. We intended our method to have usability catered towards everyone of any skill level. Hence, we use our algorithm to find completed projects associated with EMBA students. In particular, our algorithm is simple and easy enough for someone without much technical knowledge other than capability of using a search engine.

In this particular case, personal assistant Ann used the algorithm within the Google search engine to locate any potential completed projects.

1. According to her judgement, Ann listed five terms related to this case — "assignment", "EBMA", "level", "project", and "question". Ann applied term necessity rule one which resulted in "EBMA", "level", and "assignment" as central terms because they are more closely related to this case, while "project" and "question" did not satisfy this particular rule; term necessity rule two resulted in lowering the necessity of "assignment" as replaceable synonyms exist; term necessity rule three further lowered the necessity of "assignment" as co-existing synonyms exist; term necessity rule four lowered the necessity of "EBMA" as it is both an abstract and rare term. Therefore, Ann chose the necessity query term "level", more specifically, "intext:level". Ann decided to use "MBA" as her stop-word specifying "-MBA" as part of the query.

2. Ann used the "site:" parameter to focus on `freelancer.com` by specifying "site:freelancer.com".

3. Ann set the time window to be between 21st October 2013 and the 21st January 2014. Then she converted the Gregorian calendar to Julian calendar dates, which resulted in 2456587 and 2456679 respectively. Ann made use of the "daterange:" parameter by specifying "daterange:2456587-2456679".

4. To complete the query, Ann concatenated the previous four parts to construct the query: "site:freelancer.com daterange:2456587-2456679 intext:level -MBA". Ann ran the query on the Google search engine and collected the top twenty results.

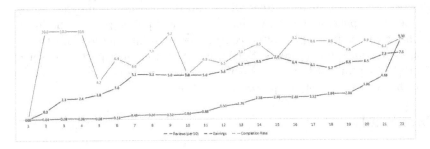

Fig. 1. Three Key Indicators of the 22 Bidders on `freelancer`

Among the twenty results, Ann analyzed the bidding information of each project. Ann found a project with ID:5231531 satisfying the best match between bidders feedback, reputation, and completion rate. The details of this project's bidding information is plotted in Figure 1. Hence, Ann recommended a further analysis of the project posted by user "waqar2001" at `http://goo.gl/XJECc2`. According to Ann's recommendation, the forensic expert Bob loaded the URL in question and noticed two specific items of interest — the project description as written by the hirer "waqar2001" and an attached archive file named

"Attachments_20131215.zip". As shown in Figure 2, the project description was constructed with poor grammar and little understanding of the English language.

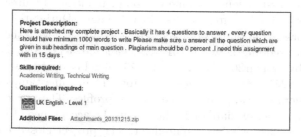

Project Description:
Here is atteched my complete project . Basically it has 4 questions to answer , every question should have minimum 1000 words to write Please make sure u answer all the question which are given in sub headings of main question . Plagiarism should be 0 percent .I need this assignment with in 15 days .

Skills required:
Academic Writing, Technical Writing

Qualifications required:

UK English - Level 1

Additional Files: Attachments_20131215.zip

Fig. 2. Project Description of the Identified Project on `freelancer`

Unfortunately, this description did not lead to further developments. Therefore Bob focused on the provided archive file. Having downloaded the file from `http://goo.gl/xMVJ0c`, Bob obtained three photographic image files in JPG format by extracting the contents of the ZIP file — 20131215_225544.jpg, 20131215 _225618.jpg and 20131215_225635.jpg. The three pictures contained four assignment questions related to 'Strategic Management', as part of the descriptor 'EBMA Diploma in Strategic Business Research and Leadership Direction Level-8'. There was a hand-written string in the form of a name "`KH. WAQAR AHMED`", part of which correlates to the username "waqar2001".

(a) 20131215_225544.eps   (b) 20131215_225618.eps   (c) 20131215_225635.eps

Fig. 3. The contents of the ZIP file

From the Exif headers of the three JPEG files, Bob identified that the device used to capture the images was a GT-I9505 camera from a Samsung Galaxy S4 smart phone. Nevertheless, the JPG pictures contain no positional or personal information relating to the user. Moreover, Bob obtained the following times: `Sunday, 15 December 2013, 22:55:44`, `22:56:18`, and `22:56:35` respectively. These times were the local time in Reading, UK where the user "waqar2001" resides. These timestamps corresponded to the time when the project was initially created and advertised, which was `Sunday, 2013-12-15 23:07:50 GMT` shifted from the server time zone. Thus Bob can conclude the images were taken just minutes before uploading them. As shown in Figure 2, "waqar2001" demanded the assignment to be completed within 15 days of the publishing of the project. The bidding window, as set by "waqar2001", actually consisted of fourteen calendar days, ending on 2013-12-22 23:07:51 GMT. Based on this end date, Bob derived that the assignment deadline was on or immediately after 2014-01-06, which is the first Monday after the New Year holidays. During this time window, twenty-two workers bid on this project before 2013-12-25, with the winning bidder "geologistt" bidding between 2013-12-15 and 2013-12-18. This winning bid was accepted by "waqar2001" on 2013-12-25 when his identity was verified, and the deposit of $247 USD was made in escrow. These timestamps were verified by the site-generated badges displayed on user profiles. The worker "geologistt" pitched for a completion date of 10 days from the acceptance of his bid, which satisfies the due date window requirement. The project closed for bidding on 2013-12-25 and was marked as fully completed on 2014-01-20.

5   Conclusions and Future Work

In this paper, we note the increased prevalence of assignments being outsourced on freelance web sites, which damages the reputability and accreditation of academic institutions. We argue that immediate attention can and must be taken by the digital forensics community. To fight against this dishonest wrongdoing, we propose a two-tiered paradigm, in which an assistant conducts a web search before the investigation is taken over by a forensic expert. To maximize the chance of retrieving related project pages, the assistant can use our step-wise algorithm to sort the query terms which are then appended to the various parameters given by search engines. Furthermore, we develop a visualization technique to filter out phantom projects based on our observations of projects on freelance sites.

Future work includes a series of experiments on a larger scale to which our method is applied to locate outsourced assignments in various topics. The feedback will then be used to improve the efficiency and useability of our method. We also would like to compare the effectiveness of employing alternative search engines. Improved 'anti-anti-forensic' techniques will also help us to increase the chance of identifying the wrongdoer.

References

1. Garfinkel, S., Nelson, A., Young, J.: A general strategy for differential forensic analysis. Digital Investigation (9, suppl.), 50–59 (2012)
2. Zhao, L., Callan, J.: Term necessity prediction. In: Proceedings of the 19th ACM International Conference on Information and Knowledge Management, CIKM 2010, pp. 259–268 (2010)

A Novel Method for Detecting Double Compressed Facebook JPEG Images

Allan NG, Lei Pan, and Yang Xiang

School of IT, Deakin University, Melbourne, Australia
{ngall,l.pan,yang}@deakin.edu.au

Abstract. Images published on online social sites such as Facebook are increasingly prone to be misused for malicious purposes. However, existing image forensic research assumes that the investigator can confiscate every piece of evidence and hence overlooks the fact that the original image is difficult to obtain. Because Facebook applies a Discrete Cosine Transform (DCT)-based compression on uploaded images, we are able to detect the modified images which are re-uploaded to Facebook. Specifically, we propose a novel method to effectively detect the presence of double compression via the spatial domain of the image: We select small image patches from a given image, define a distance metric to measure the differences between compressed images, and propose an algorithm to infer whether the given image is double compressed without referring to the original image. To demonstrate the correctness of our algorithm, we correctly predict the number of compressions being applied to a Facebook image.

1 Introduction

The general public has no easy method to check the authenticity of a Facebook image. Furthermore, image forensics fails to address the issues of a booming number of retouched images on Facebook. According to Sencar and Memon [11], image forgery detection is "the process to determine whether an image has been manipulated or processed after it was captured by an acquisition device like a digital camera". This definition fails on Facebook images because each uploaded image is compressed by Facebook image filter before publication. Moreover, the traditional viewpoint [9] that the original image and/or the device used to shoot the image should be confiscated prior to the investigation becomes rarely applicable. Hence, we need to develop a new forensic paradigm whilst handling Facebook images.

Specifically, JPEG images are difficult for digital forensic investigators because JPEG is a lossy compression algorithm which prevents the original raw image from being 100% restored from the JPEG image. Generally, there are three steps when a JPEG image is generated — firstly, a raw image is partitioned into 8×8 blocks; secondly, a two dimensional Discrete Cosine Transform (DCT) is applied to each block; thirdly, the DCT coefficients are converted to integers by using JPEG quantization table which is specific to each camera device or each image editing software tool. Hence, the retouched Facebook JPEG images are highly likely to contain digital traces left by the application of multiple DCT operations. Double compression is referred to as a process when a JPEG image file is decompressed and altered to meet an editing tool's specification before the modifications are saved to the image [12]. Detection of double compression helps to determine whether the image has been amended, according to [2] and [10].

In this paper, we solve the problem of detecting double compression in Facebook JPEG images without using its original image. Our assumptions are threefold — 1) digital forensic investigators cannot easily obtain the original photo or original device which is used to shoot the photo; 2) we can obtain or infer the camera device information to obtain the quantization table for the camera; 3) Facebook image filter invariantly compresses the uploaded JPEG images though its parameters are not disclosed to the public.

We define a novel metric to measure the distance between two JPEG images in which one image is obtained by compressing the other. Based on this metric, we could determine how many rounds of compression exist between two images. Furthermore, by using the color intensity information of the selected 8×8 patches, we construct a reference image which reaches the limit after a number of compression rounds. Hence, we estimate the presence of double compression by measuring how many compression rounds are there in the given JPEG image before reaching the maximum. We also conduct a real life experiment to demonstrate the effectiveness of our method.

The rest of this paper is organized as follows: Section 2 surveys the related work and identifies the research gap. Section 3 presents our novel distance metric for images and our double compression detection algorithm. Section 4 is a case study when we successfully and correctly determine the number of compressions applied to a Facebook JPEG image. Section 5 concludes the paper and discusses future work.

2   Related Work

Image forgery detection uncovers manipulated or tampered digital images and attempts to distinguish them from their original counterparts. A common approach to manipulating images is the copy-move method which is employed to tamper with images by altering the content within an image, commonly referring to a particular object within the scene being replaced or substituted with some other form in the same image, thus creating a new forged image. Ardizzone et al. [1] use texture descriptors to detect this type of forgery, which exploits texture as features extracted from blocks, because the block-matching process is an integral part of the copy-move method. Conversely, a process applying blind image forensics generates more robust results to detect the use of copy-move method, where the key idea is to divide the image into smaller blocks for analysis. The main process applies a Discrete Wavelet Transform (DWT) algorithm to divide a compressed image into overlapping blocks each of which has a fixed size; these blocks are firstly sorted by a lexicographic algorithm and then the duplicated blocks are identified using phase correlation [6].

Most research efforts focus on analyzing the DCT coefficient to detect double-compressed images. Fei and Xi-lan [3] measure the global blur of the image and exploits the DCT information within the image; working from sub-block to sub-block, the authors claim that we can ultimately obtain the blur region and locate the false blur regions inside the image. Lukàš and Fridrich [8] identify that the DCT coefficients lose their integer values during the quantization phase, based on which they propose to recover the missing values which are replaced by zeros according to the coefficients. Specifically, these missing values could provide a reliable indicator of identifying the primary quantization matrix used to generate the JPEG image. Moreover, Lukàš and Fridrich [8] suggest that the existence of double peaks in the DCT coefficient histogram is a good indicator of the application of double compression to an JPEG image.

Hou et al. [4] advocate detecting of double compression by extracting the first digit features of DCT coefficients. That is, the first digit should be zero in value if the image has been double-compressed. Furthermore, Popescu [9] attempts to detect double compression by observing any inconsistent patterns in the JPEG coefficient histogram, which is based on the belief that the digital trace of specific correlations of the image is often left in the image after parts from different images are merged into one JPEG file.

Furthermore, Huang et al. [5] achieve accurate results by using a random perturbation strategy to detect double compression. This method detects the double compression based on single compressed JPEG images even if the same quantization matrix is used in the process of compressing JPEG images. Lastly, Liu et al. [7] attempt to identify and re-compress the misaligned cropping pixels which will give a different reading in DCT coefficients because tampering activities such as copy and past are often done to an image patch which almost always has different DCT coefficients to the original image.

In summary, the above techniques rely on strict assumptions — the investigator has to confiscate the camera device; the investigator has prior knowledge of the original image and of the patch; the investigator has to analyze the entire image which requires excessive amount of computation and time. To address these issues, we propose a novel metric on pixel intensity in a small 8×8 patch of JPEG images in Section 3.

3   A New Metric of the Change of Color Intensity

Suppose there are two JPEG images I_i and I_j both of which are generated by compressing an original raw image I_0. Without using the original image, our method measures I_i and I_j to infer which image is compressed more and to estimate the number of the compression. To avoid confusion, we denote I_0 as the original raw image, I_1 as the first compressed JPEG image, I_2 as the double-compressed JPEG image, I_3 as the triple-compressed JPEG image, ..., and so on. Hence, I_i stands for the image which is compressed for i times.

Definition 1. *Suppose that we have two 8 × 8 JPEG image patches I_i and I_j both of which are from the same origin, the maximal difference in color intensity is defined as follows*

$$P_{max}^{i,j} = \max\{P_x^i - P_x^j \mid x \in \{0, 1, \dots, 63\}\},$$

where P_x is the RGB tuple at the position x. Similarly, the minimal difference in color intensity is

$$P_{min}^{i,j} = \min\{P_y^i - P_y^j \mid y \in \{0, 1, \dots, 63\}\},$$

where P_y is the RGB tuple at the position y.

Definition 2. *For two 8 patches of I_i and I_j, we define a new distance metric as*

$$distance(i, j) = P_{max}^{i,j} - P_{min}^{i,j}. \tag{1}$$

Example 1. We use a camera on a Samsung Galaxy S3 mobile to shoot a photo of a color-board consisting of two colors only — black and blue. Figures 1(a), 1(b) and 1(c) are raw image I_0, single compressed JPEG I_1 and doubled compressed JPEG I_2, respectively. Please note that the gradient edge is becoming smoother as more compression is applied.

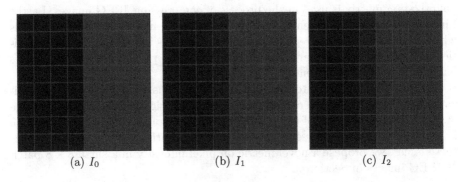

(a) I_0 (b) I_1 (c) I_2

Fig. 1. Three 8 × 8 Patches Containing Black and Blue

The red channel intensity values are all zeros for I_0; I_1 has a slight higher reading in the middle of each row so that the values become

$$\underbrace{\{0, 0, 0, 0, 7, 0, 0, 0\}}_{8 \text{ times}};$$

and I_2 has

$$\underbrace{\{4, 0, 0, 0, 13, 3, 2, 1\}}_{8 \text{ times}}.$$

The green channel is similar to the red channel: I_0 has all zeros; I_1 has

$$\underbrace{\{0,0,0,0,8,0,1,1\}}_{8 \text{ times}};$$

and I_2 has

$$\underbrace{\{0,0,0,0,11,1,3,2\}}_{8 \text{ times}}.$$

The blue channel has different readings: I_0 has

$$\underbrace{\{0,0,0,0,255,255,255,255\}}_{8 \text{ times}};$$

I_1 has

$$\underbrace{\{0,0,0,57,197,254,254,254\}}_{8 \text{ times}};$$

I_2 has

$$\underbrace{\{0,7,29,79,182,224,244,252\}}_{8 \text{ times}}.$$

The maximal difference between I_0 and I_1 occurs on the fifth column of the patches such that $P_{max}^{0,1} = 1$, and the minimal difference between I_0 and I_1 occurs on the fourth column such that $P_{min}^{0,1} = -57$. Hence the distance between I_0 and I_1 is $distance(0,1) = 58$. Similarly, we derive the distance between I_1 and I_2 as $distance(1,2) = 26 - (-29) = 55$ and distance between I_0 and I_2 as $distance(0,2) = 49 - (-79) = 128$.

Our distance metric does not always satisfy the triangular inequality. As observed in Example 1, we have $distance(0,2) > (distance(0,1) + distance(1,2))$. This is simply caused by the max and min functions. Furthermore, the distance values between the compressed images tend to converge to zero when they are more compressed. Hence, we develop the following algorithm to detect double compression of JPEG images without referring to the original picture.

Our algorithm consists of the following five steps:

1. Divide a given image I_i into 8×8 patches and randomly select a handful of the patches each of which is primarily composed of two colors. Usually, we can find these patches in the edge of objects so that approximately 32 pixels have one color and the rest have the other.
2. Compress each patch and calculate the distance values between the compressed ones and the ones obtained in **Step 1**.
3. Repeat **Step 2** until the distances converge and record the number of compression rounds k.
4. Use the same quantization table to generate a reference photo $\widehat{I_0}$ which has the color setting similar to I_i. And then repeat the first three steps for $\widehat{I_0}$. At the end of the process, we obtain the number of compression rounds $\hat{k}$ for $\widehat{I_0}$.
5. Calculate $\hat{k} - k$. If the result is greater than 2, we conclude the use of double compression on the given image I_i.

4   Case Study

To demonstrate the correctness of our detection method, we apply our algorithm on a Facebook image as shown in Figure 2. The picture is shot by using a Samsung Galaxy S3 mobile phone. We select an 8×8 patch from the boy's shoulder area which is primarily blue and black. For privacy reasons, we have blurred the image but highlighted the selected patch.

Fig. 2. A Facebook Image with a Selected Patch

We follow the second step of our algorithm by compressing the selected patch with the Facebook image filter. And we obtain a series of 6 images denoted as I_i, I_{i+1}, ... and I_{i+5}. We calculate the distances between these images by using Equation 1. The results are listed below.

	I_i	I_{i+1}	I_{i+2}	I_{i+3}	I_{i+4}	I_{i+5}
I_i	0	31	33	34	42	44
I_{i+1}		0	5	11	19	23
I_{i+2}			0	6	8	17
I_{i+3}				0	8	11
I_{i+4}					0	4
I_{i+5}						0

Each image has zero distance to itself; the distance values accumulate when the image is more compressed; the biggest distance is $distance(i, i+5) = 44$, and the smallest non-zero distance is $distance(i+4, i+5) = 4$. Furthermore, the above distance values are consistently decreasing when the image is more compressed.

Moreover, the distance value between the fifth and the sixth compressed images is zero. That is, $distance(5, 6) = 0$. Hence, we derive that the number of compression rounds is $k = 5$.

In order to construct a reference image, we observe the pattern of the row which produces the peak readings for both P_{max} and P_{min}. In our case, we identify the third row from the 6 patches as listed in Figure 3. Because blue and black are dominant colors in these patches, we set the reference image as the black and blue image as shown in Figure 1(a). And, we obtain the number of compression rounds for the reference image as $\hat{k} = 7$.

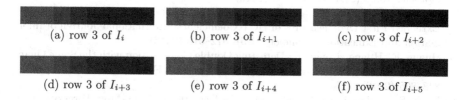

(a) row 3 of I_i (b) row 3 of I_{i+1} (c) row 3 of I_{i+2}

(d) row 3 of I_{i+3} (e) row 3 of I_{i+4} (f) row 3 of I_{i+5}

Fig. 3. The Third Row of the 6 Image Patches

Now we calculate $\hat{k} - k = 7 - 5 = 2$. Because this result is not greater than 2, we conclude that Figure 2 is not double compressed according to our algorithm. So we make a correct conclusion because this photo is single compressed.

As we observed in this case study, the intersection parts of each patch (as shown in Figure 3) are visually smoother after each compression, which matches the normal behavior of DCT-based compression. Our distance metric is a simple but reliable means to measure the differences between compressed image of the same origin. A potential drawback of our algorithm could be robustness, because malicious attackers might be able to affect our distance metric by modifying the color intensity values of the brightest and darkest pixels in each 8 × 8 patch block.

5   Conclusions and Future Work

This paper introduces a novel, simple and effective distance metric for detecting double compressed Facebook JPEG images. We also propose an algorithm to infer the number of rounds that a given Facebook image has been compressed. Specifically, our algorithm detects whether a Facebook image is modified from another Facebook image without referring to the original image. Our case study demonstrates the correctness of applying our distance metric on a real Facebook photo.

Because we rely on the color intensity, our detection algorithm works well on simple filters used by Facebook. The effectiveness of this method is unknown for sophisticated filters which is capable of sharpening the image after modification. As part of future work, we plan to conduct more testing cases on the complex filters included in professional image editing tools such as *Adobe Photoshop*.

References

1. Ardizzone, E., Bruno, A., Mazzola, G.: Copy-Move Forgery Detection via Texture Description. In: Proceedings of the 2nd ACM Workshop on Multimedia in Forensics, Security and Intelligence (2010)

2. Bianchi, T., Piva, A.: Analysis of Non-Aligned Double JPEG Artifacts for the Localization of Image Forgeries. In: Proceedings of the IEEE International Workshop on Information Forensics and Security (WIFS), pp. 1–6 (2011)
3. Fei, P., Xi-lan, W.: Digital Image Forgery Forensics by Using Blur Estimation and Abnormal Hue Detection. In: Proceedings of the Symposium on Photonics and Optoelectronic (SOPO), pp. 1–4 (2010)
4. Hou, W., Ji, Z., Jin, X., Li, X.: Double JPEG Compression Detection Base on Extended First Digit Features of DCT Coefficients. International Journal of Information and Education Technology 3(5), 512–515 (2013)
5. Huang, F., Huang, J., Shi, Y.: Detecting Double Compression with the Same Quantization Matrix. IEEE Transactions on Information Forensics and Security 5(4), 848–856 (2010)
6. Khan, S., Kulkarni, A.: Robust Method for Detection of Copy-Move Forgery in Digital Images. In: Proceedings of the International Conference on Signal and Image Processing (ICSIP), pp. 69–73 (2010)
7. Liu, Q., Li, X., Cooper, P., Hu, X.: Shift-Recompression-Based Feature Mining for Detecting Content-Aware Scaled Forgery in JPEG Images. In: Proceedings of the 12th International Workshop on Multimedia Data Mining (MDMKDD), pp. 10–16 (2012)
8. Lukàš, J., Fridrich, J.: Estimation of Primary Quantization Matrix in Double Compressed JPEG Images. In: Proceedings of the Digital Forensic Research Workshop (2003)
9. Popescu, A.: Statistical Tools for Digital Image Forensics. Ph.D. thesis, Department of Computer Science, Dartmouth College, Hanover, PhD thesis (2005)
10. Qu, Z., Luo, W., Huang, J.: Identifying Shifted Double JPEG Compression Artifacts for Non-intrusive Digital Image Forensics. In: Hu, S.-M., Martin, R.R. (eds.) CVM 2012. LNCS, vol. 7633, pp. 1–8. Springer, Heidelberg (2012)
11. Sencar, H., Memon, N.: Overview of State-of-the-art in Digital Image Forensics. Statistical Science and Interdisciplinary Research, pp. 1–19 (2008)
12. Thing, V., Chen, Y., Cheh, C.: An Improved Double Compression Detection Method for JPEG Image Forensics. In: Proceedings of the IEEE International Symposium on Multimedia, pp. 290–297 (2012)

Using Randomization to Attack Similarity Digests

Jonathan Oliver, Scott Forman, and Chun Cheng

Trend Micro, Melbourne, Australia
{jon_oliver,lane_forman,chun_cheng}@trendmicro.com

Abstract. There has been considerable research and use of similarity digests and Locality Sensitive Hashing (LSH) schemes - those hashing schemes where small changes in a file result in small changes in the digest. These schemes are useful in security and forensic applications. We examine how well three similarity digest schemes (Ssdeep, Sdhash and TLSH) work when exposed to random change. Various file types are tested by randomly manipulating source code, Html, text and executable files. In addition, we test for similarities in modified image files that were generated by cybercriminals to defeat fuzzy hashing schemes (spam images). The experiments expose shortcomings in the Sdhash and Ssdeep schemes that can be exploited in straight forward ways. The results suggest that the TLSH scheme is more robust to the attacks and random changes considered.

Keywords: Locality Sensitive Hash, similarity digests, Ssdeep, Sdhash, TLSH.

1   Introduction

Similarity digest schemes exhibit the property that small changes to the file being hashed results in a small change to the hash.   The similarity between two files can be determined by comparing the digests of the original files.

We considered the following schemes: Ssdeep [6], Sdhash [9], and TLSH [7]. We restricted the research to these schemes because they had mature implementations which were available as open source code. In addition, Ssdeep [6] is the de facto standard in the area of malware analysis. It is currently supported by NIST [12], and is the only similarity digest supported by Virus Total [16]. We did not report on the Nilsimsa [11] scheme here due to its high collision rate and false positive rate [7].

There have been several security analyses of similarity digests [2, 3, 8]. In [2], Breitinger analyzed Ssdeep and concluded that Ssdeep "is not suitable as a 'cryptographic similarity hashing function'. There are vulnerabilities that are easily exploitable". Roussev [8] concludes that Sdhash demonstrated the potential to address all five of the design requirements, where the design requirements were reasonable security requirements for similarity digests. Breitinger et al. [3] conclude that "Sdhash has the potential to be a robust similarity preserving digest algorithm".

An important property to consider for similarity digests [2, 3] is anti-blacklisting. Anti-blacklisting involves modifying a file to be semantically similar, but where a digest method assesses the files to be non-similar.

L. Batten et al. (Eds.): ATIS 2014, CCIS 490, pp. 199–210, 2014.

We have no expectation for similarity digests to match files which use an encrypted file format. For example, executable code which has been encrypted as a part of a packing process is not considered "semantically similar" to the original executable code for the purpose of this paper. Typical ways that files are modified include:

- Spam email: It is standard practice for spammers to use templates for their spam and to add randomized content to each individual message;
- Source code: It is not uncommon for the whitespace in source code to be changed by programmers, program beautifiers or editors;
- Malware: Malware uses techniques such as packing, polymorphism and metamorphism [5] to make the executable code more difficult to analyze. In this paper, we do not consider the packing issue, but we consider elements of polymorphism / metamorphism such as adding NOPs, permuting registers, adding useless instructions and loops, function re-ordering, program flow modification and inserting un-used data [5].

We focus on situations where the file is deliberately modified by an adversary using randomization as a key component. This paper offers the following new aspects to the research area: (i) we provide simple rules for modifying content to make Ssdeep ineffective, (ii) we reject the proposal in [3] that Sdhash is a robust similarity digest, and provide simple rules for modifying content to make Sdhash ineffective, and (iii) provide evidence that locality sensitive hashing schemes (such as TLSH) scheme are more difficult to exploit.

2   A Description of Ssdeep, Sdhash and TLSH

Ssdeep [6] uses 3 steps to construct the digest from file F:
(1)   use a rolling hash to split the document into distinct segments;
(2)   produce a 6 bit value for each segment by hashing the segment; and
(3)   concatenate the base64 encoded values from step (2) to form the signature.
Ssdeep assigns a similarity score in the range of 0-100 by calculating the edit distance between the two digests using the dynamic programming algorithm.

Ssdeep is vulnerable to anti-blacklisting in two ways [2]: (i) to disrupt the content identified by the rolling hash, and (ii) to modify content in all the segments. Because of these vulnerabilities, Breitinger [2] concludes that Ssdeep is insecure.

Sdhash [9] uses 3 steps to construct the digest:
(1)   identify 64 byte sequences which have a low probability;
(2)   hash the sequences identified in step (1) and put them in a Bloom filters; and
(3)   encode the series of Bloom filters to form the output signature.
Sdhash assigns a similarity score in the range 0-100 by calculating a normalized entropy measure between the two digests.

A security assessment of Sdhash is made in [3]. In [3], the authors state that the main contribution of the paper is that "Sdhash is a robust approach, but an active adversary can beat down the similarity score to approximately 28 while preserving the perceptual behavior of a file". Breitinger et al. (Section 5.1 of [3]) note that 20% of the input bytes do not influence the similarity digest, giving scope for attack.

TLSH [7] is a locality sensitive hash closer in spirit to the Nilsimsa [11] hash than the Ssdeep and Sdhash digests. TLSH uses 4 steps to construct the digest:

(1) process the input using a sliding window to populate an array of bucket counts;
(2) calculate the quartile points;
(3) construct the digest header values based on the quartile points, the length of the file and a checksum; and
(4) construct the digest body by generating a sequence of bit pairs, which depend on each bucket's value in relation to the quartile points.

TLSH assigns a distance score between two digests by summing the distance between the digest headers and the digest bodies. The distance between the digest bodies is calculated as an approximate Hamming distance between the two digest bodies. The distance between two digest headers is determined by comparing file lengths and quartile ratios. The distance score between two digests is in the range 0-1000+. The recommended threshold [7] is 100, which should be tuned for each application.

3   Analyzing Spam Image Files

We collected a sample of 1000 images which had been deliberately manipulated by spammers to avoid detection. There were 30 distinct groups of related spam images. In 23 of these groups, the spammers had systematically manipulated the images so that the image files were distinct, leaving us with a data set of 911 images. Examples of the types of manipulations are shown in Figure 1 below. The manipulations included changing the height and width, changing the font size, doing rotations of the images, adding dots and dashes to the images, and changing the background colours.

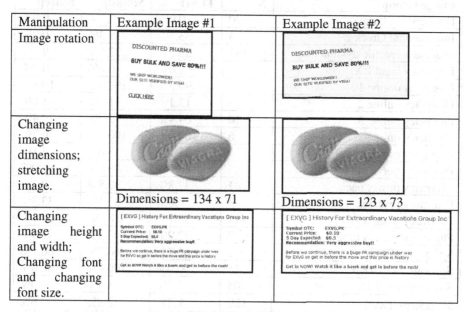

Fig. 1. Example spam images

Due to the processes used to compress jpeg and gif images, it is not a useful experiment to apply the similarity digests to the raw gif and jpeg images. So CxImage [10] was used to extract the image and save the file as a bit mapped image. The digest methods were then used on each group to determine detection rates and across distinct groups to determine a false positive rate for each of the methods.

Tables 1 shows the detection rates for each digest scheme. The Sdhash and Ssdeep methods were considered to match images if they scored any value above 0. The threshold for the TLSH digest was selected to be 100. With these thresholds, Ssdeep and Sdhash had no false positive matches, and TLSH had a false positive rate of 0.007% (29 out of 414505 image combinations). The results in Table 1, show that

- Ssdeep was ineffective at identifying images as being related, although it did have a very low false positive rate.
- The TLSH and Sdhash methods were reasonably effective at identifying that images are related, for many of the other classes of image manipulation.
- The digest methods were ineffective at certain types of adversarial image manipulations. The groups that digest methods were ineffective against included the groups where multiple types of changes were made (Pharmacy erectile dysfunction, Stockspam CYTV, Stockspam EXVG).
- TLSH was able to identify images that were rotated, while Sdhash was not able to do so (see the "Discounted Pharma" images in Figure 1).
- TLSH was able to identify images that were stretched, while Sdhash was not able to do so (see the "Pharmacy Picture" images in Figure 1).

Table 1. Detection rates for each group of images

Image Group	N	TLSH	Sdhash	Ssdeep
Discounted Pharma	20	80.0%	3.7%	0.0%
International Greek	3	33.3%	33.3%	0.0%
Pharmacy erectile dysfunction	147	22.1%	22.6%	9.6%
Pharmacy legal RX	22	0.0%	0.0%	0.0%
Pharmacy online 1	22	90.5%	100.0%	10.8%
Pharmacy online 2	63	12.1%	11.2%	1.0%
Pharmacy online 3	10	64.4%	62.2%	4.4%
Pharmacy online 4	6	100.0%	100.0%	6.7%
Pharmacy picture	8	57.1%	3.6%	7.1%
Pharmacy pop a pill	5	80.0%	100.0%	60.0%
Pharmacy power pack	41	47.8%	47.8%	20.7%
Pharmacy research	3	0.0%	33.3%	33.3%
Pharmacy Viagra Pro	11	32.7%	38.2%	29.1%
Pharmacy Viagra Pro2	7	42.9%	42.9%	42.9%
Software OEM	6	66.7%	66.7%	66.7%
Software SOBAKA	11	100.0%	100.0%	100.0%
StockSpam CYTV	105	1.7%	1.4%	0.0%
StockSpam EXVG	389	1.2%	2.8%	0.6%

4   Analyzing Text Files and Web Pages

In the case of image files, we had real world data where images had been altered to try to stop a filter from determining that they were similar. For text and Html files, we randomly made changes to them to simulate the adversarial environment.

4.1   Performing Random Changes

Procedure "greedy_adversarial_search" takes two inputs a file F(0) and a digest scheme DS. At iteration n, it considers "random changes" to F(n-1), and creates F(n) by applying the change that results in the lowest score according to digest scheme DS. This creates a sequence of files F(0) ... F(n) where for each i > j, score(F(i), F(0)) < score(F(j), F(0)) according to scheme DS. It will perform these changes until F(n) is considered a non-match or up to 500 iterations. In the case of the TLSH scheme, the scores of the sequence are increasing rather than decreasing. We define a single "random change" as one of the following actions:

  I. insert a new word (selected randomly);
  II. delete an existing word (selected randomly);
  III. swap two words (each word selected randomly from within the document);
  IV. substitute a word for another word (each word selected randomly) ;
  V. replace 10 occurrences of a character with another character;
  VI. delete 10 occurrences of a character;
  VII. swap two lines (selected randomly)
VIII. append a low entropy token of length 10 at the end of the document (a single character is selected randomly) (for example append "1111111111"); and
  IX. append a high entropy token of length 10 at the end of the document (for example append the token "Qo*\ezN)8$").

We used the procedure on 500 text and html files to identify vulnerabilities in the digest methods. Across the sample of files we measure the following:
- •File Size: the size of original files in bytes,
- •Number of Files Broken: the number of files where greedy procedure returned successfully (i.e, the greedy procedure was successful at defeating the digest within 500 iterations),
- •Iteration Required to Break Digest: When the greedy procedure ends in success, we record the iteration number,
- •Relative File Change: This was measured by comparing the original file with the manipulated file at the final iteration of the greedy procedure. The comparison is made by converting the original and final manipulated file into two sorted lists of tokens (by replacing all sequences of whitespace by a newline character) and using the Linux "diff" command to determine the ratio of tokens that have changed to the original number of tokens in the file.
- •List of Random Changes: The sequence of changes performed by the greedy procedure.

Table 2 gives the results of applying the greedy procedure to the 500 text and Html files. The table splits the results into 5 file size ranges, and for each range gives the average results for the criteria measured.

Table 2. Results after applying the greedy procedure to 500 text and Html files

File Size	Average Relative Change	Digest Attacked	% Broken	Average Iterations to Break Digest
0-10000	34.3%	TLSH	20.6%	83.7
0-10000	34.3%	Ssdeep	100.0%	6.9
0-10000	34.3%	Sdhash	100.0%	14.5
10000-20000	21.8%	TLSH	12.7%	84.5
10000-20000	21.8%	Ssdeep	100.0%	7.1
10000-20000	21.8%	Sdhash	100.0%	26.3
20000-40000	14.4%	TLSH	2.8%	78.7
20000-40000	14.4%	Ssdeep	100.0%	7.9
20000-40000	14.4%	Sdhash	97.2%	44.9
40000-80000	10.4%	TLSH	0.0%	
40000-80000	10.4%	Ssdeep	100.0%	10.3
40000-80000	10.4%	Sdhash	32.9%	68.0
80000-	7.9%	TLSH	0.0%	
80000-	7.9%	Ssdeep	96.9%	12.4
80000-	7.9%	Sdhash	0.0%	

The greedy procedure was highly successful at breaking the Ssdeep and Sdhash digests when the file size was below 40,000 bytes. The Ssdeep digest method was particularly vulnerable - on average being broken with less than 10 iterations. The difference in the robustness of the digest approaches to adversarial manipulation is highlighted with file sizes in the range 20,000-40,000; in this range manipulating an average of 14% of the original file will break Ssdeep and Sdhash most of the time, while the TLSH scheme is still able to identify the files as being related files.

The Ssdeep method was consistently broken by procedure greedy_adversarial_search. The random changes selected most frequently by the procedure were the swap-line, change-char and delete-char modifications. The characters selected the most often to be changed or deleted were

'S', 'N', newline, space

This is particularly disturbing for the Ssdeep method since the changes which are very effective at breaking the digest method are those that humans are unlikely to notice, such as changing the spacing and the line length.

The Sdhash method was also consistently broken by procedure greedy_adversarial_search, though on average Sdhash required 25 more iterations to break than Ssdeep. The random changes selected most frequently by the procedure were the change-char, delete-char and swap-line modifications. The characters selected the most often to be changed or deleted were:

'c', 'd', 'u', 'r', 'e', 'm', newline, 'f', comma, 'S'

This is also disturbing for the Sdhash method - some changes which are very effective at breaking the digest method include those that do not change the meaning of the document - namely changing the length of lines in a document.

4.2   Anti-blacklisting for C/C++ Source Code

Task (1) is to modify source code in such a way that:
- The modified source code still compiled and produced an executable program identical to the original source code, and
- Each modified file of source code resulted in a similarity digest which was judged to not match the digest of the original source file.

This could be achieved with the sed [1] script: "s/;[\t]*$/& / s/{[\t]*$/& /".

This sed script adds a space after each semicolon (;) and open brace ({) at the end of lines. We note that there is a multitude of ways that further changes can be made before we start to consider the types of program transformations which do not alter the meaning of the program, but change its representation. We tried it on a range of source code projects, and found the script to be 100% effective at breaking both Ssdeep and Sdhash.

4.3   Anti-blacklisting for Html files

Task (2) is to modify Html files in such a way that:
- The modified Html file had the same appearance and browser functionality to the original Html file, and
- The modified Html file had a similarity digest which was judged to not match the digest of the original Html file.

This could be achieved with the sed [1] script:

```
s/<[a-zA-Z0-9]*[ \t]/& /g
s/[\"]>/" >/g
s/[ \t][a-zA-Z0-9]*>/ &/g
s/<([a-zA-Z0-9]*)>/<\1 >/g
s/>[ \t]/& /g
s/,[ \t]/& /g
s/[;}>][ \t]*$/& /
s/[a-zA-Z0-9]$/& /
```

The intent of the script is to exploit the following features of Html:

- It is permissible to put additional whitespace to further separate attributes inside Html tags [13], (lines 1-4).
- It is permissible to put an additional whitespace after end tags and commas in the text in the Html page will result in an identical output page being displayed, (lines 5-6).
- It is permissible to put an additional whitespace at the end of lines where the last token is an end tag or a word, which will result in an identical output displayed (lines 7-8).

We applied the technique to 500 HTML files and got the following results:

Digest Method	Number of manipulated Html files identified as matching original file
TLSH	291
Sdhash	16
Ssdeep	11

5   Analyzing Executable Files

We expect that similarity digests will behave differently when applied to executable files than when applied to image files, text files and html files. The reason for this is that text files and image files have no requirement to share common components. However, we fully expect executable files to share standard components. For example we expect C and C++ programs to share components such as the stdio library and the preparation of the argc and argv parameters to the main() function. Thus we need to establish a baseline threshold for each similarity digest scheme. In Section 5.1, we determine suitable thresholds for the digest schemes for Linux executable programs. We use these thresholds in Section 5.2 in our efforts to break the digest schemes.

5.1   Suitable Thresholds for Linux Executable Files

We analyzed the binary files from /usr/bin of a standard Linux distribution. There are 2526 files in /usr/bin, and we removed all those files which were either symbolic links or less than 512 bytes (since the Sdhash scheme requires a minimum of 512 bytes to create a digest). This left 1975 executable files. We applied the similarity digest schemes doing 1975 * 1974 / 2 = 1,949,325 file comparisons. We begin this analysis using the tentative thresholds of <= 100 for TLSH, and >= 1 for Sdhash and Ssdeep. Using these thresholds resulted in the following number of file matches:

Digest	Number of matches
TLSH • 100	35733
Sdhash • 1	25408
Ssdeep • 1	836

Manual inspection of the files showed that:
- A threshold of 100 was not useful for TLSH – it was making many unjustified matches near the threshold of 100 – for example matching "time" and "xtrapchar".
- A threshold of 1 was not useful for Sdhash – it was making many unjustified matches near the threshold of 1 – for example matching "ap2" and "xkill".
- A threshold of 1 was appropriate for Ssdeep.

To improve the thresholds for Sdhash and TLSH, we consider thresholds where there is similar discriminatory power. We found the thresholds which where closest to assigning 1 in 1000 and 1 in 100 of the possible 1,949,325 file combinations as matching:

	Threshold	Number of matches
1 in 1000	Sdhash $\geq$ 13	2215
1 in 1000	TLSH $\leq$ 52	2130
1 in 100	Sdhash $\geq$ 2	19029
1 in 100	TLSH $\leq$ 85	19307

We found that for the thresholds of 13 for Sdhash and of 52 for TLSH, file pairs near the thresholds are very likely to be related executable files. For the thresholds of 2 for Sdhash and of 85 for TLSH, file pairs near the thresholds are almost always unrelated executable files.

Based on this, we will take a conservative approach and use a threshold of 2 for Sdhash and 85 for TLSH as the basis of anti-blacklisting testing. By this, we mean that if an executable program can be modified (while keeping its functionality the same) in a way which causes the TLSH distance between the original and modified program to be >= 86, then we have broken the digest scheme.

5.2   Anti-blacklisting for Executable Programs

Task (3) is to modify an executable program in such a way that:
- The modified source code still compiled and produced identical program behavior (determined by finding no difference on various output runs), and
- The modified executable program had a similarity digest which was judged to not match the digest of the original program.

To achieve this, we performed modifications to the source code and applied the digest methods to the executable program created by compiling the source code. Each change considered was designed to leave unchanged the semantic meaning of the program, while creating small changes in the object code. The semantic meaning of the code was verified using unit-test programs. The changes introduced to the source code, were typical of the changes performed by polymorphic malware and metamorphic malware [6]. The changes implemented are given in Table 3.

Table 3. 10 Modifications for source code

Modification	Description
And-Reordering	Changing the order of clauses in an "if" statement if the condition is a conjunction
Or-Reordering	Changing the order of terms in an "if" statement if the condition is a disjunction
Control-Flow-If-Then-Else	Change control flow of an if-then-else statement
Control-Flow-If-Then	Change control flow of an if-then statement
New Integer Variables	Introducing new integer variables
New String Variables	Introducing new string variables
Re-ordering Functions	Changing the order of functions within the source code
Adding NOPs	Adding variables definitions and adding NOPs related to those variables.
Adding Random Binary Data	Adding character strings with randomized content.
Splitting Strings	Split the control string within printf statements

We applied these changes to 3 programs:
- C4.5 [4],
- SVMlight [14],
- greedy_adversarial_search (the program from Section 4.1)

We applied the modifications listed to each source file in turn. Some of the modifications were not applicable to some source files, and some of the modifications could cause syntactic or semantic errors. Where this occurred the modification was discarded.

Table 4. Scores after a single modification on the C4.5 source code

	Number of source files modified	TLSH	Sdhash	Ssdeep
And-Reordering	5	13	28	32
Or-Reordering	5	26	25	0
If-Then-Else	9	13	46	27
If-Then	12	9	81	69
New Integer Variables	6	12	35	30
Reorder Funs	1	9	79	71
Add NOPs	4	13	16	29
Add Random Data	3	11	70	60
Split Strings	1	13	24	33
New String Variables	14	62	1	0

Table 4 gives the scores of the various digests schemes when we apply a single manipulation from Table 3 to the source code of C4.5 [4]. The column "Number of source files modified" is the number of source code files that the manipulation is applicable to and produces no errors. For the C4.5 source code, applying a single type of manipulation broke both the Sdhash and the Ssdeep digest schemes.

We applied the same approach to SVMlight:
- •5 of the manipulations reduced the Ssdeep score to 0.
- •The "New String Variables" manipulation reduced the Sdhash score to 0 and increased the TLSH score to 50.

Applying the "New String Variables" manipulation followed by the "And-Reordering" manipulation increased the TLSH score to 34 and reduced the Sdhash and Ssdeep scores to 0.

We applied the same approach to greedy_adversarial_search:
- •Again 5 of the manipulations reduced the Ssdeep score to 0 (it was a different set of 5 manipulations).
- •The "Add NOPs" manipulation reduced the Sdhash score to 2.
- •The "New String Variables" manipulation increased the TLSH score to 23.
- •The "Add NOPs" manipulation reduced the Sdhash score to 2.

Applying the "New String Variables" manipulation followed by the "New Integer Variables" manipulation increased the TLSH score to 38 and reduced the Sdhash and Ssdeep scores to 0.

6   Conclusion

Research into similarity digests and locality sensitive hashes for security applications should be done in an adversarial environment, where the people developing the digest schemes are actively trying to break their own work and the work of other such schemes.

Our work demonstrated that different types of manipulations can have very distinct effects on the scores of similarity digests. Researchers should also explore the manipulations which are mostly likely to adversely affect the scheme.

Different thresholds need to be considered for different file types. The experiments described in this paper show that executable files appear to be a more difficult discrimination task for similarity digests than Html, text files and images, requiring careful selection of suitable thresholds.

Our work also demonstrates that similarity digests should not use a restricted range, such as 0 to 100. This gives adversaries a target to strive for; once a Sdhash or Ssdeep digest has been reduced to zero, then these schemes cannot adjust their threshold any further. An open ended distance criteria makes the job of an adversary more difficult.

Based on the analysis in this paper, we make the following conclusions:
- Ssdeep: We concur with the previous assessments [2, 8] that Ssdeep is not suitable as a 'secure similarity digest'.
- Sdhash: We disagree with the security assessment in [3] that "Sdhash is a robust approach". Sdhash has significant vulnerabilities that can be exploited.

- TLSH: Based on the experiments done here, TLSH appears significantly more robust to random changes and adversarial manipulations than Ssdeep and Sdhash.

Acknowledgments. We would like to thank Jennifer Rihn for her helpful comments on drafts of the manuscript, Charlie Hou and Yanggui Chen for their assistance, and Liwei Ren for his support and ideas about the research. We also thank our anonymous reviewers for their feedback which was very helpful.

References

1. Barnett, B.: Sed - An Introduction and Tutorial,
   http://www.grymoire.com/Unix/Sed.html
2. Breitinger, F.: Sicherheitsaspekte von fuzzy-hashing. Master's thesis, Hochschule Darmstadt (2011)
3. Breitinger, F., Baier, H., Beckingham, J.: Security and Implementation Analysis of the Similarity Digest sdhash. In: 1st International Baltic Conference on Network Security & Forensics (NeSeFo), Tartu, Estland (2012)
4. C4.5 source code, http://www.rulequest.com/Personal/
5. Hosmer, C.: Metamorphic and Polymorphic Malware, Black Hat USA (2008),
   http://blackhat.com/presentations/bh-usa-08/Hosmer/BH_US_08_Hosmer_Polymorphic_Malware.pdf
6. Kornblum, J.: Identifying Almost Identical Files Using Context Triggered Piecewise Hashing. In: Proceedings of the 6th Annual DFRWS, pp. S91–S97. Elsevier (2006)
7. Oliver, J., Cheng, C., Chen, Y.: TLSH - A Locality Sensitive Hash. In: 4th Cybercrime and Trustworthy Computing Workshop, Sydney (November 2013),
   https://www.academia.edu/7833902/TLSH_-A_Locality_Sensitive_Hash
8. Roussev, V.: An Evaluation of Forensics Similarity Hashes. In: Proceedings of the 11th Annual DFRWS, pp. S34–S41. Elsevier (2011)
9. Roussev, V.: Data Fingerprinting with Similarity Digests. In: Chow, K., Shenoi, S. (eds.) Advances in Digital Forensics VI. IFIP AICT, vol. 337, pp. 207–226. Springer, Heidelberg (2010)
10. CxImage, http://www.codeproject.com/Articles/1300/CxImage
11. Nilsimsa source code,
    http://ixazon.dynip.com/~cmeclax/nilsimsa.html
12. NIST, http://www.nsrl.nist.gov/ssdeep.htm
13. Stackoverflow Blog, White space inside XML/HTML tags,
    http://stackoverflow.com/questions/3314535/white-space-inside-xml-html-tags
14. SVMlight source code, http://svmlight.joachims.org/
15. TLSH source code, https://github.com/trendmicro/tlsh
16. Virus Total, http://www.virustotal.org/

Research of Password Recovery Method
for RAR Based on Parallel Random search

Liang Ge[*] and Lianhai Wang

Shandong Computer Science Center (National Supercomputer Center in Jinan),
Shandong Provincial Key Laboratory of Computer Networks, Jinan, Shandong, China
`ge1@sdas.org, wanglh@sdas.org`

Abstract. Password recovery of RAR encrypted file is an important problem in computer forensics. It is difficult to deal with this problem by the traditional methods such as guess, dictionary, rainbow table and brute force. We give a new method based on parallel random search. The new method use a parallel stochastic approach on word selection in the dictionary attack. It can greatly improve the success rate of password recovery. And the experiment shows that the new approach is effective in the password recovery of RAR file.

Keywords: parallel computing, random search, password recovery, RAR file, compute forensics.

1   Introduction

Nowadays, with the development of mobile Internet, cloud computing and the Internet of things, the computer and the network are playing a more important role in people's life; but at the same time, the illegal and criminal activities associated with the computer and network also emerge in an endless stream. It also promoted the development of the new branch of information security --computer forensics[1]. Computer forensics is an important research area of information security, while password recovery is an important part of computer forensics. The RAR encrypted files are often encountered in the process of computer forensics, Its password cracking is a difficult problem in computer forensics. RAR is a proprietary file format, used for data compression and archiving package. It has become a very popular file compression format. At the same time, due to the relative perfect encryption technology that compress data while encrypt data, the RAR format is widely used to preserve the privacy file. The corresponding password recovery has also become an important research direction in the field of computer forensics. There are two encryption schemes for the RAR file in history [2]. Before the vision of 3.0, the RAR file used the private encryption scheme, and from the vision of 3.0, the RAR file started to use the new encryption scheme which used the SHA-1 algorithm to generate the key and used the AES algorithm to encrypt the file. All of the two schemes are hardly to crack. In this paper we will mainly deal with the cracking of the newest encryption scheme.

---

[*] Corresponding author.

L. Batten et al. (Eds.): ATIS 2014, CCIS 490, pp. 211–218, 2014.
© Springer-Verlag Berlin Heidelberg 2014

At present, there are four methods for encrypted document password recovery in the field of computer forensics, such as guess [3], dictionary attack [4], brute force cracking [5-8] and rainbow table crack [9]. Guess method is mainly dependent on experience and the target user familiarity to guess the password. In real life, a lot of people's password is a simple combination of name and date of birthday , and even people with such as "12345" and "password" extremely dangerous password. At this time, the guess method has a high efficiency. The principle of the dictionary method is through the establishment of a word dictionary which contains a large amount of vocabulary, phrases, sentence and then use the software one by one to try until the correct password. The brute method tries all permutations and combinations in order to find the correct password. A rainbow table which is a large, pre-calculated encryption set for all the possible combinations can be used to crack many kinds of passwords quickly. But since the RAR encrypted file increase the salt in the encryption process, the rainbow table will be too large to generate. Additionally, the guess method is too dependent on luck to be used in practice. Brute force method takes too long time to get the password in the validity. Comparatively, the dictionary method is more efficient used for the cracking of RAR encrypted file. If the correct password is contained in the dictionary, the time only depends on the search strategy and the location of password. For the sequence search, the success rate is 1/N (where N is the number of password in the dictionary). When the dictionary is very large, the efficiency of dictionary method is still very low. In short, the password recovery of encrypted RAR file is still a difficult problem in computer forensic. At present there is no effective password cracking method.

Parallel and randomized method is an important method in the algorithm design at present. They can often achieve more computational efficiency than the serial deterministic algorithm for some practical computational problem, where the parallel computational method has been widely applied in password recovery. In this paper, we obtain a new password recovery method for the encrypted RAR file based on the parallel and random search method. The algorithm of this method is given, and the experiment shows that this method can accelerate the time of password recovery. It also provides a new way for other related password cracking for the computer forensics.

The article is divided as follows: in the next section we present an overview of the encrypted algorithm of RAR. Then we describe the random search method and our new parallel random search method for password recovery. In the fourth section the experiment shows the validity of the algorithm. Finally, we give the conclusion of the method.

2   RAR Compressing File Decryption Mechanism

In this section we will show the decrypt method of RAR compressed encrypted file. The decryption of RAR has used the AES algorithm, the SHA-1 algorithm and the CRC algorithm [2]. The process is shown as follow:

(1) Password amplification: each password is expanded from one byte to two bytes—PASSWPRD_EXPANSION, where the extension is filled by 0;

(2) Join the SALT: obtain the SALT value from the file header and connect to the PASSWPRD_EXPANSION to obtain the TEMP_KEY_STRING;

(3) Mosaic: the 262144 TEMP_KEY_STRING are connected together to form the TEMP_KEY_BUFFER;

(4) SHA-1 operation: let TEMP_KEY_BUFFER be the input of the SHA-1 operation. Each SHA-1 operation deals with 512bits. It will take tens of thousands times SHA-1 operation. Times increases with the password length. In the last the key of AES is obtained from the SHA-1 operational value AES_KET;

(5) Decryption: use the key AES_KEY to decrypt the ciphertext to obtain the data COMPRESSED_TEXt.

(6) Decompression: use the improved LZSS compressing algorithm to decompress COMPRESSED_TEXT to obtain PLAINTEXT;

(7) CRC operation: get the CRC checksum value from the CRC operation for the PLAINTEXT;

(8) Password determination: compare the CRC checksum value with the value saved in the header of file. If equal, then the password is right; else error.

3   Password Recovery Method for RAR File Based on Parallel and Random Search

In this section we will give the parallel random password recovery for RAR file. It contains two parts: random search and parallel password cracking. First we will give the random search method.

3.1   Password Recovery Based on Random Search

The basic idea of random password cracking method is to crack the key by randomly selecting the possible keys from the key space [10]. Firstly a random number generated by the random number generator Rand() is mapped to the key space to give a key k_i by the map function f(), then the key is used to encrypt the plaintext P to obtain the ciphertext C'. If the C' is equal to the known ciphertext C, the key k_i is the seeking key, otherwise continue to generate the next random key k_{i+1}. The pseudo-code of password random search algorithm is as followed:

```
Loop: kᵢ =f(Rand()) ;
        C'=Encrypt(kᵢ);
            If(C'==C)
            Break;
            Else
            Goto Loop;
```

The probability to hit the proper key of each random search is 1 meanwhile the probability of each sequential search is 1/N (N is the size of the key space). So theoretically the random search has a high success rate.   But in practical application, since the random search takes longer time to search a key than the sequential search, the random search is actually useless when the key space is big. Since the high performance computing technology will greatly speed up the search efficiency, we will give a new parallel random search algorithm which makes the random search to be useful and use this algorithm to crack RAR file password in this paper.

3.2   Parallel Random Number Generation Method

Parallel computing refers to the simultaneous use of multiple computing resources to solve the computational problem [11]. It is an effective mean to improve the computing speed and processing ability of computer system. In this subsection we will give the parallel random number generation method. There have been many random number generation strategy. Based on the study of the existing methods, we find that the existing methods mainly use the linear congruence random number generation algorithm. namely $x_{n+j}=(a^j \times x_n)$ mod m. In order to generate the random number parallel, we will use the double linear congruence method and the master-slave mode of the parallel computing in this paper. The algorithm is shown as follow, where a is the multiplier, M is the remainder, x_0 is the initial value and P is the number of computing nodes.

1. In Master
    Input: a, x_0, M, P

    Output : A_j, x_j, j=1,2,...,P

    Let A_0=a;
    For   j=1; j<=P; j++

    A_j=a×A_{j-1} mod M

    x_j=a×x_{j-1} mod M

2. In Slaver
    Input: A_j, x_j, M, n
    Output: R_j^k, k=1,2, ..., n; j=1,2, ...,P
    Let R_j^0=x_j
    For   k=1; k<=n; k++
    R_j^k =$A_j \times R_j^{k-1}$ mod M

In the above algorithm, the parallel technology is used to the generation of random numbers. In addition, the linear congruence parameters of random number generator for each slave node are derived from the same master. So random number generated can't repeat. This can greatly improve the efficiency of random search.

3.3   Password Recovery Based on Parallel Random Search

The parallel random password cracking method given in this paper is shown as follows:

Algorithm: parallel random password cracking process

Input: the initial value of random search, the number of processes, random search times of each process, related parameters of encryption

Output: password

Begin

Initialize: the master process generate the initial random search value of each slave process and the multiplier.

Task allocation

Parallel perform the following operations for each calculation process

Loop: generate the random number

Use the function f( ) to map the random number to the key space.

Use the key and plaintext to obtain the ciphertext uder the RAR's

encryption algorithm.

If the ciphertext is equal to the stored ciphertext, terminate the computation process

Else go to Loop until the specified number of search.

The communication of parallel data

MPI_Send () and MPI_Recv () are used to swap data between the master and the slaver.

Show the output

End

In this algorithm P+1 threads are started based on the MPI computing environment. Firstly the random number is generated by the method shown in 3.1 and mapped to the key space to obtain the key by the function f( ). Then the ciphertext is computed by the plaintext, key and the encryption algorithm. Once again the ciphertext is compared with the stored ciohertext to confirm the key is correct. The functions MPI_Send() and MPI_Recv() are used to swap data between the master and the slaver when the computation is running. Finally the correct password is output.

4   Experiment

4.1   Test Platform

The experiment is performed on the shen wei lan guang computing system in the national supercomputing center in JiNan. There are 8704 Shenwei 1600 CPUs which have 16 cores in the shen wei lan guang computing system. We only used a CPU in this test.

4.2   Contrast between Parallel Random Search and Sequential Search

First of all since the parallel communication time between parallel process is too low to negligible compared with the password searching time, we only compare the times of password searches. Then the key space is divided into 11 parts, the procedure in each parts is repeated for 1000 times in order to obtain greater precision in measurement. The average value of search times is used in comparison of the sequential and the random process. In the first, searched word is located in the first 1/6 of the wordlist. In the next test case, the word is located in the first 2/6 of the wordlist, and so on. In the last test case the searched word is located in the last 1/6 of the whole wordlist. Table 1 shows locations of the searched word for all 11 test cases.

Table 1. Ranges of picked words

Test case	Parts of wordlist taken for selection					
1	1/6	1/6	1/6	1/6	1/6	1/6
2	1/6	1/6	1/6	1/6	1/6	1/6
3	1/6	1/6	1/6	1/6	1/6	1/6
4	1/6	1/6	1/6	1/6	1/6	1/6
5	1/6	1/6	1/6	1/6	1/6	1/6
6	1/6	1/6	1/6	1/6	1/6	1/6
7	1/6	1/6	1/6	1/6	1/6	1/6
8	1/6	1/6	1/6	1/6	1/6	1/6
9	1/6	1/6	1/6	1/6	1/6	1/6
10	1/6	1/6	1/6	1/6	1/6	1/6
11	1/6	1/6	1/6	1/6	1/6	1/6

Two sizes of wordlists have been used for the testing purposes, containing 0.3×10^6 words and 0.6×10^6 words. Although the selected word is located in the special part of the wordlist, the search range of the parallel random search and sequential search is all of the wordlist. The result is shown in Fig1 and Fig 2.

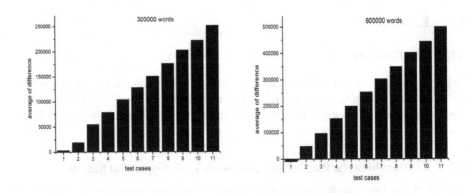

Fig. 1. Difference between the parallel random search and sequential search

The difference between the parallel random search and sequential search of all the 11 cases for the two wordlists are shown in Fig1. On the X axis there are 11 test cases from 1 to 11, and on the Y axis an average value of difference between the parallel random search and sequential search is shown. The parallel core number which we use is 11. From Fig 1 we can see that the times of each core in the parallel random search is lower than these in the sequential search. And the gap is really more of a chasm with the experimental space gradually moving backward.

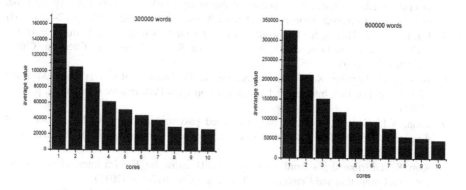

Fig. 2. Change of average search number over the increase of the parallel cores

The change of average search number over the increase of the parallel cores for the sixth test case of two wordlists is shown in Fig2. On the X axis there are 11 cores from 1 to 10, and on the Y axis an average value of the parallel random search is shown. From Fig 2 we can see that, with the increase of cores, the search times are reduced, and the parallel acceleration effect is very obvious.

It can be concluded that the parallel random search is much better than the sequential search.

5   Conclusion

In current password recovery of RAR file is an important research direction in computer forensics. In this paper for the encrypted RAR file, a parallel random password recovery method based on MPI is proposed. This method could be used to the cracking of the widely used RAR 3.x and over encrypted file. The test results show that this method can effectively improve the speed of the password search.

Acknowledgments. Special appreciative to reviewers for useful advices and comments. This study is supported by the Shandong Province Outstanding Young Scientists Research Award Fund Project (Grant No. BS2013DX010), by the Natural Science Foundation of Shandong Province, China (Grant No. ZR2011FQ030, ZR2013FQ001, ZR2013FM025), and by the Shandong Academy of Sciences Youth Fund Project (Grant No. 2013QN007) .

References

1. Simson, L.: Digital forensics research: The next 10 years. Digital Investigation 7, S64–S73 (2010)
2. RARLab.:RAR version 3.20 Technical information, http://www.win-rar.com/index.php?id=24&kb_article_ind=162
3. Ding, Y., Horster, P.: Undetectable on-line password guessing attacks. SIGOPS Operating Systems Reviex 29(4), 77–86 (1995)
4. Delaune, S., Jacquemard, F.: A Theory of dictionary attacks and its complexity. In: Proc. of 17th IEEE Computer Security Foundations Workshop, Cambridge, UK, pp. 2–15 (2004)
5. Hu, G., Ma, J., Huang, B.: Password recovery for rar files using CUDA. In: Proc. of 8th IEEE Int. Conf. on Dependable, Autonomic and Secure Computing, Chengdu, China, pp. 486–490 (2009)
6. Apostal, D., Foerster, K., Chatterjee, A., Desell, T.: Password Recovery Using MPI and CUDA. In: The 19th International Conference on High Performance Computing, pp. 1–9 (2012)
7. Zhan, X.J., Hong, J.X.: Study on GPU-based password recovery for MS Office 2003 document. In: The 7th International Conference on Computer Science & Education, pp. 517–520 (2012)
8. Kim, K.: Distributed password cracking on GPU nodes. In: The 7th International Conference on Computing and Convergence Technology, pp. 647–650 (2012)
9. Narayanan, A., Shmatikov, V.: Fast dictionary attacks on passwords using time-space tradeoff. In: Proceedings of the 12th ACM Conference on Computer and Communications Security, pp. 364–372. ACM (2005)
10. Martinovic, G., Horvat, L., Balen, J.: Stochastic Approach on Hash Cracking. MIPRO, 887–891 (2012)
11. Pacheco, P.: An Introduction to Parallel Programming. Morgan Kaufmann (2011)

Sybil-Resist: A New Protocol for Sybil Attack Defense in Social Network

Wei Ma[1], Sen-Zhe Hu[2], Qiong Dai[1], Ting-Ting Wang[1], and Yin-Fei Huang[3]

[1] Institute of Information Engineering, Chinese Academy of Sciences, Beijing, 100093, China
[2] Beijing Special Vehicle Institute, Beijing, 100072, China
[3] Shanghai Stock Exchange, Shanghai, 200120, China
{mawei,daiqiong,wangtingting}@iie.ac.cn,
husenzhe@126.com, yfhuang@sse.com.cn

Abstract. Currently, most of the existing social networks on Internet are distributed, decentralized systems, and they are particularly vulnerable to Sybil attack in which a single malicious user introduces multiple bogus identities and pretends to be multiple and real users in the network. With these controlled identities, the malicious user can create a Byzantine failure in collaborative tasks by 'out vote' the real identities. This paper conducts a survey on the network security of social networks to provide the overview of the current online security of the social networks and the corresponding defend methods. Based on the survey, this paper proposes Sybil-Resist, a *Random Walk*-based Sybil attack defense protocol devoting to identifying the Sybil nodes and the Sybil region efficiently. The simulation results obtained by a more realistic simulation topology show that the proposed scheme outperforms existing solutions in terms of detection accuracy and running time.

Keywords: Network security, social networks, Sybil attack and detection.

1 Introduction

The rapid development of various on-line social networks has changed the way people live around the world. Compared with the traditional social life, social network acts as a kind of platform where people can communicate and discuss. Actually, not socializing face-to-face is originally a major part of our social life, so it means that social network will definitely bring a huge impact on traditional world. Many social networks adopted Client/server model at the beginning, but with the sharp increase of users, there is a huge amount of data needs to be handled by the data center, so it requires the ISP to have many powerful servers, storage devices and broadband network to support these services. In order to solve this problem, many networks adopt peer-to-peer or distributed systems. Then, Sybil Attack becomes a serious problem for those systems, by which a malicious user could create a lot of fake identities (also called Sybil identities) to compromise the running of the network or to pour fake information into the network.

Sybil attack is a very serious threat to the proper operation of an online social network. For computer security, Sybil attack is an attack wherein a reputation system is

L. Batten et al. (Eds.): ATIS 2014, CCIS 490, pp. 219–230, 2014.

subverted by forging identities in peer-to-peer networks. By creating a large number of pseudonymous identities, the attacker subverts the reputation system of a peer-to-peer network and gains a disproportionately large influence. The vulnerability of a reputation system to a Sybil attack depends on how cheaply the identities can be created. An entity on a peer-to-peer network is a piece of software, and it has access to local resources. By using an identity, an entity can advertise itself on the peer-to-peer network and also can mapping to many identities. Aiming at resource sharing and reliability, entities use multiple identities in peer-to-peer networks. There are four kinds of communication models of Sybil attack:

1) Direct communication: The Sybil node communicates directly with the honest node. When an honest node broadcasts a message in the network, the Sybil node which shares a link with that node will listen to this message.

2) Indirect communication: in this kind of Sybil attack, there isn't any honest node can be reached by the Sybil node. On the contrast, one or some Sybil nodes declare that they could reach the honest region. So they will use a Sybil node which has a relationship with an honest node to transmit their messages.

3) Simultaneous communication: In some cases, an adversary can fabricate many Sybil identities. For example, if the identity of a node is a 32 bit integer, then the adversary can assign a 32 bit value to the Sybil node as its identity. But if there is a mechanism that can verify the identity of the Sybil node, like naming space, then the adversary can't fabricate fake identities. So, in that case, the adversary needs to assign a legal identity to the Sybil node. This kind of identity theft is hard to be detected if the adversary invalidates the original node. Simultaneous communication means the adversary let its all Sybil identities take part in one network communication. So if one node only be allowed to use its identity once, the adversary can recycle some of its Sybil identities to make that Sybil node seems like many honest identities.

4) Non-simultaneous communication: if the attacker uses some of the Sybil nodes only in a specified time period and other Sybil nodes in another time period, then it will look like the regular action of the honest nodes.

Although Sybil attacks could be alleviated by using a trusted central authority by issuing credentials of the real users or requiring some kinds of payments, it is hard to achieve because it is difficult or impossible to establish a single entity that all the users of the website are willing to trust. Some other ways, like binding every user to IP address or requiring users to solve a simple puzzle, cannot make effective protections, because the adversary is able to harvest IP addresses which is quite different to each other, thereby it is difficult to filter them. So we need to build up a scheme to analysis the characteristics of the Sybil attack and defend it by some computer-based algorithms.

2   Related Work

In the past few years, there was an increasing interest in creating defense methods for Sybil attack. H. Yu et al. (2006) proposed SybilGuard, after that they proposed the SybilLimit (2008). G. Danezis (2009) proposed the SybilInfer. More recently, N. Tran et al. (2011) proposed the SybilResilient, and W. Wei et al. (2012) proposed the SybilDefender. Although some of the pervious schemes have a nice performance when the topology is small, their algorithms aren't computationally efficient, and it can't handle the situation when the topology contains millions of users. For example, Sybil-Guard H.Yu et al. (2006), only allows $O(\sqrt{n}logn)$ Sybil nodes per attack edge. But the theoretical factor should be $logn$ per attack edge. What's more, the pervious schemes can only allow one node to be identified at a time. So finding the Sybil region will be time-consuming, because they have to examine the whole graph.

In a social network, each user is regarded as a node in the network graph. If two users are friends which means one should make a request and another should make an acknowledgement, they share with an undirected link, such as Facebook or RenRen. The relationship established between users in other kinds of websites like WeiBo or YouTube, in which users can plus interest on anyone in the website unilaterally, is directed link. To prevent a malicious user from initiating Sybil attack, all previous Sybil defense schemes based on the assumption that there is only limited links between the honest nodes and the Sybil nodes, are also called as attack edges. As a result, even although an adversary can fabricate a lot of Sybil nodes and put many links between them, we can still find a small cut between the Sybil region and the honest region. The small cut can disconnect the Sybil nodes from other honest nodes in the whole topology, which means it intersects all the attack edges. To limit the number of attack edges, the previous works assume that the relationships between the users are all trusted and users sharing a link are friends in the real world, and a Sybil node can't make many 'friends' who are honest users. However, some real-world social networks have been showed that they don't follow that rules.

In this paper, we proposed the Sybil-Resist scheme based on the existing work SybilDefender, which introduces that a Sybil node can only reach the honest region through a small cut, but the honest node isn't restricted. So it is highly possible that the random walks start from the Sybil node tend to be restricted in its own Sybil region. Then we could use this random walk theory to determine the Sybil region and defend the Sybil attack.

3   The Proposed Scheme

In our design, we take the social network as a graph G which consists of edges E and Vertices V. The majority of V are honest users which are also called as honest nodes. There are also several adversaries in the social network and each of them has a number of Sybil identities. Each Sybil identity is regarded as a Sybil node in graph G. And if two identities are friends, then there is an edge between those two nodes which represents their relationship. The edges we discussed in this paper are undirected. There is also another definition we use is attack edge, which refers to the edge between a Sybil node and an honest node. All the honest nodes consist of an honest region while all the Sybil nodes consist of a Sybil region. And the Sybil region is controlled by the malicious user, thus there can be any number of edges among the Sybil nodes.

3.1   Assumptions

There are several assumptions as shown in the following.

- The honest region is fast mixing.
- There is one known honest node. We assume that there is one honest node that we know in advance which is set as the start point of the proposed algorithm.
- Given the social network topology before testing, we can process the nodes and get their information. So this scheme is a centralized defending mechanism. And it is valid according to the fact that all the existing online social networks are under centralized control.
- The size of the honest region is much larger than the size of Sybil region. Given the fact that the current online social networks do have large user bases, Facebook (over 500 million), Twitter (over 200 million), Orkut (over 120 million), we can tell that a malicious user isn't able to create such many Sybil identities, because creating a new identity in the online social network by computer program is not possible. Many processes like verifying an email address, providing some information or solving CAPTCHAs, require human effort.
- There are only a limited number of attack edges. Although the adversary may create any number of edges within the Sybil region, there will be a small cut which can traverse all the attack edges and it disturbs the fast-mixing property: the mixing between the honest nodes is fast, while the Sybil nodes are opposite. The previous schemes assume that the honest nodes only share links with their real-world friends. But it has been proved to be wrong by Bilge *et al.* (2009), who shows that people will accept 20% of requests from fake identities on Facebook. And all these relationships will be attack edges when the adversary launches an attack.

The proposed algorithm consists of four main parts and four supporting functions: Preprocessing algorithm is used to pre-process the topology and get some characteristic values of the honest node; a Sybil identification algorithm to identify the suspect nodes; a walk length estimation algorithm to set some value for Sybil region algorithms; And a Sybil region detection algorithm to detect the Sybil region among the detected nodes.

3.2   Pre-processing

In this algorithm, we treat social network as a social graph G (V, E), the honest node we know as h. And these two parameters are taken as inputs of the pre-processing algorithm. Random walks play an important role in this scheme. A random walk on a graph refers to a movement that a node randomly selects one of its neighbors to move. If node i has the degree d_i, then the probability that the node will make a movement to one of its neighbor is $1/d_i$.

This program first performs f random walks with length $l_s = \log n$ starting from the known node h. Since we use the assumption that the honest region is fast mixing, the f ending nodes follow the stationary distribution. Then these nodes are treated as honest nodes and we use these nodes as the following starting points to obtain the characteristic values of honest nodes as judging criterion in algorithm 2. And there is a little possibility that there may be Sybil nodes in J. But in our evaluation, it won't influence the effectiveness. The random walk starts from the minimum length, and adds an interval in every loop until. For each l, the algorithm performs R (200 in our evaluation) random walks starting from every node in J. Then we count the frequency of every node and select all the nodes whose frequency is no smaller than a threshold t (a constant with value of 5). At last, we calculate the mean value and standard deviation of the $f+1$ values for each l and output them.

```
Algorithm 1: Pre-Processing (G, h)

J = {}
for i = 1 to f
    perform a random walk with length lₛ = log n starting from h
    J = J ∪ {the ending node of the random walk}
End
l = l_min
while l ≤ l_max
    for i = J(1) to J(last)
        Perform R random walks with length l starting from node i
        Get nᵢ as the number of nodes with frequency no smaller than t
    end
    Out = {l, mean({nᵢ : i ∈ J}), stdDeviation({nᵢ : i ∈ J})}
    l = l + interval
end
```

3.3 Sybil Identification

The second part is to determine whether a suspect node u is a Sybil node, and the pseudo-code is shown in algorithm 2. Firstly, the algorithm performs R random walks with an initial length l_0 starting from u. l_0 is a value that no smaller than l_{min} used in PreProcessing. Secondly, the algorithm makes a comparison between the number of nodes whose frequency is bigger than or equal to t and the mean value in tuple {l, mean, stdDeviation} in Algorithm 1. And if the inequality mean $-$ m $>$ stdDeviation $* \alpha$ is valid, we can judge that u is a Sybil node and end this algorithm. Otherwise, we will double the value of l and do the loop again until l is larger than the upper limit of l, l_{max}. And if the inequality mean $-$ m $>$ stdDeviation $*$ α is still false, we suppose that the node is an honest node. To set the value of t, we perform R random walks starting from h with length l_{max}, the number of nodes with frequency bigger than or equal to t should be larger than $|V|/2$. This defending scheme adopt adaptive test model to identify the suspect node in order to guarantee that it can fit all sizes of Sybil regions: the short random walks can be used in small Sybil region, while long random walks are required for large Sybil regions.

```
Algorithm 2 SybilIdentification(G, u, output of Alg.1)
```

1. $l = l_0$
2. while $l \leq l_{max}$
3. perform R random walks with length l starting from u
4. m = the number of nodes whose frequency is no smaller than t
5. Let the tuple corresponding to length l in the *output of Alg.1* be
6. {l, *mean*, *stdDeviation*}
7. if $mean - m > stdDeviation * \alpha$ then
8. Output u is a Sybil node
9. end
10. $l = l * 2$
11. End
12. Output u is an honest node

3.4   Sybil Region Detection Algorithm

```
Algorithm 3 WalkLengthEstimation(G, s)
```

1. $l = l_0/2$
2. *deadWalkRatio* = 0
3. **while** $deadWalkRatio < \beta$
4. $l = l * 2$
5. *deadWalkNum* = 0
6. **for** $i = 1$ to R
7. Perform a partial random walk starting from s with length l
8. **if** the partial random walk is dead before it reaches l then
9. *deadWalkNum* ++
10. **end**
11. **end**
12. $deadWalkRatio = deadWalkNum/R$
13. **end**
14. output l

Once a Sybil node is detected, this algorithm will detect the Sybil region among that node. This Sybil region detection Algorithm takes a social topology G (V, E) and a known Sybil node s as inputs. We define a Sybil region as a sub graph of G which doesn't have a small cut, and it consists of all the Sybil nodes.

This algorithm introduces a definition of partial random walks, which behaves the same as the standard random walks except that it doesn't traverse the same node twice. So if a partial random walk reaches a node with all its neighbors have been traversed, this partial random walk is 'dead' and cannot proceed. This character makes that a partial random walk starting from a Sybil node is more likely to be 'trapped' in Sybil region than standard random walk. Thus we could detect the Sybil region by examining the nodes that traversed by the partial random walks. However, we should estimate the required length of the partial random walks at first, and the algorithm is shown in Algorithm 3.

The algorithm performs R partial random walks starting from s and counts the ratio of dead walks with the initial length l_0. If this ratio is smaller than β a threshold value near to 1 (probably 0.95), we double the current length and perform the loop again. The loop won't end until the dead walk ratio is bigger than or equal to β.

Algorithm 4 SybilRegionDetection(*G, s, l from Alg.3*)

```
1. initialize the frequency of all the nodes to be 0
2. for i = 1 to R
3.    perform a partial random walk originating from node s with
      length l
4.    s.frequency ++
5.    for j = 1 to l
6.       Let the j^th hop of the partial random walk be node k
7.       k.frequency++
8.    end
9. end
10.   traversedList = Sort the traversed nodes by their frequency in
      decreasing order
11.   counter = 0
12.   S = ∅
13.   while true
14.      counter = conductance(S)
15.      for i = traversedList(1)to traversedList(last)
16.         if conductance ({i} ∪ S) ≤ conductance(S)
17.            S = {i} ∪ S
18.         end
19.      end
20.      if counter ≤ conductance(S)
21.         break
22.      end
23.   end
24.   output S
```

The Algorithm 4 has three inputs: G (V, E), s and the estimates length l as inputs and outputs all the sybil nodes around the s (which is the Sybil region). Considering that there may some honest nodes have been traversed by the partial random walks as some walks entering the honest region through the attack edges, and we should select the Sybil nodes from the set. This algorithm introduces a metric called conductance, which introduced by R. Kannan (2000), the definition is at below. Let d be the sum of the degrees of all the nodes in set S, and a be the number of edges with one endpoint in S and another endpoint in $\bar{S}$. The conductance of S equals to a/d, and it measures the quality of cut between S and $\bar{S}$: the bigger the conductance is, the bigger the cut is. And using the conductance matrix to solve the problem is quiet appropriate because we make the assumption that there is a small cut at the middle of honest region and Sybil region.

Algorithm 4 firstly performs R partial random walks originating from the known Sybil node s, and the initial value is what we got in algorithm *WalkLengthEstimation*.

Then this algorithm sorts all the traversed nodes by their frequency in decreasing order and stores them in set *traversedList*. Then, starting from the first node (always s), this algorithm iterates the nodes in *traversedList* and adds newly encountered node to S as long as it won't increase the conductance of S. After all the nodes in the *traversedList* have been examined, it records the current conductance value and begins a new loop. This loop won't stop until the conductance doesn't change in two consecutive loops. Then the algorithm will output S as the detected Sybil region. The intuition is that all the Sybil nodes in Sybil region among that node will be covered by the partial random walks starting from the detected node. What's more, Sybil nodes tend to be at the top of the *traversedList*.

4   Performance Analysis

4.1   Social Topology Establishing

In the performance analysis, the topology consists of honest part and Sybil part. We choose the Facebook topology in Stanford Large Network Dataset Collection created by Jure Leskovec &B. Schoelkopf (2013) as our honest region, which is a small part of the whole Facebook topology which consists of 4039 nodes and 88234 edges. To manipulate the topology, we use NodeXL which is a free, open-source template that makes it easy to explore network graphs. And about the Sybil region, we use the ER model. The Sybil region built upon this model is random networks with no particular bias and emulates the arbitrary structures. The average degree of the ER model Sybil region is between 2 to 3, which represents a sparse matrix compared with the honest region.

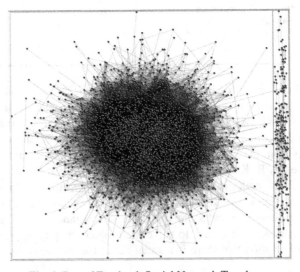

Fig. 1. Part of Facebook Social Network Topology

Fig. 1 shows a part of Facebook topology which generated by the software No-deXL. Black nodes represent honest nodes (3999 in total) while blue nodes (240 in total) represent Sybil nodes. And all the black nodes make up the honest region where each node has comparably more relationships with other nodes, and there are ten main users having bigger degree than other nodes in the topology. And here, we adopt ER model to build the Sybil region, and we use Python language to generate it. Each node has a number (select 4239 number from 1 to 4439, there will be some nodes that have no connection with other nodes, and it can't launch Sybil attack, so we exclude them) act as the identity of a real user. There are ten attack edges between the Sybil region and the honest region while a small cut pass across all of them.

Table 1 shows the general information of the part of Facebook social network to-pology, the characteristics contains Graph Type, Vertices, Unique Edges, Edges with Duplicates, Total Edges, Self-Loops, Maximum Vertices in a Connected Component and so on. With this information, we can get a better understanding on the distribution of the nodes in the topology.

Table 1. The General Information of the Topology

Parameters	Value(s)
Graph Type	Undirected
Vertices	3999
Unique Edges	87071
Edges With Duplicates	0
Total Edges	87071
Self-Loops	0
Connected Components	3
Single-Vertex Connected Components	0
Maximum Vertices in a Connected Component	3995
Maximum Edges in a Connected Component	87069
Maximum Geodesic Distance (Diameter)	11
Average Geodesic Distance	4.173561
Graph Density	0.010892043
NodeXL Version	1.0.1.229

The minimum degree of the nodes in the topology is 1, while the maximum is 769. And the average value is 41.174, the median value is 23. So we can see that there is a large deference between the Sybil nodes and the honest nodes. The range of degree of the Sybil nodes is from 1 to 5, while the range of degree of the honest nodes is from 1 to 769, and the average value of the degree is 44.

4.2 Detection Rate of Sybil Identification Algorithm

In this section, we will show the performance of the Sybil identification algorithm. In our Sybil identification algorithm, we think that because of the existence of a small cut between the Sybil region and honest region, there will be a difference between the coverage of random walks originating form a Sybil node and from an honest node.

In the test we perform 20 random walks starting from each source node which is randomly selected. The parameters we set in our experiments are showed as low: $l_{min} = 10$, $l_{max} = 100$, $l_0 = 10$, $t = 5$, $\alpha=2.8$, $f = 20$, $R = 200$. Now, we make two definitions, first one is false positive rate, which means the percentage of the honest nodes identified to be Sybil node; second is false negative rate, which means the percentage of the Sybil nodes identified to be honest.

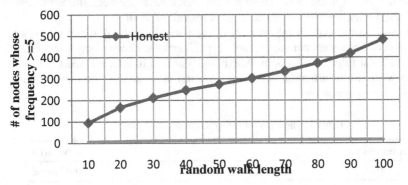

Fig. 2. Difference between the coverage of random walks originating from honest nodes and from Sybil nodes

The upper curve in Fig.2 shows the number of nodes traversed by random walks starting from an honest node which is not smaller than 5 times, and the lower curve is the number of nodes traversed by random walks starting from a Sybil node which no smaller than 5 times. And each value of the points in the curves represents the mean value of 50 experiments. We can see the difference is larger than 100 nodes since the beginning. So as we described in Algorithm 2, we use $mean - m > stdDeviation * \alpha$ as the threshold to identify Sybil nodes. So in our evaluation, the value of α is a relatively small value (2.8 in the experiments) to limit the number of falsely identified honest node.

Table 2. False Positive and negative rates of the Sybil Node Identification Algorithm

	24 Sybil nodes per attack edge (240 Sybil nodes) Facebook ER model of Sybil Region	
	F+	F-
200RWs	6.125%	2.167%
300RWs	4.245%	1.025%

Table 2 shows the result when there are 24 Sybil nodes per attack edge with ER model, and the value is the mean value of 50 times results. So as it shows in the table, our algorithm achieves comparably low false positive and negative rates in all cases. When using the same topology, the average false positive rate of Gatekeeper is 11.721%, and its average false negative rate is 17.625%.

Besides, we used the same computer to run the Sybil node identification algorithms of My Sybil defense scheme—Sybil-Resist and of SybilLimit to compare the average running time. Our algorithm can achieve an average running time 4.0 seconds to test one Sybil node, while the average running time to test one honest node by SybilLimit is 8.11 seconds.

4.3   Evaluation of Sybil Community Detection Algorithm

In this section, we show the performance of our Sybil community detection algorithm. So, we perform 20 times of the experiments on the part of Facebook topology, and the parameters we used in the experiments are as follows: $l_0 = 10$, $\beta = 0.95$, $R = 200$. The number of the attack edges in the topology we used is 10, and each attack edge introduces 24 Sybil nodes on average. The goal of our Sybil community detection algorithm is to detect the Sybil region among the known Sybil node, so we randomly select a Sybil node as the input and get the percentage of the Sybil nodes that can be detected, also we can get the number of honest nodes that are detected falsely. We perform the experiments for 50 times to get the result, which are showed in Table 4.

Table 3. The Performance of the Sybil region detection algorithm

	24 Sybil nodes per attack edge (240 Sybil nodes) Facebook ER model of Sybil Region	
	Percentage of found Sybil Nodes	Number of falsely detected Honest Nodes
Mean Value	98.6%	0.63%
Maximum Value	99.2%	1.85%
Minimum Value	96.3%	0.2%
Median Value	98.3%	0.71%

As we can see from the Table 3, our Sybil region detection algorithm can detect the majority of the Sybil nodes around the known Sybil node. In the most ideal experiment, it can detect almost every Sybil nodes in the topology (99.2% detection rate). Also the algorithm can achieve a less than one node honest node falsely detected rate on average (0.63% false detection rate). What's more, this Sybil region detection algorithm can achieve high accuracy with relatively short running time (58 minutes on average). The undetected Sybil nodes are usually the Sybil nodes that have direct relationships with the honest node, also called as compromised nodes.

5   Conclusions

In this paper, we study the defending scheme for Sybil attack which uses social topology to mitigate the Sybil attacks in large social networks. The performance analysis results show that the proposed scheme has a better performance in the self-made part of Facebook social network topology than some of the previous schemes which can effectively identify the Sybil node even when the number of Sybil nodes introduces by each attack edge reaches the theoretically lower bound of detectable. And it can also detect the Sybil region among the known Sybil node with some sizes. However, there are many different structures of the Sybil region, and every time the structure changes, the performance of the algorithms change. In the experiments, we only analyze the ER model as our Sybil region architecture. So in the future, there may be a scheme can self-correct when the structure of Sybil region changes. And that may achieve a more accurate detection rate.

References

1. Danezis, G., Mittal, P.: Sybilinfer: Detecting Sybil nodes using social networks. In: NDSS (2009)
2. Mao, H., Shuai, X., Kapadia, A.: Loose tweets: an analysis of privacy leaks on twitter. In: Proceedings of the 10th Annual ACM Workshop on Privacy in the Electronic Society, WPES 2011, pp. 1–12. ACM, New York (2011)
3. Yu, H., Kaminsky, M., Gibbons, P.B., Flaxman, A.: Sybilguard: defending against Sybil attacks via social networks. In: SIGCOMM (2006)
4. Yu, H., Gibbons, P.B., Kaminsky, M., Xiao, F.: Sybillimit: A near optimal social network defence against Sybil attacks. In: IEEE Symposium on Security and Privacy (2008)
5. Douceur, J.R.: The Sybil Attack. In: Druschel, P., Kaashoek, M.F., Rowstron, A. (eds.) IPTPS 2002. LNCS, vol. 2429, p. 251. Springer, Heidelberg (2002)
6. Leskovec, J., Schoelkopf, B.: Structure and Dynamics of Information Pathways in Online Media. In: ACM International Conference on Web Search and Data Mining WSDM (2013) http://snap.stanford.edu/snap/index.html
7. Bilge, L., Strufe, T., Balzarotti, D., Kirda, E.: All your contacts are belong to us: automated identity theft attacks on social networks. In: WWW (2009)
8. von Ahn, L., Blum, M., Hopper, N.J., Langford, J.: CAPTCHA: Using Hard AI Problems for Security. Computer Science Department. Paper 136 (2003)
9. Mitzenmacher, M., Upfal, E. (2005). Probability and Computing. Cambridge University Press (2005)
10. Tran, N., Li, J., Subramanian, L., Chow, S.S.M.: Optimal Sybil-resilient node admission control. In: IEEE INFOCOM (2011)
11. Bazzi, R., Konjevod, G.: On the establishment of distinct identities in overlay networks. In: ACM PODC (2005)
12. Kannan, R., Vempala&, S., Vetta, A.: On clustering: Good, bad and spectral. In: FOCS (2000)
13. Morselli, R., Bhattacharjee, B., Srinivasan, A., Marsh, M.: Efficient lookup on unstructured topologies. In: ACM PODC (2005)
14. Lee, R., Nia, R., Hsu, J., Levitt, K.N., Rowe, J., Wu, S.F., Ye, S.: Design and implementation of faith: an experimental system to intercept and manipulate online social informatics. In: 2011 International Conference on Advances in Social Networks Analysis and Mining (ASONAM), pp. 195–202 (July 2011)
15. Isdal, T., Piatek, M., Krishnamurthy, A., Anderson, T.: SIGCOMM 2010, New Delhi, India, August 30-September 3 (2010)
16. Ng, T.S.E., Zhang, H.: Predicting internet network distance with coordinates-based approaches. In: IEEE INFOCOM (2002)
17. Wei, W., Xu, F., Tan, C.C., Li, Q.: Sybildefender: Defend against Sybil attacks in large social networks. In: INFOCOM (2012)

PAITS: Detecting Masquerader
via Short-Lived Interventional Mouse Dynamics

Xiao-jun Chen[1], Jin-qiao Shi[1], Rui Xu[1], S.M. Yiu[2], Bing-xing Fang[3], and Fei Xu[1]

[1] Institute of Information Engineering, Chinese Academy of Sciences, Beijing, China
[2] Department of Computer Science, The University of Hong Kong, Hong Kong
[3] Beijing University of Posts and Telecommunication
{chenxiaojun,shijinqiao,xufei}@iie.ac.cn,
xurui@nelmail.iie.ac.cn, smyiu@cs.hku.hk, fangbx@bupt.edu.cn

Abstract. It is relatively easier for an insider attacker to steal the password of a colleague or use an unattended machine (logged in by other users) within a trusted domain to launch an attack. A simple real-time authentication by password may not work if they have the password. By comparing the stored mouse behavioral profile of the valid user, the system automatically authenticates the user. However, long verification time in existing approaches based on mouse dynamics which mostly last dozens of minutes and probably make masquerader escaped from detection mechanism. In this paper, we proposed a system called PAITS (Practical Authentication with Identity Tracing System) to do re-authentication via comparison of mouse behavior under a short-lived interventional scenario. Mouse movements under the special scenario where the cursor is a bit out of control can capture the user's unconscious reaction, and then be used for behavioral comparison and detection of malicious masquerader. Our experiments on PAITS demonstrate best result with a *FRR* of 2.86% and a *FAR* of 3.23% under probability neural network with 71 features. That is a comparative result against the previous research results, but at the same time significantly shorten the verification time from dozens of minutes to five seconds.

Keywords: insider threat, re-authentication, mouse dynamics, behavioral model.

1   Introduction

Insider threats [1] [2] to organizational security has been one of the most difficult challenges to address and are receiving increased attention in academic, commercial and government research communities. Masqueraders are one kind of malicious insiders who commit a penetration to an organization's network, system or data through identity theft. One most common example is forgotten lock-screen attack when the legal user leaves for dinner without locking screen, his malicious workmate enters his computer with the administrator access privilege. So he could do any crimes such as reading confidential business documents or filching personal privacy information or keep a back-door on the victim's computer via clicking a prepared webpage with trojan horses for successive attacks.

L. Batten et al. (Eds.): ATIS 2014, CCIS 490, pp. 231–242, 2014.

Identify theft broke the traditional authentication mechanism under which authentication is performed once at the starting of each login session. Re-authentication system monitors user's operation continually to do re-authenticate to the current user such as executed command sequence, file access logs and especially Human-computer interaction (HCI) behavior. As a kind of HCI behavioral biometrics, mouse dynamics has received more and more focus.

Mouse dynamics describe an individual's behavior via extracting unique biological characteristic of mouse operations, such as moving speed, accelerations etc. Some mouse dynamics prototype system has been developed and claimed that they achieved very low false rejected ratio (FRR) and false accept ratio (FAR). For example Pusara et al. [4] showed a FRR of 2.4649 and a FAR of 2.4614 in their experiments, and Gamboa et al. [6] implement their solution with a FAR of 2%.

But existing approaches of mouse dynamics are criticized in several aspects, especially in practicability. Too long verification time failed to capture attacks from malicious insiders efficiently, such as 14-30 minutes in Pusara's method and 10 minutes in Gamboa's system. Long verification time is not acceptable for practical authentication system against insider threat.

In this paper, by using meticulous designed short-lived Interventional scenario, we implemented PAITS in which a new technique is used to address the verification time gap described in existing approaches. Specifically, there are three main contributions as following:

- Three short-lived interventional scenarios under which the users are a bit out of control of mouse device during five seconds are designed to collect the user's anxious and subconscious mouse moves. To the best of our knowledge, this is the first work to plant such short-lived interventional scenarios in re-authentication system.
- To quantitatively examine the mouse movement behavior under the specified scenarios, we go deep into the cursor track data and extract 71 features to make different individuals' mouse behaviors distinguishable.
- To validate our approach, we developed a practical and identity-traceable re-authentication system using the proposed approach. Experimental results showed that our re-authentication system can achieve comparable *FAR* and *FRR* to previous works but shorten the verification time to five seconds.

The remainder of the paper is organized as follows. In the next section, we provide related work on mouse dynamics for authentication. In Section 3, we present the system architecture of PAITS. Short-lived interventional scenarios design is presented in section 4, followed by a discussion of system implement which include data preprocessing, features extraction and the classifications algorithms for behavior comparison in Section 5. In Sections 6, we describe our experiments and discuss results obtained and then conclude the paper with some remarks in Section 7.

2   Related Work

As a new kind of behavioral biometric, mouse dynamics was first investigated in 2003 and developed rapidly during the past few years. The basic idea is to collect mouse actions when the users interact with a graphical user interface and extract bio-metrics to build profiles for users, aiming at verifying the current user's identify and privileges ultimately.

Hocquet et al.[3] designed a game in which participants are asked to click the left button of the mice to hit the moving square, and then they compute features of the action with mice such as speeds, accelerations, angular velocities, curvature etc. Authentication is made by comparing the current features sample again the normal behavioral profile and an error rate of 37.5% is achieved in their experiment. Pusara et al. [4] collected the raw cursor movement data and extract features such as distance, angle, and speed between data points for different user and different application to the same user. They found that the same user will have different mouse behavior for different applications. Separate normal behavior models for each application per user are set up and an average *FAR* of 0.43% and *FRR* of 1.75% are achieved. Their performance benefit from the careful behavioral models for every application and each user but too many models are commonly impractical to build. Ahmed and Traor [5] presented a biometric technology based on mouse dynamics using artificial neural networks. Their experiments extracted features like movement speed, average movement speed per movement direction etc. and achieved a *FAR* of 2.46% and a *FRR* of 2.46%.

In order to make mouse dynamics to be used for re-authentication in practical, we need to overcome two mainly challenges. Firstly, verification process under a static and explicit scenario will warn the malicious insider to behave more gingerly or give up their attack intent. Secondly, most approaches need too long mouse events collecting duration to complete the verification. Long session time will failed to detect the masqueraders because they can complete their attack within few minutes. Compared with other existing approaches, PAITS can complete the identity verification under an implicit scenario that be insensible to user, and with a low equal error rate (*EER*) comparable with the methods described above. And more importantly, PAITS only needs 5s to re-authenticate a current user's identify, which is a great improvement.

3   System Architecture

3.1   Design Goals

We designed PAITS to meet a number of goals. Order by priority, the goals are listed as follow:

1. Fast verification process. Since the masquerader could make and complement their crime (such as steal the personal privacy or secret document) in very short time, it should capture the malicious insider's within short duration. Our system achieve this goal by designing a special short-lived interventional scenarios.

2. Comparable low equal error rate. Obviously it should achieve high accuracy, that is to say low error rate. Quantitatively, it should reach a comparable low ERR with the past methods if not better than them.

3. Identity traceability. When a masquerader was detected, this system should find out that real identity of him. That goal can be achieved by behavior classification ability of it and wide deployment of it in the target organization.

4. Suspicious criminal actions recording. When a masquerader was detected, this system can record his successive attack actions. That will help administrator's auditing job and estimate the harm of attacks.

3.2   Architecture Overview

PAITS consists of: (i) Data capturing module which implements three short-lived interventional scenarios (Cursor-Stopping, Cursor-Disappearance and Cursor Slowing) and collect user behavior based on these scenarios. This module will be triggered according to some security measures (e.g. the machine has been idle for a few minutes) and (ii) a feature selection module which receives raw mouse movement data and extracts abstract features, and feeds features into the for training or testing and (iii) a behavior comparison module which use probability neural network and one-class SVM to detect masquerader and trace real identity of attacker(iv) suspicious operation recording module in which when an anomaly is detected, current user's suspicious operation sequence data will be sent back by data capturing component and is stored in server for forensics later. Fig.1 describes the details of PAITS.

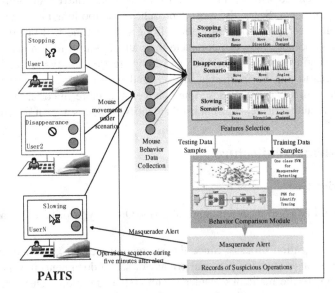

Fig. 1. System architecture of PAITS

4   Short-Lived Interventional Scenarios

In this section, we introduce a special type of scenario named short-lived interventional scenario. It's the most import idea of this system. Past research had to enlarge the time of behavioral session to capturing enough mouse movements for discriminating normal user and malicious users. Long verification time is the essential problem for practicability of mouse dynamics methods. Our short-lived interventional scenario is design to collect more mouse movement data in a short time.

Concretely, we deliberately let current user enter a short-lived scenario where the cursor is a bit out of control (such as cursor stopping, disappearing or slowing) when he/her enter the owner's sensitive applications. That's the mean of 'interventional', our collecting tools would make the cursor seemed to be stopping or disappearing or slowing when the user want to move it. And we think this short-time will disturb a bit on-going work of the current user and make him or her to generate a plenty of subconscious move movements to. This reasoning is a very intuitionistic idea but will be proven sound and common phenomenon for most individuals.

Totally three short-lived interventional scenarios are designed that include Cursor-Stopping, Cursor-Disappearance and Cursor-Slowing scenarios. In Cursor-Stopping scenario, the cursor is fixed on the center of the screen for five seconds. In Cursor-Disappearance scenario, the cursor gets invisible for five seconds. In Cursor-Slowing scenario, the cursor move shorter distance with one mouse moving action than the normal situation. We expect the user could show some different behavioral biometrics under different scenarios and we can analyze their difference to find the best method for re-authentication.

Cursor-Stopping scenario is implemented by a transparent full-screen popup window in the middle of which a normal mouse icon is drawn. The origin cursor is set to invisible by calling WINAPI ShowCursor(FALSE). The sensor keeps the window on the top the Z order by calling WINAPI BringWindowToTop (sensorWnd) for five seconds and records all real mouse movement of the user. When this scenario ends, user can get control of the cursor back.

Cursor-Disappearance and Cursor-Slowing scenario are implemented in a similar way. They both set the origin cursor invisible but the latter also draws the trajectory of cursor by scaling down the speed of movement. For example, if the user moves the cursor 100 pixels, a cursor move with 60 pixels distance along with the same direction will be draw on the pop window.

5   Implementation

5.1   Data Capturing and Preprocessing

This section we give the design of our mouse-move-sensor and how to implement three short-lived interventional scenarios mentioned above. Data preprocessing will be discuss upon it.

Data Interception

We develop a mouse-move-sensor which register a mouse hook function into the operating system and generate one record when the hook function is called every time. The mouse-move-sensor is activated periodically, or when some high-level security activities occurred such as opening the personal email client software (Microsoft Outlook, Foxmail etc). When the sensor is activated, the user will enter one short-lived interventional scenario which is polled from the three pre-determined scenarios, Cursor-Stopping, Cursor-Disappearance and Cursor-Slowing.

We can collect many move events which are called one movement session in every occurrence of any scenario. Every move event is a quadruple consisted of timestamp, button_click (indicator for left button or right button), and point location pair (x,y). We will process the raw movement session further and extract features in the section 5.2.

Data Preprocessing

The accuracy of the behavior modeling can be affected by the nature of the data provided. We do the data preprocessing from the following three ways.

- Merging tiny moves: The original records describe the point location every execution of hook function. Our computer system will send out plenty of MOUSE messages when the user moves his cursor. That will generate many tiny moves which can bring some problems when extracting feature. For example, the user moves the cursor from $p_1(100,100)$ to $p_n(115,130)$. There may exist three adjacent point locations which are $p_1(100,100)$, $p_2(101,100)$ and $p_3(101,101)$. When calculating the angle between the two moving vectors (p_1, p_2) and (p_2, p_3), we will get two $\pi/2$ which brings distortion for the real situation. In order to eliminate the distortion, we merge the tiny moves into a longer moves not less than five pixels.
- Movement session filtering: a movement session is defined as all mouse moves gathered in one scenario. If user generated too few events when one scenario occurred, the move session will be regarded as invalid and be discarded as a noise point. In PAITS, 50 mouse moves is the minimum value for one session.
- Normalization: Different features have different scale, such as the move distance is about from 100 pixels to 2000 pixels, but the move speed is from 500 pixels/s to 20000 pixels/s. We applied Max-Min Normalization method on all features.

5.2   Features Selection

71 features are extracted from the raw mouse moves which are organized in three categories as following: movement range, movement direction & Speed and angle between moves.

Movement Range

The first impression from Fig.1 is that the range of cursor movement is different between individuals. To depict this characteristic, we define X-Range as the average difference value between the max x value and the min x value, and Y-Range at the same way. We also calculate the gross distance in one session.

Table 2 shows the statistical result. Most of users is seemed to move the cursor in a wide range of the screen, the X-Range is above on 1000 pixels and Y-Range is between 450 pixels and 800 pixels, that all cover more than half of the screen. The gross distance in one session reveals the frequentness of the moves, and reflects the level of anxiousness of users. Left figure of Fig.2 shows the gross distances in one session in a bar for 7 users. Obviously user4 is the most impatient one who move the cursor average 35,844 pixels distance in every scenario.

To reveal the favored areas of mouse movement and in order to facilitate capture the relation of these favored areas, we divide the full screen into a few zones according the x coordination and y coordination. Along x-axis, we count the distance and number of moves occurred in 8 zones which are x<200, 200<=x<400, 400<= x<800... until to x>1400. And we count the same features in 6 zones along y-axis which are y<200, 200<=x<400... until to y>1000. The distributions of distance and number of moves for all zones are shown in right figure of Fig.2. As we can see, most user show average move distance for x-zones but prefer moving their cursor in the lower part of the screen.

Table 1. Movement Range and Distance (pixels)

User	X-Range	Y-Range	Gross Distance
User1	1.3626e+03	794.7000	1.4870e+04
User2	924.8056	553.8889	7.5070e+03
User3	1.2827e+03	449.0982	8.5484e+03
User4	1.9973e+03	753.5444	3.5844e+04
User5	2.0403e+03	756.4342	2.3708e+04
User6	1.8674e+03	794.7460	2.0142e+04
User7	1.3649e+03	732.8571	1.7393e+04

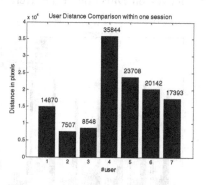 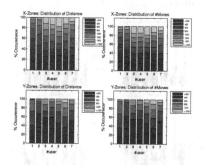

Fig. 2. Movement range distribution. The left figure shows the average distance in one session and the right figure shows moves distribution on different zones.

Movement Direction and Speed

The next group of features is about movement direction and speed. As same as Ahmed's approach [5], we classify all moves into 8 directions which divide equally the whole circle. An interesting but common observable is that user usually moves the cursor more alone the horizontal direction, and less alone the vertical direction. So we define two more general direction that Direction_I is defined as a set of horizontal direction 1,4,5,8 and Direction_II is defined as a set of vertical direction 2,3,6,7. More statistical characteristics also are on the two general direction.

Table 2. Average distance and speed on direction I and direction II (pixels or pixels/s)

user	Distance(I)	Speed(I)	Distance(II)	Speed(II)
U1	179.30	4156.63	37.74	1804.74
U2	95.48	2654.46	18.06	823.7323
U3	160.31	2915.08	22.03	868.72
U4	371.31	10605.31	35.59	3096.64
U5	319.74	8203.18	46.11	3184.51
U6	224.22	21342.46	96.90	10961.58
U7	142.39	5209.28	64.45	3468.69

Table 3 give the average movement distance and speed on Direction_I and Direction_II. As mentioned above, both the move distance and move speed on Direction_I are longer and faster than those on Direction_II.

The left figure of Fig.3 shows the details about distributions of average move distance and average move speed on the two directions. Based on statistical data and empirical knowledge we divide distance on Direction_I into 7 sectors from 0 to over 800 and divide distance on Direction_II into 5 sectors from 0 to over 80. Speed on Direction_I is divided into 5 sectors from 0 to over 8000 and speed on Direction_II is divided into 4 sectors from 0 to over 1600. From the first two figures in top, most user's one cursor move distance is short, over 50 percent of moves on Direction_I are less than 50 pixels, and over 60 percent of moves on Direction_II are less than 20 pixels for the first four users, but the others' moves on Direction_II are averagely distributed.

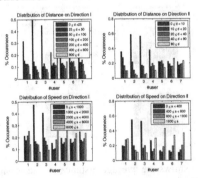 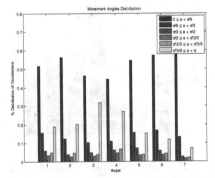

Fig. 3. Distribution on movement direction and angles. The left figure shows movement distribution on directions and the right figure shows angels distribution.

Angles between Two Consecutive Moves

Angels between two consecutive moves is another group important characteristics. They measure the curvature of consecutive moves. We calculate the angel between two consecutive moves (m1: <x1, y1> <x2, y2>, m2: <x2, y2> <x3, y3>) as following formula. In this formula, *ind* indicates weather the two consecutive moves turn back or not on horizontal direction. If the two consecutive moves turn back on vertical direction, property of function *argtan* can guarantee correct calculation. So the value range of angel is $[0, \pi]$.

$$A = | \arg \tan(\frac{y_3 - y_2}{x_3 - x_2}) - \arg \tan(\frac{y_2 - y_1}{x_2 - x_1}) | + ind * \pi / 2$$

$$ind(m_1, m_2) = \begin{cases} 0, if (x_3 - x_2) * (x_2 - x_1) > 0 \\ 1, if (x_3 - x_2) * (x_2 - x_1) < 0 \end{cases}$$

More moves with large angel change may reflect the level of anxiousness of users. From the right figure of Fig.3, we can see that most of users move their cursor from left to right, and generate more moves with small angel change $[0, \pi/6)$ and large angel $[\pi5/6, \pi]$. Different users can show difference on details.

5.3   Behavior Comparison

We try three classifier algorithms to find the best result for mouse movement behavior comparison that include decision tree (C5.0), support vector machine (SVM) and Probabilistic neural network (PNN).

Decision Tree

A decision tree is a tree structure where each internal node denotes a test on a feature, each branch indicates an outcome of the test, and the leaf nodes represent class result. C5.0 is one of best implement of decision tree [7]. And See5 is an excellent implement version of C5.0 [8]. An important feature of See5 is that it can generate classifiers called rulesets which consist of collection of if-then rules. Ruleset generated from a decision tree usually has fewer rules than the tree has leaves and can make better prediction See5 also implemented adaptive boosting algorithm based on research of Freund al [9]. The basic idea is that See5 will generate several classifiers rather than one in the stage of training, when a new sample is to be classified, final class is given by counting the every classifier's votes. Boosting can increase the accuracy of classifier that would be shown in the experiments.

Support Vector Machine

Support Vector Machine (SVM) [10] was provided by Corinna Cortes and Vapnik at 1995, and it can be used for classification and regression analysis. The main idea of support vector machine is to constructs a hyper plane as decision hyper plane, which can separate the two categories by the largest distance of the nearest data point of each class. Parameters choosing is very important for results of SVM classifier, the Particle Swarm Optimization (PSO) has been commonly used to improve the learning and generalization performance of SVM. PSO is an evolutionary computation technology based on swarm intelligence, by searching particle followed with optimal particle in the solution space.

Probabilistic Neural Network

Probabilistic Neural Network (PNN) is a feed-forward neural network, was provided by Dr. D.F. Specht in the early 1990s [11]. In practical applications, especially in solving classification problem, PNN has the advantage of using a linear learning algorithm to accomplish the work done by non-linear learning algorithm, while maintaining the high accuracy and other characteristics of the non-linear algorithm. Due to the weights corresponding to PNN is the distribution pattern of samples, PNN does not require training, which is possible to meet the requirements of real-time processing.

6   Performance Evaluation

6.1   Experiment Environment and dataset

We designed a mouse monitor program and implemented the program on 12 user computers which they use for daily work. The mouse monitor program will automatically run in the background right after the computer system start-up. The program is transparent to user and has no influence or restrictions on user's normal operation.

In our experiment, there are 7 normal users and 5 malicious users. In the training period, each user's mouse movement characters are collected. Then we deliberately devised the 5 malicious users to use 7 normal user's mouse now and then during the experiment, and we try to find out when and which malicious user accessed normal user's computer by analyze the data we collected from the program.

We asked 12 volunteers to use the system over a one month period of time and collected 1038 mouse sessions in total, an average of 86 sessions per user. Among all these sessions, there are 757 sessions in cursor stopping scenario, 144sessions in cursor disappearance scenario and 137 sessions in cursor slowing scenario.

6.2   Masquerader Detection with Identify Tracing

Three classifier algorithms C5.0, SVM and PNN mentioned above are used for masquerader detection. We selected half of sessions in dataset for training different classifiers. Another half of sessions and half of training dataset are formed the testing dataset. For every classifier algorithm, we used the original 71 features to train or test, also employed a feature filter algorithm joint mutual information (JMI) to test which is available in FEAST toolbox[11]. Result comparison can be see in the following table 4.

The first eight rows show the experimental results of C5.0. Expect that JMI is applied or not, experimental results of C5.0 with default setting also are compared with C5.0 with Boosting and ruleset. From table 5, we are given that boosting and ruleset can increase accuracy of classifier. Besides that, we may can draw a conclusion that feature filtering algorithms may lost some key information and reduce accuracy of classifier. For example, results of C5.0 with boosting and ruleset on original 71 features can achieve best FRR of 5.71 percent and FAR of 2.42 percent. The other FRR and FAR are obviously higher than it. Same phenomenon can be observed in the other two groups of classifier.

The middle four rows show the experimental result of SVM. The FRR and FAR of SVM testing are very high but there exists an exception that SVM testing algorithm on original 71 features achieved FAR of 0.81 percent. We think it is a good choice where the FAR is very important for the security administrator, although the FRR is nearby 15 percent. After all a false accusation would be a high-cost accident that will harm the wrongly accused employee and even the enthusiasm of other normal colleagues.

Among three group classifiers, PNN shows the better accuracy than the others. Especially, PNN on original 71 features shows the best accuracy with FRR of 2.86 percent and FAR of 3.23 percent when spread value is set 0.3.

Table 3. Experimental result

Type	Setting	Feature Filter	FRR	FAR
C5.0	Boosting Ruleset	71	5.71	2.42
		JMI-40	17.14	4.84
		JMI-20	17.14	3.23
		JMI-10	8.57	8.06
	Default	71	25.71	3.23
		JMI-40	28.57	1.61
		JMI-20	28.57	4.03
		JMI-10	20.00	13.71
SVM	PSO method	71	14.29	0.81
		JMI-40	17.14	10.48
		JMI-20	17.14	4.84
		JMI-10	22.86	7.26
PNN	**Spread=0.3**	**71**	**2.86**	**3.23**
	Spread=0.22	JMI-40	5.71	8.87
	Spread=0.21	JMI-20	11.43	5.65
	Spread=0.14	JMI-10	20.00	7.26

7   Conclusion and Future Works

In this paper, we introduced a new re-authentication system based on mouse dynamic, PAITS. It addresses two shortcomings mentioned in previous works. Most significantly, PAITS considerably reduced the time of verification process to five seconds. And experiment results show that it can achieve an *FRR* of 2.86% and FAR of 3.23% by using probability neural network on 71 features set.

Besides the scenarios we designed in this paper, future work will extend the size of the user population involved in the experiment. Future work will also investigate how our proposed mouse biometrics can be integrated efficiently with existing insider threat detection techniques.

Acknowledgments. This work is supported by National High Technology Research and Development Program of China, 863 Program (Grant No.2012AA013101), and Strategic Priority Research Program of the Chinese Academy of Sciences (Grant No. XDA06030200).

References

1. Anderson, R.H., Brackney, R.: Understanding the insider threat. RAND Corporation (2004)
2. Chen, X., Fang, B., Tan, Q., et al.: Inferring attack intent of malicious insider based on probabilistic attack graph model. Chinese Journal of Computers 37(1), 62–72 (2014)
3. Hocquet, S., Ramel, J.Y., Cardot, H.: Users Authentic-ation by a Study of Human Computer Interactions. In: Proc. Eighth Ann. (Doctoral) Meeting on Health, Science and Technology (2004),
   http://www.univ-tours.fr/ed/edsst/comm2004/hocquet.pdf
4. Pusara, M., Brodley, C.E.: User re-authentication via mouse movements. In: Proceedings of the 2004 ACM Workshop on Visualization and Data Mining for Computer Security, pp. 1–8. ACM (October 2004)
5. Ahmed, A.A.E., Traore, I.: IEEE Transactions on A new biometric technology based on mouse dynamics. Dependable and Secure Computing 4(3), 165–179 (2007)
6. Gamboa, H., Fred, A.L.N., Jain, A.K.: Webbiometrics: user verification via web interaction. In: Biometrics Symposium 2007, pp. 1–6. IEEE (September 2007)
7. Quinlan, J.R.: C4. 5: Programs for machine learning (vol. 1). Morgan kaufmann (1993)
8. Rulequest. See5: An Informal Tutorial,
   http://www.rulequest.com/see5-win.html (August 25, 2014)
9. Freund, Y., Schapire, R.E.: A desicion-theoretic generalization of on-line learning and an application to boosting. In: Vitányi, P.M.B. (ed.) EuroCOLT 1995. LNCS, vol. 904, pp. 23–37. Springer, Heidelberg (1995)
10. Suykens, J.A., Vandewalle, J.: Least squares support vector machine classifiers. Neural processing letters 9(3), 293–300 (1999)
11. Specht, D.F.: Probabilistic neural networks. Neural Networks 3(1), 109–118 (1990)
12. FEAST. A Feature Selection Toolbox for C and Matlab,
    http://www.cs.man.ac.uk/~gbrown/fstoolbox/ (August 25, 2014)

Social Engineering through Social Media:
An Investigation on Enterprise Security

Heidi Wilcox, Maumita Bhattacharya, and Rafiqul Islam

School of Computing & Mathematics
Charles Sturt University, Australia - 2640
{hwilcox,mbhattacharya,mislam}@csu.edu.au

Abstract. Social engineering attacks the weakest organizational security link – the human. The influx of employees using social media throughout the working environment has presented information security professionals with an extensive array of challenges facing people, process and technology. These challenges also show enormous impact on the confidentiality, integrity and availability of information assets residing within the organization. This paper aims to provide an in-depth insight into classification and mitigation of social engineering security issues faced by enterprises in adopting social media for business use.

1 Introduction and Background

The confluence of technology merging with readily accessible and promotive data is imbued in every possible facet of our business and personal lives. The distinction between personal and organizational social circles is becoming increasingly blurred with the introduction of social media in various forms throughout the organization. [11]. Traditional security countermeasures are not keeping up with these changes in the workplace as more businesses are encountering breaches targeting the human elements, such as social engineering. Social engineers exploit human behaviour idiosyncrasies to form an attack from the outside that leads them to gain inconspicuous entry into protected areas of the company for their own illicit use.

Protecting the confidentiality, integrity and availability of information assets is a significant global business challenge for information security recognized by researchers [7], and [18]. Using these technologies preface new information risks, particularly through social engineers and their use of these technologies to harvest information for targeted attacks [3, 12, 8, 21].

Failure to protect company information may result in data leakage, business continuity failures and compliance breaches; reputational risks through loss of valuable intellectual property, consumer confidence and competitive advantage [3, 6, 20]. There are currently more cyber-attacks associated with exploiting humans than previously recorded, and they are more challenging to control [9].

Numerous studies have shown that there is a growing correlation between social engineering and social media sites such as Facebook and Twitter, due to the wealth of personal and organisational information to be found within these environments

L. Batten et al. (Eds.): ATIS 2014, CCIS 490, pp. 243–255, 2014.

[5, 10, 4, 13]. The top three social media issues negatively experienced by organisations include: employees sharing too much information, the loss of confidential information and increased exposure to litigation [16]. Other equally important results include losses concerning employee productivity and increased risk of exposure to virus and malware [1].

Organisations that protect information assets through effective security policies will more effectively manage the business risks of the future. Social media policies and guidelines provide advice on how social media participation will be applied to all of the members of an organization [2, 17, 19]. It is also reported that the most effective security countermeasure against social engineering is to increase employee awareness of the many tricks employed by social engineers against them in the workplace. The rest of the paper is organised as follows. In Section 2 we introduce a lifecycle for social engineering and present an interpretation of social engineering in the context of social media use. Section 3 presents a comprehensive classification of the relevant challenges based on three identified parameters, namely, threat vectors, threat contributors and threat impacts. We also propose a set of solutions addressing these challenges in Section 4 and finally, some concluding remarks are presented in Section 5.

2   What Is Enterprise Social Engineering?

Social engineering is the art of manipulating people into performing a specific task for the engineer rather than the engineer gaining entry into systems or networks using the traditional technical hacks. [14]. Social engineers employ the following approach when initiating and completing these attacks.

2.1   Social Engineering Lifecycle

1. Fact - Finding - A variety of techniques can be used by an aggressor to gather information about the targets. Once gathered, this information can then be used to build a relationship with either the target or someone important to the success of the attack.
2. Entrustment - An aggressor may freely exploit the willingness of a target to be trusting in order to develop rapport with them. While developing this relationship, the aggressor will position himself into a position of trust which he will then exploit.
3. Manipulation - The target may then be manipulated by the "trusted" aggressor to reveal information (e.g., passwords) or perform an action (e.g., creating an account or reversing telephone charges) that would not normally occur. This action could be the end of the attack or the beginning of the next stage.
4. Execution: Once the target has completed the task requested by the aggressor, the cycle is complete.

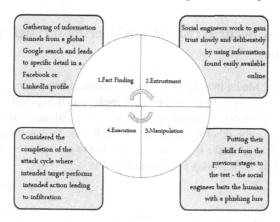

Fig. 1. Closing the circle through Social Media – The Social Engineer

2.2   Social Engineering in Context of Social Media Use

Web based attacks are consistently found to be the leading transport vectors for cyber-attacks; social media and social gaming provides the perfect vehicle or attack surface for delivering lures and payloads. The classification of threat agents into groups of hacktivists, espionage spies, cyber criminals, cyber terrorists or social engineers no longer holds distinct value due to the merging of 'skills' to complete the sophistication of today's exploits. To place into context regarding the topic of this investigation – social engineering through social media within enterprise – the following workflow in Figure 2 has been concluded.

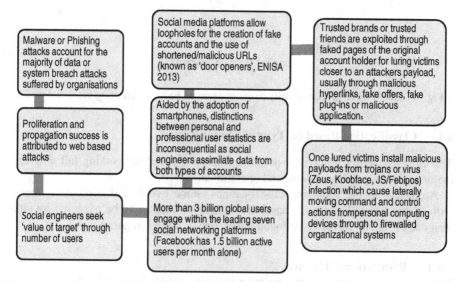

Fig. 2. Social Engineering through Social Media workflow

3   Enterprise Security: Social Engineering through Social Media Challenges

The advent of Social Media into the corporate environment brings along multiple risks to the data, technology, people and the organization itself. Social Engineering predominantly targets the people within the organization either directly or indirectly, however these risks have major impact to the other environments as well. Figure 3 is an illustration of the significant types of social media risks that are occurring in enterprise currently, along with an identification of the contributing factors and impacts.

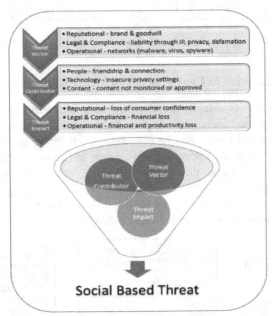

Fig. 3. Classifying enterprise security issues concerning social engineering via social media

3.1   Classification Based on Type of Threat Vector

The most frequently observed risks from enterprise social networking fall into three major groups: reputational, legal and operational.

According to the following classifications, some events and conditions interact with each other and generate causal relationships. A risk may be triggered by more than one event and therefore be found within one or more categories.

3.1.1   Reputational Threats

The hardest challenge to mitigate from the use of social media is the risks to an organization's reputation or brand. Reputation can be damaged if the company is seen to be technically inept – for example, if social networking or corporate blog accounts are hijacked by malware from social engineers which then spreads to customers, partners and other contacts.

On social networks like Facebook and Twitter, a common form of attack is to entice users through social engineering to authorize some third-party application which is then given permission to access the user's data and post information on his or her behalf, or to click on a link that invisibly installs some malware.

Additionally, employees are key to an organization's reputation. They are the organization's best asset but if they post inappropriate or incorrect comments, especially if in contradiction to a corporate message, they can also cause damage with enormous consequence to reputation. Another aspect concerning loss of reputation that could occur outside of official or professional accounts, is the damage caused by forum activity where consumers talk about likes or dislikes of companies. Public comment can be sometimes detrimental alone, however, social engineers can also hijack personal accounts and perform very damaging attacks to the organization while appearing to be an official representative of the company. Public conversations relating to the organization need to be routinely monitored to prevent these conversations escalating to cause severe reputational damage, as companies like BP have found to their cost. [15].

3.1.2   Legal and Compliance Threats

The primary legal and compliance risks include: privacy, security, intellectual property (IP) and media content. Any breach arising from social media engagement could force the organization to face liability.

The legal risks associated with social media usage should be carefully assessed by risk management strategies prior to adopting an enterprise social media framework. Social engineers can infiltrate social networks through the use of malware or phishing sites that pose as the online presence for the organisation. Legal liability is risked if employees are manipulated into providing sensitive personal data or confidential company information. Infringement of intellectual property or copyright claims can result to the organisation from posted or re-posted information that belongs to others, and is used without their permission. It could also place the company potentially in breach of some contractual arrangements, if owned by an existing client. Furthermore, employee conversations on social media sites could reveal third-party trade secrets that the company is legally required to protect, and that can lead to misappropriation and other contractual claims.

Defamation claims are yet another legal risk that may result from social media activities. Companies need to be aware of potential liability for any defamatory statements made by their employees about competitors. Liability can also be a consequence for defamatory statements made by the public on the companies' third-party social media accounts.

There are many ways in which social engineers may manipulate users to compromise or leak sensitive company information (or client information) that could have legal consequences. These are: through crowdsourcing sites (the company posts a problem and asks for solutions from the public, with the unintended consequence that trade secrets are indirectly revealed); through inadvertently compiled client lists (a vice president's contacts on LinkedIn, say, could equate to a complete client list, visible by competitors); and through the inadvertent disclosure of "competitive intelligence" while discussing products, customers, and strategic decisions on various social networking sites. (Some businesses act in a social engineering capacity where they actively gather information about their competitors through social media sites, and analyse that information to gain a competitive advantage. If trade secrets or other proprietary information has been inadvertently revealed in this way, legal headaches could ensue.)

3.1.3   Operational Threats

The use of social media sites for business use places great risk to the organization's traditional networks due to the employee unknowingly downloading malware or spyware from malevolent links or applications added to these sites. Unsuspecting users are enticed into clicking tailored hyperlinks or interesting applications by social engineers, any of these methods could transport users to faked pages or accounts in use for malicious downloads and subsequent entry into secured networks. The user is none the wiser, thinking they are participating with the actual company. The result is that the entire organization's systems could be compromised and taken over by cyber-attackers. As technical security measures are designed to cover developing technical threats, social engineers are increasing attacks via social media due to the low priority these channels are given in security strategies, Technical security alone is ineffective against the nature of social engineered attacks.

3.2   Classification Based on Primary Contributors to Threat

Social media risks via social engineering - such as those listed above - are associated with the people involved in the organization as well as with the information and the technology the organization utilizes so as to perform its operations and meet its objectives. In line with this, social media risk contributors can be classified under the three following categories:

3.2.1   Contributors That Are Associated with People: Sociability and Friendship with Strangers

Social media takes advantage of the social behaviors and motivations of its users by providing a medium for sharing and connecting, even with total strangers. Social media users bond through similar interests where all users must interact through respecting and trusting online relationships. Social engineers can abuse that overall community trust by using the psychological deception of starting a 'friendship' with the employee in order to build trust between the attacker and the victim. The main goal of any social engineer is to manipulate this trust to launch a well-planned and premeditated attack. These types of attack could lead to the social engineer gaining sensitive information from the victim or to get them to perform a specific action that unwittingly causes some damage to their organization.

These online social platforms allow social engineer's to create any number of fake accounts to befriend a target and make it easy for the engineer to invite friendship and establish a direct connection. 'Friending' allows the attacker and victim to engage in conversations relating to interests, problems or dislikes which help the engineer to inch closer to their victim on a personal level. Furthermore, being in a 'friend list' of a victim, allows the social engineer to spy on posts or activities that the victim makes to others. It is not uncommon for users to accept large numbers of 'friends' recommended by the social channel itself based on common elements. This also creates reverse engineering attacks which target the intended victim's 'friend' group first, hoping that the victim gets tricked into inviting the social engineer into their own page of their own accord.

Threat	Threat Contributor
Reputational	**Techniques used**
Account or Brand Hijacking	Create fake business or profile pages on Facebook to obtain details or logins
Phishing	Create fake pages of an actual Facebook or Twitter login page to capture username and password
Malware	Lured to accepting or clicking malicious links, URLS or downloads from third parties
Comments, photos, forum posts	Employees postings can link personal user accounts to their workplace
Information leakage/Loss of data	Employees persuaded to reveal information assets or sensitive organisational data
Legal/Compliance	**Techniques used**
Privacy	Encourage employees to overshare blurring personal, professional and official social media account management
Security	Attackers cause employees to bypass security settings such as protected login details or passwords information
Intellectual Property (IP)	gathered can contribute to identity theft
Media Content	Information gathered from employees using personal accounts to post work information or company secrets that can violate infringement or contractual breach
	Hijacked accounts or socially engineered employees can cause legal liability through posting inappropriate or copyrighted content
Operational	**Techniques used**
Malware/Spyware	Installed through malicious applications or browser extensions by employee through social media site or by spear phishing email
Botnet Command and Control	Twitter URL obfuscation allows attacker to initiate peer to peer conversation with victim or group under a malicious URL and
Faked Pages	infection leads to attacker being able to listen to user conversations
Driveby web download	Attackers using 'look a like' pages that parallel an authentic, they can also compromise friends profiles to trick victims to error
Phishing	Research frequently used websites of employees and inject with malicious code causing infection when visited
Bandwidth	Attackers lure victims with fake offers, links, profiles, plugins, apps or notifications employed on Facebook or Twitter
	Attackers can initiate DoS exploit if systems compromised, employees are allowing unsecured wireless mobile devices to access social media applications and company bandwidth

Fig. 4. Types of threats and their chief contributors

3.2.2 Contributors That Are Associated with Technology: Vulnerable Security Domains

Most social networks classify users in relation to others, as a 'friend,' 'friend of friend,' or 'public'. If users group these social circles effectively they can also provide different levels of security through the privacy settings which will determine what they can see when it is posted by the user. Research has found, however, that these privacy settings are set at a default level by the site itself and most users do not bother with changing these details. Over 100 million Facebook users use these default settings, allowing access to anyone within the social network but also through publicly accessible search engines such as Google. The users of social media sites are also highly willing to reveal private or personal information on their profiles. This information includes their names, birthdays, work, locations, phone or mobile numbers, addresses, e-mails or photos. Users, with the information they reveal online, expose themselves to social engineers who can use this information to launch various physical and cyber-attacks. Their home addresses and e-mail addresses, for example, can be used in phishing. Photos, names, birthdays, and addresses can be valuable information for pretexting, identity theft, impersonation, and other kinds of threats.

3.2.3   Contributors That Are Associated with Content Information: Insecure Content Creation

Rich media content is available from all user's profiles, Facebook for example, shares more than 30 billion pieces of content each month in the form of posts, tags, photos, videos and hyperlinks. Lack of content security and privacy over personal, professional or official accounts leads to many organizations falling prey to actions of social engineers through their own employees. The increase in sophistication of phishing attacks by email or social networking makes it extremely hard for users to distinguish between real or fakes sites. Harmless looking hyperlinks can really be links to malware, virus or worms; ready and waiting for the unsuspecting user to transfer to traditionally secured company networks. A common example of a phishing attack appearing innocuously within a social media page is either a story, offer, or alert message that are attractive enough for the user to download an attachment or click on an embedded hyperlink.

3.3   Classification Based on Those Negatively Impacted by Such Threats

Social engineering issues faced from enterprise social media usage were categorized previously by the type of threat encountered, the following classification appends to this group with those that are impacted negatively by the introduction of these types of threats.

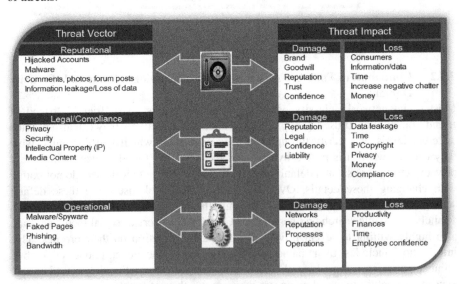

Fig. 5. Mapping threat vectors to organizational impact

3.3.1   Reputational Damage Impact

A company's brand, reputation, and goodwill are an asset. These assets can suffer extreme negative impact from social engineering exploits, to the point where consumer's lose faith or confidence in the organization and will no longer conduct business with them. General online chatter should be monitored to assess whether public comment regarding the organization has positive or negative connotations. When public opinion mentions management or employees, or general business operations with negative implications, the company needs to minimize the ripple effect created by the immediacy of social media. Impacts caused by damage to reputation include the costs of trying to repair damage and recover. Considerable time, money and effort are required to restore customer confidence, especially to show that it won't happen again. Since these breaches may happen, there are also costs for proactive behavior in order to prevent the breach from re-occurring. Examples of specific risks include use of personal accounts to communicate work-related information, or posting photos or information that link users to their employers so social engineers can gather information.

3.3.2   Legal and Compliance Damage Impact

Information held by an organization is an asset. Information may belong to the organization itself or may be owned by another entity and held by the organization as a custodian of that information. Even the personal information of an organization's customers may require protection. Data leakage, loss of intellectual property or copyright, defamatory or incorrect content are negative consequences of using social media within the organization. Social engineers can manipulate employees to reveal such information online, or indeed hijack and manipulate company accounts through phishing techniques. If this asset is impacted in a negative way, usually referred to as a breach, it may lead to financial losses. Reputation may be depreciated due to loss of customer confidence. If the information falls under regulatory compliance, there may be costs for compliance failure.

3.3.3   Operational Damage Impacts

Social engineers favor online social networks as an easy vehicle to create company and employee attacks through phishing and malware. These attacks use employee online social network accounts to inject company systems with fake sites infected with malware and viruses. From a technological or operational aspect this impacts on company financially through costs to mitigate attacks and also those involved through loss of employee productivity. Additionally, excessive employee use of social media in the workplace [9] can also lead to operational impacts. When social media sites are accessed with corporate assets or from the corporate network, technical resources are consumed. These resources are in the form of CPU cycles and network bandwidth. For the worker, loss of productivity may be incurred in the workplace even when using personal assets (e.g. worker uses personal smart phone or tablet to access social media).

4   Proposed Solutions

Within the previous section, a classification of three main security risk areas suggested groupings involve threat vectors, threat contributors and threat impacts. The primary issues for organizations concerning risk management and based on these previous classifications are damage to reputation, legal and compliance issues and operational processes and security. This section addresses these concerns and proposes countermeasures to aid in prevention of these risks occurring.

Threat Vector	Threat Contributor	Threat Impact	
Reputational	**Social Engineers via Social Media**	**Damage**	**Loss**
Hijacked Accounts Malware Comments, photos, forum posts Information leakage/Loss of data	Reputational damage and loss is caused by online social engineers gathering information to cause further attack on organisations. Social engineers exploit users desire to create and share via a friendship or trusted connection. Insecure privacy settings of user's personal social media accounts contribute to information gathering and level of success.	Brand Goodwill Reputation Trust Confidence	Consumers Information/data Time Increase negative chatter Money
Legal/Compliance	**Social Engineers via Social Media**	**Damage**	**Loss**
Privacy Security Intellectual Property (IP) Media Content	Organisations can violate many laws and regulations due to employees being socially engineered online. Social media can result in many organisational risks from attacks to the privacy and security of accounts. Liability can be caused from attackers creating fake pages with misinformation or damaging malware. It is also common for employees to be lured to reveal company data or secrets to contribute to identity theft.	Reputation Legal Confidence Liability	Data leakage Time IP/Copyright Privacy Money Compliance
Operational	**Social Engineers via Social Media**	**Damage**	**Loss**
Malware/Spyware Faked Pages Phishing Bandwidth	From a technical perspective, enormous damage to networks and systems can be attributed to online social engineers. Payloads such as trojans, worms and virus from phishing lures are installed bypassing traditional security and detection. The patience and persistence of the attacker is rewarded with organisational access gained from an employee opening the door.	Networks Reputation Processes Operations	Productivity Finances Time Employee confidence

Fig. 6. Putting it all together – threats, contributors, impacts

Figure 6 is a pictorial representation explaining the relationships between threat vectors and contributors and how these impact the organization. Threat vectors for social engineering through social media can belong to one of three categories (reputational, legal/compliance, operational) and social engineers can exploit these areas through more specific avenues of attack, shown as threat vector examples in the figure. Contributing factors illustrates how social engineers can take advantage of social media to form attacks on employees and their organization. The resulting impacts of these types of attacks cause monumental costs from damage or loss in a number of areas relating to people, processes and technology. Figures 7, 8, 9, form recommendations to mitigate damage and loss according to the individual threat vector. Threats to an organzation's reputation are most suited to mitigation strategies that focus on the employee. Effective policies should be provided to complement awareness training, alerting employees to the high costs involved with brand and reputation damage. Legal or compliance risk can be managed primarily by well-designed policies that focus on maintaining provision for current regulations and requirements. Effectiveness is improved through advocating employee awareness and understanding of the policy issues.

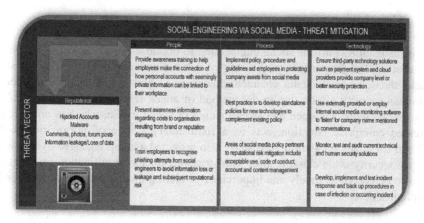

Fig. 7. Threat Mitigation for Reputational threats

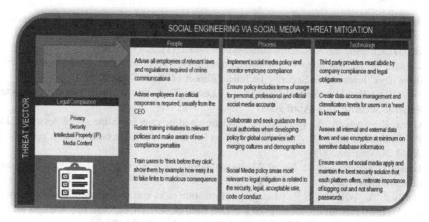

Fig. 8. Threat Mitigation for Legal/Compliance threats

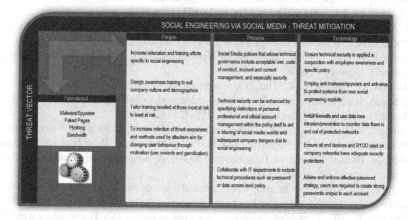

Fig. 9. Threat Mitigation for Operational threats

5   Conclusion

Our investigation confirms social engineering to organizational employees as one of the most challenging information security threats; and explored the link to such attacks through social media channels. It examined how social engineering defies traditional security efforts due to the method of attack relying on human naïveté or error. Furthermore, the open and shared nature of social media, which is now seeing increased enterprise adoption, acts as a rudimentary source of information to be gathered for attack escalation. The study also provided a comprehensive overview of primary security issue classification with strategies for threat mitigation and control. It is also perceived as timely and important considering the current media attention to this predicament.

References

1. Almeida, F.: Web 2.0 technologies and social networking security fears in enterprises. arXiv preprint arXiv:1204 (2012)
2. Bell, J.: Clearing the AIR. Communication World 27(1), 27–30 (2010)
3. Colwill, C.: Human factors in information security: The insider threat–Who can you trust these days? Information Security Technical Report 14(4), 186–196 (2009)
4. Furnell, S.: End User Security Culture – A Lesson That Will Never Be Learnt? Computer Fraud & Security, 6–9 (April 2008)
5. Gross, R., Acquisti, A.: Information revelation and privacy in online social networks. In: Proceedings of the 2005 ACM Workshop on Privacy in the Electronic Society, pp. 71–80. ACM (November 2005)
6. Gudaitis, The Impact of Social Media on Information Security: What every company needs to know (2013)
7. Hardy, C.A., Williams, S.P.: Managing information risks and protecting information assets in a Web 2.0 era. In: Proceedings of the 23rd Bled eConferenceeTrust: Implications for the Individual, Enterprises and Society, Bled, Slovenia, June 20-23 (2010)
8. He, W.: A review of social media security risks and mitigation techniques. Journal of Systems and Information Technology 14(2), 171–180 (2012)
9. ISACA. Social Media: Business Benefits and Security, Governance and Assurance Perspectives. An ISACA emerging technology whitepaper (2010)
10. King, P.: Cyber Crooks Target Social Networking Sites, Point for Credit Research & advice, 9 (January 1, 2008)
11. Meister, J.C., Willyerd, K.: The 2020 workplace. HarperCollins, New York (2010)
12. Rudman, R.J.: Framework to identify and manage risks in Web 2.0 applications. African Journal of Business Management 4(13), 3251–3264 (2010)
13. Sanders, B.G., Dowland, P.S., Furnell, S.: An Assessment of People's Vulnerabilities in Relation to Personal and Sensitive Data. In: Proceedings of the Third International Symposium on Human Aspects of Information Security & Assurance (HAISA 2009), Athens, Greece, June 25-26, p. 50 (2009)
14. Savage, M.: Target the human. Cybercriminals are using social engineering fueled by social media to attack users and break into companies. Information Security (May, 2011)
15. Shogren, E.: BP: A textbook example of how not to handle PR. The message makers: inside PR and advertising, NPR (2011)

16. Symantec. Social Media Protection Flash Poll Global Results. Powerpoint Presentation (2011)
17. Turner, R.: The dawn of a new approach to security. Computer Fraud & Security 2010(4), 15–17 (2010)
18. Workman, M., Bommer, W.H., Straub, D.: Security lapses and the omission of information security measures: A threat control model and empirical test. Computers in Human Behavior 24(6), 2799–2816 (2008)
19. Wright, D.K., Hinson, M.D.: An analysis of the increasing impact of social and other new media on public relations practice. In: 12th Annual International Public Relations Research Conference, Coral Gables, Florida, vol. 7 (March 2009)
20. Young, K.: Policies and procedures to manage employee Internet abuse. Computers in Human Behavior 26(6), 1467–1471 (2010)
21. Zerfass, A., Linke, A.: Future trends in social media use for strategic organisation communication: Results of a Delphi study. Public Communication Review 2(3) (2012)

Efficient Key Pre-distribution for 6LoWPAN

Ruben Smeets[1], Nele Mentens[1,2], Kris Aerts[1], Dave Singelée[2], An Braeken[3],
Matthias Carlier[3], Laurent Segers[3], Kris Steenhaut[3], and Abdellah Touhafi[3,*]

[1] KU Leuven, Technologiecampus Diepenbeek, ES&S, Wetenschapspark 21,
3590 Diepenbeek, Belgium
{firstname.lastname}@kuleuven.be
[2] KU Leuven, ESAT/COSIC and IBBT, Kasteelpark Arenberg 10,
3001 Leuven, Belgium
{firstname.lastname}@esat.kuleuven.be
[3] VUB, INDI and ETRO, Pleinlaan 2, 1050 Elsene, Belgium
{firstname.lastname}@vub.ac.be

Abstract. The Internet of Things is imposing an evolution of the capabilities of wireless sensor networks. The new IP-based 6LoWPAN standard for low power sensor networks allows an almost seamless connection of local sensor networks to the Internet. On the other hand, the connection to the Internet also opens doors for unauthorized nodes to become part of the local network. The most important challenge in preventing this, is the implementation of a key management architecture, keeping in mind that the sensor nodes are constrained in power consumption and data storage capacity. This paper builds on a previously proposed symmetric key management scheme for 6LoWPAN networks presented by Smeets et al. in [1]. The original scheme is based on wired bootstrapping for the enrollment of new nodes, while the paper at hand proposes a wireless method. We analyze the original wired scheme and propose an improved wireless scheme, elaborating on the practical implementation on Zolertia Z1 nodes running Contiki-OS. We show that it is possible to provide end-to-end security using wireless bootstrapping within the constraints of the tiny nodes at hand.

Keywords: 6LoWPAN, Sensor Network Security, Zolertia Z1, Contiki.

1   Introduction

6LoWPAN is a communication standard for wireless sensor networks [2]. The standard is based on IPv6, which allows an easy integration between local sensor networks and the Internet. This way, complex gateways to allow the communication of 6LoWPAN sensor nodes with data processing servers connected to the Internet become obsolete. On the downside, connecting local sensor networks to the Internet makes them vulnerable for all known security attacks in IP networks, besides the vulnerabilities already present in local wireless sensor networks [3]. Whereas traditional computers in traditional IP networks have a large capacity

---

* This work was funded by IWT-TETRA project 120105 "6LoWPAN".

L. Batten et al. (Eds.): ATIS 2014, CCIS 490, pp. 256–263, 2014.

for the implementation of security architectures, the nodes in wireless sensor networks are limited in data storage and power budget. In this paper, we present a scheme that provides end-to-end security in 6LoWPAN networks using the Zolertia Z1 hardware platform. We use the open source operating system Contiki [4], which is developed to operate on constrained sensor nodes. Contiki allows multitasking and is C-based. It uses the μIPv6 stack for 6LoWPAN communications. The scheme builds on a previously proposed scheme using wired bootstrapping for the enrollment of new network nodes [1]. We identify the shortcomings of this scheme and propose a new method for wireless key pre-distribution. We obtain a higher level of security by pre-configuring the sensor node firmware with a unique secret key that is used during key transfer of the bootstrapping phase. In addition, we augment the user friendliness by allowing multiple nodes to connect at the same time. We also show that there is no performance drop compared to the wired approach in terms of memory usage on the constrained nodes. In Sect. 2, we discuss background information. Sect. 3 shows the proposed key management architecture based on a wireless key pre-distribution mechanism. The implementation and the performance of the scheme are dealt with in Sect. 4 and Sect.5, respectively. Conclusions are drawn in Sect. 6.

2   Background

This paper builds on the scheme that was presented in [1]. We refer to that scheme as the 'original scheme'. This section explains the topology of the original scheme and the wired bootstrapping method. Further, we elaborate on the sensor network platform that has been used in both the original and the new scheme.

The original key management scheme infrastructure consists of a tablet PC, a portable Physical Unclonable Function (PUF), a trusted central entity (CE), a 6LoWPAN edge router (ER) and individual sensor nodes. The original scheme is a distributive scheme that uses parts of the SPINS protocol [5] and the Zigbee 2007 security scheme [6]. It consists of a bootstrapping phase, a discovery phase and a pairing phase. In the bootstrapping phase, the tablet and the PUF generate cryptographic strong keys for the entire network. The CE receives these keys through a secure connection and stores them in the database. Then, the ER sends a request to receive a network key over an encrypted tunnel. Sensor nodes are added to the network through a wired interface to the CE. Through the installer laptop, a key request packet is sent over an encrypted tunnel to the central entity, after which the node information is stored in the database. After authorization of the node by the user (through the tablet), the node receives the network key and a unique sensor key. In the discovery phase and the pairing phase the sensor nodes determine their routes and establish a session key, respectively. This paper focuses on the improvement of the bootstrapping phase.

Our selected hardware platform comprises of the Zolertia Z1 [7] sensor nodes running the Contiki OS with the μIP communication stack. The nodes are equipped with a MSP430F2617 microcontroller [8] that offers 8 kB of RAM and 92 kB of Flash memory. The wireless communications are handled by the CC2420 transceiver from Chipcon [9] operating in the 2.4 GHz range. The CC2420 is compliant with the IEEE802.15.4 standard [10] offering MAC and baseband modem support. In addition, it has an AES128 co-processor [11] that operates in three different block cipher modes: CBC-MAC, CTR and CCM [12]. During communications the AES core can perform in-line security operations unburdening the load of the microcontroller. Furthermore, it can also be used freely by the application for higher level security operations.

Similar work has been done by V. A. Pérez in [13], presenting a solution based on a public-key scheme, which has the advantage that new nodes do not need preparation by the vendor. On the other hand, public-key schemes are less light-weight than symmetric-key schemes in terms of power consumption and memory requirements. Our solution only uses symmetric-key cryptography and needs preparation of the nodes by the vendor.

3   Proposed Wireless Key Pre-distribution Mechanism

In this section, we present our wireless key pre-distribution mechanism for efficient security bootstrapping of wireless sensor nodes. This work aims to improve the user friendliness and security trade-offs for the wired bootstrapping mechanism described in [1], which has the following shortcomings: (1) *scalability*: in larger networks the key bootstrapping becomes tedious and unmanageable due to the limitation of configuring one node at a time; (2) *applicability*: nodes without a serial interface are not able to participate in the network and additional resources are needed for the wired interface; (3) *security*: due to the unencrypted key transfer between the node and its access point, the scheme is vulnerable for eavesdropping attacks [3]. The general structure of our wireless solution can be divided into two separate preparation phases. The first phase is handled by the sensor node vendor and the second by the user during deployment.

Vendor Preparation. The sensor node vendor supplies the user with the sensor node hardware and firmware. In our solution, the vendor is required to extend the firmware with an unique pre-installed Bootstrap Key (Kb) that is linked to the node's MAC address or node ID. The Kb's are used only temporary during the "user preparation" phase for secure key transfer between the Central Entity (CE) and the sensor node. Every Kb is derived from a Master Bootstrap Key (Kmb) using a Key Derivation Function (KDF) such as [14] in combination with a node's MAC address. By using the node ID as additional KDF input we ensure that each Kb is unique and related to the specified sensor node. These firmware preparations are illustrated in Fig. 1. Providing the KDF with the Kmb and a list of all the node IDs, the vendor firmware generator is able to create firmware files containing an unique Kb. This results in an unique firmware file for each sensor node. Moreover, the vendor collects all the Kb's with their associated node ID in a list that is used during the "user preparation" phase.

User Preparation. After the "vendor preparations" the nodes containing the required firmware are ready for deployment. The user starts by updating the CE

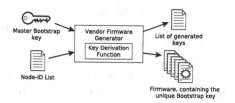

Fig. 1. Vendor firmware preparation

security database with the list of generated Kb's from the vendor. This is done by uploading the list into the tablet and transferring the keys to the security database through a secure connection as is shown in Fig. 2. Once the database is up-to-date the CE is ready to accept key requests from the sensor nodes. If a node wants to join a network it sends out a key request packet through its wireless radio. The packet is unencrypted and contains information about the node. The user has to ensure that, during the key request, the nodes are within a range of 10 centimeters of the 6LoWPAN edge router (ER). This allows the ER to ignore unencrypted packets from which the signal strength is below a predefined value. Other initialized nodes in the network will automatically drop the unencrypted packets by default. Fig. 3 illustrates the various components of the setup. Once the ER receives and identifies a valid key request, it is transferred through an encrypted tunnel to the CE for further processing. The CE analyses the node information from the key request packet and checks whether the node ID is linked to a valid Kb in the security database. Upon a valid check the request is stored and awaits approval from the user through the tablet. Otherwise, the key request is dropped. In case multiple key requests from the same node arrive, only the first one is stored. Similar to the original scheme the user makes use of the tablet interface to either acknowledge or decline a request [1]. For each approved request the CE creates a unique security device in its database. This information is encrypted using AES [11] by the CE using the individual Kb. After completion a reply packet is created containing the encrypted message and sent back to the ER for broadcasting in the 6LoWPAN network. Finally, the requesting node receives a reply from the CE through the ER and decrypts the packet with its own Kb, after which the security information is stored and the node is ready to participate in network communications.

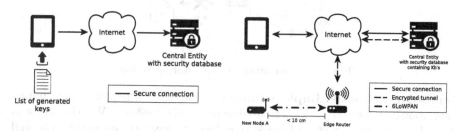

Fig. 2. Central Entity (CE) database preparation

Fig. 3. Adding new nodes

Evaluation. We use the same criteria that were used for the evaluation of the wired solution: (1) *scalability*: due to the absence of a physical connection the nodes are able to request keys in parallel, greatly reducing the deployment time; (2) *applicability*: devices without a wired interface can participate in secure network communications; (3) *security*: our solution provides confidentiality, integrity and authenticity during key transfer as well as replay protection. Further, the system has good resilience against node capture. If multiple nodes are physically compromised and the Kb's are extracted, other nodes are not affected because every node has an unique Kb. Furthermore, revoking Kb's is trivial due to the centralized topology of the network and obtaining Kmb with information from the individual Kb's should be very difficult because of the KDF.

4   Implementation of the Wireless Bootstrapping Mechanism

The implementation of the wireless bootstrapping mechanism consists of the vendor firmware generator, the Contiki implementation on the individual sensor nodes, the extension of the wireless access points and the CE server configuration.

Vendor Firmware Generator. The vendor is responsible for providing the sensor nodes with unique firmware files containing the Kb. In addition, the vendor should provide a list of key value pairs linking the node ID to a matching Kb. We use the standardized KDF1 key derivation function [14] in combination with the NIST recommended SHA3-256 hashing algorithm [15] through the open source Java Bouncy Castle crypto library [16]. We used scripting to create the vendor firmware generator. The script derives a Kb from the specified Kmb using a copy of the node IDs as additional input for the KDF. Each generated Kb is then copied to a placeholder in one of the sensor node's source files and compiled to a unique firmware file as illustrated in Fig. 4. The script also creates an XML file containing a list of the node IDs and their derived Kb's.

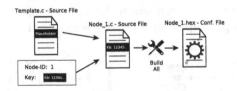

Fig. 4. Vendor firmware generator operation

Sensor Node Contiki Implementation. The wireless bootstrapping implementation on the sensor nodes is focused on area and robustness. We tried to use as many built-in components of Contiki to reduce the memory consumption as well as the complexity. The bootstrapping functionality is mainly situated in the MAC layer of the μIP stack and makes use of its broadcast capabilities. Consider a blank sensor node without associated key material wanting to join a network. Starting with a system reset, the node checks its memory for key material. For a blank node, this check fails and the node initiates the bootstrap procedure. Immediately after initialization, the node sends out a single unencrypted hello message containing the node ID and a one-byte message code indicating a key request packet. Because the node has no knowledge of the surrounding entities or the CE, the packet is broadcasted on MAC level using the existing Contiki functions. The node waits for a reply message coming from the CE. The hello reply message is an encrypted packet containing the requesting node's key material. The packet is encrypted using the AES block cipher in combination with the node's Kb, providing packet confidentiality. The integrity is preserved by calculating and appending a MIC tag of 8 bytes to the message. Authenticity is provided by the fact that only two entities have knowledge over the Kb, being the node in question and the CE. Packet freshness is implemented by incorporating a nonce counter in the message. The node tries to decrypt the reply packet using its Kb as decryption key for the dedicated AES core in CCM mode. In case the message authentication fails, the node drops the packet and returns to its wait state. Otherwise, the packet is parsed and the key material is extracted and stored in the node's memory. Once the keys are stored, the program performs a software reset forcing re-initialization. This time the node detects the key material and normal operations are started.

Wireless Access Point Contiki Implementation. The wireless bootstrapping mechanism is implemented as an extension of the wireless access point or Edge router (ER) functionality. In contrast to the wireless sensor nodes, the ER has to cope with both normal security operations and the wireless bootstrapping operations at the same time. Therefore, we chose to extend the Contiki process on the ER in order to handle these additional requirements. The implementation resides in the MAC layer and application layer of the μIP stack. Starting with the MAC layer, the nodes send out an unencrypted key request packet as a MAC broadcast message. In normal circumstances these packets would be ignored by the ER due to failed integrity check at MAC level. However, by verifying the signal strength and the message length the ER allows these packets to flow through for further processing. In our case we chose a minimum signal strength value that translates in a distance of approximately 10 centimeters. The unencrypted packets that flow through are considered to be key request messages and are handed over to the ER process. The ER process resides at the application layer and has access to a UDP connection. Since the nodes do not know the CE's address, the ER process is responsible for forwarding the packet to the CE. This is done by extracting the key request payload and formating it to a UDP packet designated for the CE. Upon completion, the UDP packet is transmitted through an encrypted tunnel to the CE. Once the key request has been processed a reply is generated by the CE. The hello reply is forwarded over the UDP connection, through the encrypted tunnel, back to the ER. The ER process translates the reply message payload to a MAC broadcast packet and hands it over to the wireless radio for transmission. Note that the requesting node should be in a one-hop radius from the ER to receive the reply packet.

Central Entity Server Configuration. Since the CE holds the cryptographic key material of the entire network, additional care must be applied when extending its functionality. Therefore, we focused on providing a robust implementation of the CE's key pre-distribution mechanism. The complete mechanism is written as a stand-alone Java UDP server that listens to incoming packets coming from the encrypted tunnels. The server stands in direct contact with the security database through a secure connection, giving access to the key material. In case of an incoming key request, the packet is parsed and followed by an immediate identity check through the presence of a Kb record in the database. Upon an invalid result the packet is dropped. Otherwise, the server continues with verifying if the request was already processed before storing it in the database. Once the request is stored, it awaits approval from the user. A separate thread, that makes use of the same UDP connection, handles the approved requests. For each request, the server creates a new security device in its database and selects new key material according to the origin of the request. The origin is verified by checking the address of the ER where the request was registered. Finally, a reply packet is created and encrypted using the corresponding Kb as encryption key for the AES-CCM core, implemented through Bouncy Castle.

5   Performance Analysis

Due to the limited availability of processing power/energy and memory it is difficult to implement complex functionality on the sensor nodes. For that reason we compared the memory requirements of our implementation with those of the wired bootstrapping interface. The results are shown in Fig. 5. The measurements are normalized to the total available memory of the Zolertia Z1 platform, which is 92 kB ROM and 8 kB RAM. The sensor node measurements are given for a UDP client example program. We list the UDP client implementation without security as a reference. Then we give the results of the wired and wireless bootstrapping implementation. Note that the differences in memory requirements between the wired and wireless implementations are fairly minimal. However, if we consider the gains in user friendliness, the obsoleteness of a wired interface and the stronger security, our wireless solution is more favorable. The memory requirements of the edge router extension in show that extending the functionality with the wireless bootstrapping mechanism has a small impact on memory

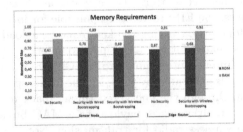

Fig. 5. Memory requirements of the sensor node and ER Contiki implementations

requirements. Note that the results of the vendor firmware generator and the CE Java server are not included, because they are irrelevant in this comparison.

6 Conclusion

We presented our wireless bootstrapping mechanism as an improvement on the wired bootstrapping mechanism described by Smeets et al. [1]. We aim at achieving both higher security and increased user friendliness without the need for additional hardware. Our solution is integrated in the Contiki OS and evaluated on the Zolertia Z1 platform with the focus on a robust implementation. The results show that by using wireless bootstrapping we achieve reduced memory costs in comparison to the wired mechanism with the advent of stronger security. In the future we plan to examine the effect of various attacks against the wireless bootstrapping mechanism and we also plan to increase the resilience against Denial-Of-Service attacks.

References

1. Smeets, R., Aerts, K., Mentens, N., Singelée, D., Braeken, A., Segers, L., Touhafi, A., Steenhaut, K., Niccolo, D.: A cryptographic key management architecture for dynamic 6LowPan networks. In: Proc. of the 9th ICAI (2014)
2. Shelby, Z., Bormann, C.: 6LoWPAN: The Wireless Embedded Internet. John Wiley & Sons Ltd (2009)
3. Çayırcı, E., Rong, C.: Security in Wireless Ad Hoc and Sensor Networks, pp. 107–283. John Wiley & Sons Ltd. (2009)
4. Dunkels, A., Gronvall, B., Voigt, T.: Contiki - a Lightweight and Flexible Operating System for Tiny Networked Sensors. In: Proc. of the 29th Annual IEEE International Conf. on Local Computer Networks (2004)
5. Perrig, A., Szewczyk, R., Tygar, J.D., Wen, V., Culler, D.E.: Spins: Security protocols for sensor networks. Wirel. Netw. 8(5), 521–534 (2002)
6. Yüksel, E., Nielson, H.R., Nielson, F.: ZigBee-2007 Security Essentials. In: Proc. of the 13th NordSec (2008)
7. Zolertia, http://zolertia.sourceforge.net/wiki/images/e/e8/Z1_RevC_Datasheet.pdf
8. MSP430F2617 datasheet, http://www.ti.com/lit/ds/symlink/msp430f2617.pdf
9. Chipcon: CC2420 datasheet, http://www.ti.com/lit/ds/symlink/cc2420.pdf
10. IEEE 802.15.4: Wireless Medium Access Control (MAC) and Physical Layer (PHY) Specifications for Low-Rate Wireless Personal Area Networks (2003)
11. Daemen, J., Rijmen, V.: The Design of Rijndael: AES - The Advanced Encryption Standard. Springer (2002)
12. NIST: Recommendation for Block Cipher Modes of Operation, SP800-38A (2012)
13. Pérez, V.A.: Efficient Key Generation and Distributionon Wireless Sensor Networks, Master Thesis, KTH (2013)
14. ISO/IEC 18033-2:2006: Information technology - Security techniques - Encryption algorithms - Part 2: Asymmetric ciphers. Ed. Victor Shoup (2006)
15. Bertoni, G., Daemen, J., Peeters, M., Van Assche, G.: The Keccak SHA-3 submission (2011), http://keccak.noekeon.org/Keccak-submission-3.pdf
16. The Legion of the Bouncy Castle: Cryptography APIs, http://www.bouncycastle.org

Author Index